CHINA'S NIGHTMARE, AMERICA'S DREAM

CHINA'S NIGHTMARE, AMERICA'S DREAM

India as the Next Global Power

William H. Avery

AMARYLLIS

This edition first published 2012

AMARYLLIS

An imprint of Manjul Publishing House Pvt. Ltd.

Editorial Office:
J-39, Ground Floor, Jor Bagh Lane,
New Delhi 110 003, India
Tel: 011-24642447/24652447 Fax: 011-24622448
Email: amaryllis@amaryllis.co.in
Website: www.amaryllis.co.in

Registered Office:
10, Nishat Colony, Bhopal 462 003, M.P., India

This edition is for sale in the Indian subcontinent only.

The opinions and characterisations in this book are those of the author, and do not necessarily represent official positions of the United States Government.

ISBN: 978-93-81506-07-3

Printed and Bound in India by
Manipal Technologies Ltd, Manipal

To Carla and Sofie

We have hard work ahead. There is no resting for any one of us till we redeem our pledge in full, till we make all the people of India what destiny intended them to be.

Jawaharlal Nehru, 14 August 1947

CONTENTS

ACKNOWLEDGEMENTS

The following people provided support and encouragement during the writing of the book: Annie Avery, Costa Avery, Genie Avery, Harry Avery, JoAnn Avery, Raj Bhatt, Alison Gross, Jerry Gross, Tim Harris, Bhaskar Majumdar, Lawrence Monagle, Rita Payne, Kishore Rao, Ashok Swarup, and Frank Wisner. I am grateful to them all.

Deeparghya Mukherjee, my able research assistant, provided valuable help in locating sources and documenting them in the endnotes. The staff of the British Library, especially the staff of the Business and Intellectual Property Centre and of the Asian and African Studies Reading Room, provided assistance with locating and retrieving sources from the library's magnificent collections.

I alone am responsible for any errors or shortcomings in the book.

AUTHOR'S NOTE

I wrote this book for two reasons.

First, I believe India is capable of being a true world power, not just an aspiring one. A timidity among India's political leadership for much of the time since Independence sixty-four years ago has meant that India has been denied that power, and that Indians have been denied opportunities to share the wealth that state power brings. I hope that this book stimulates some measure of debate within India about the country's economic and geopolitical future, and what needs to happen (or happen faster) to achieve security and prosperity for all Indians.

Second, the world *needs* India to become a true global power. The United States has been the primary defender of democratic and free market principles since it emerged as a superpower a century ago. As we begin the second decade of the twenty-first century, it is clear that the United States cannot continue to play this role alone. It needs a partner that shares its values, and will fight to defend those values when needed. It needs a strong and assertive India, and the world needs both nations.

India is not yet ready to join the United States in this role. But there are no natural impediments standing in India's way; the only thing missing is will and action. It has all the advantages the United States had in its infancy: size, diversity, a strategic location, a stable government and a thriving economy. Now India needs to convert these advantages into raw power. The prescriptions in this book are meant to be a guide for India to become, in the coming decades, a global power.

Critics may charge, with some justification, that this work overlooks India's many faults in favour of its vast potential. They may also charge that the book would remake India in the image of the United States. I certainly believe that India can learn from recent American history in key areas: defence policy, university education, and fostering of innovation. Yet India should not simply become another United States: It can become a new kind of global power, one that is well suited to the world of the twenty-first century.

If India and the United States join together to defend and promote their common values, both nations will become stronger and wiser through the alliance. In the process the shared values will find greater expression and new adherents. This will be good for the world, as well as for the United States and India.

★

The book covers a wide range of subjects relating to India: history, economics, domestic politics and international relations, among others. To help illuminate India's past, present and future, the book also touches on historical and contemporary matters from other nations, notably the United States, China, the United Kingdom,[1] and countries in Continental Europe, as well as developing nations. Specialists may find the book's treatment of these fields, nations or periods of history insufficient. If so, their criticisms are welcome. One of the aims of the book is to stimulate debate about India's place in the world, and to do so among thinkers from different nations and different disciplines.

---

[1] In this work, the term United Kingdom is used to refer to the British Isles after the establishment of the United Kingdom in 1801. For references to time periods before 1801, either the term Britain or British Empire is used. The term Britain (or British Empire) is also used when referring to periods of time that span both pre- and post-1801, as well as for references to historical legacy of the British Isles and the specific phrase 'America's New Britain'.

INTRODUCTION

This is India's moment. Like the United States a century ago and China thirty years ago, it is clear that India is on the verge of achieving great power status. But the world will not grant India that role simply because of its size and economic potential; India has to reach out and grab it. The problem, however, is that India has not yet demonstrated the will to do so.

What defines a great power? It is a status that, by definition, at most only a handful of nations at any one time, can hold. Throughout human history, there are only a few indisputable great powers. Rome was the first, followed by Spain, Britain, and most recently, the United States. Others, like the Ottoman Empire and the Soviet Union, could arguably meet the definition of great powers as well, at least for short periods of time.

Today the world is undergoing a shift in economic activity from the West (the United States and Europe) to the East (Asia). As this shift accelerates, a small number of Asian nations will have the opportunity to convert their increased wealth into increased power. Once the shift is complete, a greater share of global power will be concentrated in the hands of those Asian nations who dared to grasp this opportunity; the rest will be consigned to second tier or regional power status.

This book is about what India needs to do, as this shift takes place in the coming decades, to emerge as a great power. It tells the story of where India has come from (great wealth over much of the last two millennia); how far it has declined (hitting rock bottom in 1991); where it is today (still an emerging power, but full of natural advantages); and what it must do now to reclaim its rightful place in the world (convert those advantages into raw power).

China is well on its way to building the economic and military strength required to become a great power. Its leaders may be hoping that, having achieved this level of power, it will be able to dominate Asia. India is the only Asian nation standing in its way. An India that pursues and achieves great status power is China's worst geopolitical nightmare.

The United States, meanwhile, faces a future where an increasingly assertive, and perhaps increasingly aggressive, China will challenge American global military and economic supremacy. Furthermore, the United States knows it can no longer rely on the United Kingdom to help extend Anglo-American power far and wide. The United States longs for a new partner for the twenty-first century, one that, like the United Kingdom, shares its core values. An India that amasses the power needed to fill the void left by the United Kingdom would be an American dream come true.

★

Jawaharlal Nehru, independent India's first prime minister, saw that great power would one day be within India's reach. His speech to Parliament on the eve of Indian independence on 14 August 1947 emphasised both the opportunity India had before it and the necessity for India to take action to realise that opportunity. For Nehru, the opportunity was for India to claim 'her rightful place in the world', which would require 'incessant striving'. As Nehru said, '...the achievement we celebrate today is but a step, an opening of opportunity, to the greater triumphs and achievements that await us.'

Nehru's speech is as much about India's past as about its future. He felt that newly independent India had a responsibility to honour its history as a people and a culture; 'redeeming the pledge' as he put it. Nehru also acknowledged on the night of 14 August 1947 that India had not, simply by becoming independent, honoured its history 'in full measure'. That would have to come later.

Nehru's later is now. With resolve India can claim today its rightful place in the world. It has a responsibility to become a global power, not only for itself but for the world. It is time to redeem the pledge in full measure.

★

The book is organised into three parts. Part One is a brief review of India's history. It shows that India's recent economic and political weakness is a temporary phase, and sets the context for the central argument of the book: that – with the right policies and leadership – India can return to its historical position of wealth and power. Chapter One describes how and why India, wealthy for much of its history, became impoverished by the time of Independence. Chapter Two recounts India's *annus horribilis* of 1991, when two crises – the assassination of Rajiv Gandhi and a balance of payments (BOP) shortfall – converged to push the nation to the edge of political and economic ruin. Chapter Three covers India's emergence from global obscurity, from the 1998 nuclear test through to the December 2001 attack on Parliament and onto the 2008 Indo-American nuclear agreement.

Part Two focuses on India today, and details the actions India needs to take both at home and abroad to claim global power status. Chapter Four describes India's current economic advantages relative to much of the rest of the world, driven by its positive demographics and its strong industrial base; these advantages offer India a window of opportunity to become one of the world's leading economies. The next two chapters cover the economic and commercial steps that India's government and private sector must take to seize this opportunity.

Chapter Five takes the conventional assessment of India's outsourcing industry and turns it on its head: Outsourcing is not the pride of India, but rather a low-value use of India's considerable skills that is retarding India's economic growth. In order for the nation to become an economic power, corporate India will have to move away from 'back' office work to 'front' office work, in which it develops its own intellectual property and markets its own brands. To do so, India must build a world class university system that will direct brains and capital to innovation-intensive industries.

Chapter Six focuses on corporate India's role in the nation's transition to global power status. India's corporate sector is one of the nation's greatest economic advantages. If India is to become an economic superpower, its corporate sector will have to first conquer world markets. Corporate India's depth, breadth, efficient capital markets and talented management teams mean that there are hundreds of multinationals-in-waiting, poised to help India secure a top place among the world's economies. The chapter also exposes the risks for Indian companies in using acquisitions to go global, and lays out ten rules for them to follow when considering growth through acquisition.

Chapter Seven moves beyond economic power to consider the tasks ahead in order for India to develop global political and military strength. It surveys India's foreign policy in recent decades, and finds that policy timid to the point of neglecting national security. While China has been building military strength and establishing footholds in India's backyard, India has been distracted by its hollow arguments for a seat on the United Nations Security Council (UNSC) and enfeebled by its continued association with the Non-Aligned Movement (NAM). To close the power gap with China, India will have to accelerate its currently planned increases in military spending and adopt an aggressive stance towards any incursion by China or any other power in its sphere of influence.

Former United States President Theodore Roosevelt once quoted an African proverb: 'Speak softly and carry a big stick; you will go far.' India has the 'speak softly' part mastered. Now it needs to find a big stick, fast.

India's power cannot be a theoretical construct. Even if India is able to develop the tools of economic and military power described in Part Two, it will need to exercise that power in the real world in competition with other states. Part Three offers a framework for how an increasingly wealthy and assertive India can exercise real power in the twenty-first century: through an alliance with the United States.

Chapter Eight argues that the Indo-American alliance can be to the twenty-first century what the Anglo-American alliance was to the twentieth century. In the span of one decade (from India's 1998 nuclear test to the 2008 Indo-American nuclear agreement), the two nations moved from mutual mistrust to cooperation. Now India and the United States must broaden their partnership beyond nuclear matters to joint intelligence and military operations. One key to the Indo-American alliance, as it is with the Anglo-American alliance, will be people-to-people contacts. The United States' increasingly influential Indian diaspora will underpin the Indo-American alliance, as will the United States' growing commercial interests in India.

Chapter Nine places the Indo-American alliance in the context of the security threats that are likely to characterise the twenty-first century. India and the United States are heirs to a common tradition of values stemming from Britain: democracy, the rule of law, and free enterprise. The United States and the United Kingdom were the main defenders of those values in the twentieth century. India, for its part, spent its first fifty years of independence developing a stable, pluralistic democracy that earned it moral authority in the eyes of the world. Now India must supplement that moral standing with raw power, and the willingness to use that power to stop the spread of tyranny. If there is a Third World War, it will likely start in Asia. If there is a Third World War, the United States and India, as heirs to the values of the British Crown, will have to win it together; the future of freedom depends on it.

Prologue

THE BOMB

Once upon a time there were two kingdoms, one in the East, and one in the West.

The kingdom in the East was an ancient and proud kingdom, thousands of years old.

The kingdom in the West was a much younger kingdom, only hundreds of years old, and also proud, for it was the richest and most powerful kingdom in the world.

The kingdom in the East was also once rich and powerful. Long ago, its palaces were the finest anywhere, and visitors came from other kingdoms to marvel at their splendour. For centuries the kingdom lived in prosperity.

Meanwhile, far away, great changes were taking place and new kingdoms were emerging. These new kingdoms were making rapid advancements in science – advancements that allowed them to build factories to produce large quantities of goods. These factories created great wealth, which the kingdoms used to fund new technologies that bred yet more riches. It was in this period that the kingdom in the West was born, and it quickly amassed tremendous wealth and power.

The kingdom in the East was unaware of this new system of mass production, and before it realised what was happening, it was no longer one of the richest kingdoms in the world. In fact, it had become one of the poorest. The kingdom in the East gradually fell under the domination of another kingdom, and its new rulers ensured it remained poor and powerless.

The kingdom of the West had the greatest scientists in the world. One day they invented a new weapon that could instantly destroy the cities of other kingdoms. The kingdom of the West used this weapon to win what had been a long war against its rivals, and with its victory became the most powerful of all kingdoms.

Around this time, the kingdom in the East succeeded in winning its freedom, but it emerged from centuries of foreign rule poorer than ever, and far behind other kingdoms in development.

The kingdom in the West, newly dominant, and the kingdom in the East, newly independent, had much in common. They spoke the same language, and ran their kingdoms in the same way. In spite of these similarities, the two kingdoms did not enjoy good relations. They were not enemies, but they were not friends either. The people of both kingdoms thought that was a pity, because they quite liked each other.

Meanwhile, other kingdoms had discovered the secret of the powerful weapon, and could threaten the kingdom of the West with instant destruction. This made the kingdom in the West feel more unsafe than it ever had before.

One day, the kingdoms that possessed the weapon's secrets decided they would prevent other kingdoms from developing this new weapon. The kingdom in the East thought this was unfair, and put its own scientists to work in unlocking the weapon's secrets.

After many years of hard work, the scientists were ready with the new weapon. They had tested it once before during its development, and now they needed a final test to ensure it would work properly in case they had to use it on an enemy kingdom. Deep in the desert, the scientists prepared to test the weapon underground, so that it would not hurt anyone.

The kingdom in the West was strongly opposed to the kingdom in the East mastering the new weapon. When it learned from it spies about the test that the kingdom in the East was preparing, it was gravely concerned. The kingdom in the West sent its emissary immediately to the kingdom of the East. And that is where our story begins.

★

New Delhi, 15 December 1995[2]

Ambassador Frank G. Wisner II stepped into the backseat of the car, and the thick bullet proof door shut behind him with a thud. It was a short drive from the United States Embassy to the Prime Minister's Office (PMO) at South Block, and the car – with police escort and an American flag fluttering atop each front fender – made its way quickly through Delhi's traffic.

Wisner looked out the window at the grand buildings of Imperial Delhi, and considered the task before him. The evidence was clear: India was preparing to test a nuclear bomb. Now it was his job to get it to stop.

★

Frank Wisner was something of a legend in the United States Foreign Service. India was his fourth ambassadorship. He had reached the highest level of the Foreign Service, the rank of career ambassador. A handful of Foreign Service officers held that rank at any one time; he was the civilian version of a four star general.

Wisner, in fact, looked more like a general than a diplomat. From the neck below he was built like a tank. He did not, however, give the impression of someone who needed to lift weights to build muscle. He had an intensity about him that made one thing clear: The energy he expended in simply *being* Frank Wisner was a daily workout.

Wisner always spoke slowly and deliberately, unlike most Americans who rush to the end of their sentences. The voice itself was deep and resonant, with just a hint of the refinement that some Americans have. It was not so much an accent as the absence of one – no Midwestern nasal

---

[2]The following description of the events of December 1995 is based on two sources, supplemented by the author's own narrative interpretation of events:

Strobe Talbott, *Engaging India: Diplomacy, Democracy and the Bomb*, Brookings Institution Press, 2004, pp 37-38.

George Perkovich, *India's Nuclear Bomb: The Impact on Global Proliferation*, University of California Press, 1999, pp. 367-71.

twang, no Southern drawl, only words enunciated clearly in a manner that unmistakably signified good education.

Wisner was made from a mould that is unknown in contemporary India. Maybe centuries ago Indian warriors were built like him, but no longer. And certainly not the typical Indian government official: thin and wiry – often; big and flabby – sometimes; big and muscular – never. It is safe to say that in December 1995, nowhere in the vast Indian government was there a human being with the raw force of Frank Wisner. Wisner versus the Indian government was an unfair fight; the Indians never had a chance.

★

Wisner had just returned to Delhi after several days of consultations in Washington. During his visit there, American spy satellites had detected suspicious activity at a nuclear facility in India's north. The Pokhran[3] test site, deep in the desert of Rajasthan, was a place Washington kept a close eye on; India had conducted its first nuclear test at Pokhran in 1974 (under the regime of then prime minister, Indira Gandhi), and Washington knew that if the Indians tested again, it would be there.

So when the satellites picked up a vast increase in the level of activity at Pokhran, Washington feared the worst. Wisner went to the Central Intelligence Agency (CIA) to look at the evidence, arranged for the Agency to send satellite photos to the United States Embassy in Delhi, and caught a flight back to India.

When Wisner landed in Delhi, another surprise awaited him. He was handed a dispatch from the State Department that had been sent to the Embassy in Delhi. The cable carried the text of a report that the *New York Times* had run while Wisner was airborne: 'U.S. Suspects India Prepares To Conduct Nuclear Test'.[4]

---

[3]Pokhran in Hindi means 'the land of five mirages', an apt name for a nuclear test site in the desert.

[4]Tim Weiner, 'U.S. Suspects India Prepares To Conduct Nuclear Test', *New York Times*, 15 December 1995.

Wisner scanned the text. Someone had spoken to the press. The report referred specifically to the satellite images and quoted an unnamed American 'government official' saying, 'we're not sure what [the Indians] are up to'. The report also carried the requisite denials from the Indian government.

The press leak meant Wisner's hopes of averting the test without the glare of publicity were dashed. That made his job doubly difficult. Indians preferred to discuss sensitive state-to-state matters in discreet diplomatic channels. Now they would assume the United States was trying to intensify international pressure on India not to test. (The Opposition party at the time, the Bharatiya Janata Party [BJP] accused the United States of precisely that, dismissing the *New York Times* story as an American 'ploy'.)

Still, the leak was not all bad. It contained enough doubt about Indian motives – were they preparing for a nuclear test or simply running some experiments? – to offer the Indians a face-saving way to call off the test. It had also taken the element of surprise away from the Indians, and increased the price they would have to pay if they did test. With the news public, any test by the Indians now would look that much more defiant, leading to even greater international condemnation than would have been the case with a surprise test.

With the news of India's test preparations public, there was no time to lose. Fresh off the plane, Wisner immediately arranged a meeting with Amar Nath Verma, principal secretary to Prime Minister P.V. Narasimha Rao. Verma's position undoubtedly made him one of the most powerful men in India. He was a bureaucrat, not a politician, but he wielded what one of India's leading news weeklies called 'awesome power', a power greater than many members of the Cabinet. He had been principal secretary since 1991, the year when Rao came into office. Verma controlled access to the prime minister, and was known to keep ministers waiting for days for an appointment with his boss.[5]

Seeing Verma was as good as seeing the PM himself – better, in fact. Verma was a true professional. Wisner knew he could be direct with him,

---

[5]Prabhu Chawla, 'The Importance of Being Brajesh Mishra', *India Today*, 2 April 2001. http://www.indiatoday.com/itoday/20010402/cover-brajesh.shtml

without Verma taking offence, and that the message would reach the top within minutes.

As Wisner's car pulled up to South Block, he was prepared to do whatever it took to achieve his objective. He clutched the folder of photographs. He had had a lot of tough meetings in his career, and this would be one of the tougher ones. But it had to be done: The Indians could not be allowed to conduct a nuclear test.

One of Verma's assistants was waiting for Wisner as his car pulled up. He whisked the ambassador through the corridors of South Block and into Verma's office. Verma was sitting at his large desk, surrounded by stacks of paper – and typically of Indian government officials in those days – several vintage, fixed line telephones of different shapes and colours.

Verma greeted him warmly, and the obligatory tea and biscuits were served. Wisner got right to the point. He slid one of the CIA's Pokhran satellite pictures out of the folder and onto the table in front of Verma. Verma had a brief glance at the photo before Wisner slid it back into the folder.

Verma, who had seen a lot in his long career, kept a steady face. He had known from the *New York Times* story that the United States had satellite imagery of Pokhran, and no doubt guessed why Wisner wanted to see him. Yet, despite his outward calm, the episode must have astounded him: Here was an American who had strode into his office, and produced an eight-by-ten inch glossy photo of the most sensitive activities at India's most sensitive military site.

Wisner went on to say that the test was a bad idea, and would hurt India's overall interests. He mentioned specifically the sanctions that the United States would, under law, be obliged to impose on India if it chose to test. The message was clear: The United States would come down hard on India if it went ahead. Verma listened intently, showing he absorbed the message, but offered no reaction.

It was a brief meeting. Wisner shook Verma's hand, and was again led by Verma's assistant through the corridors of South Block. Soon he was in his car headed back to the United States Embassy.

Wisner was confident he had got his point across. But would it be enough to stop the Indians? He decided his government could not take any chances: President Bill Clinton would have to call Prime Minister Rao personally to make the case against a nuclear weapon test.

Secretary of State Warren Christopher agreed with Wisner's recommendation, and the request for the call went to the Oval Office. The president also concurred. However, when Clinton did place the call, he did not get the assurance he had been hoping for from Rao. Rao merely responded to Clinton's appeal in opaque Indian fashion by saying that India would not act irresponsibly.[6]

In a few days it became clear that Wisner and Clinton had in fact been successful. American satellites saw activity levels at Pokhran return to normal; India had called off the test, and official Washington breathed a sigh of relief.

The prospect of American sanctions was part of the reason Rao had decided not to test.[7] After Wisner's visit and Clinton's call, Rao had summoned his economic advisors to forecast the economic repercussions of a test. They told him that the Indian economy would suffer, and in particular that inflation was likely to rise. Fear of inflation, and its effect on India's poor, was a main factor in Rao's calculation. He felt that the Indian economy needed to be stronger to withstand the inevitable fallout from a test.

India's entry onto the world stage would have to wait.

The scuttled test was a painful episode for India's political leadership. India was a proud nation, and it considered itself a responsible actor in world affairs. It had had nuclear technology for decades, and neither used it to menace others nor sold it for profit. India had shown restraint despite having two potentially dangerous neighbours – one a declared nuclear power and the other a putative nuclear power, both of whom had committed armed aggressions against India.

---

[6]Talbott, 37.

[7]There were likely additional factors in Rao's decision not to test, apart from the threat of sanctions. Rao may have wanted to preserve a strategic ambiguity that India's pre-Pokhran nuclear status carried. Or, perhaps, with general elections scheduled to begin in five months (April 1996), Rao decided that a decision to test towards the end of his five-year term was not prudent.

Yet India's attempt to safeguard its security by developing a credible nuclear deterrent was met with patronising scorn by the outside world, especially the United States. The gap between how India saw itself and how the world saw it – the gap between its ambitions and the reality of global power – was as frustratingly wide as ever.

But India had learned its lesson. Two-and-a-half years later, in 1998, when India was once again ready to test, it made its preparations while the American eye in the sky was not watching. Next time, India would not be surprised by press reports and satellite photos. Next time, it would be the world's turn to be surprised.

PART ONE

Decline, Fall and Rebirth

A Nazi and a non-Nazi version of the present war would have no resemblance to one another, and which of them finally gets into the history books will be decided not by evidential methods but on the battlefield.... History is written by the winners.

— GEORGE ORWELL, *As I Please*, 4 February 1944

1

RICHES TO RAGS

India's Image Problem

A human being lives about seventy-five years on average in developed economies. His impressions are necessarily formed based on what he has learned and observed himself during his lifetime.

For India, today, the limited human frame of reference presents a problem. Its image in the world is based on what human beings have learned and observed about it during their lifetimes: that India is poor in comparison to the wealth of Europe and the United States.

This image, of course, is partially accurate: Poverty is an enormous problem in India, as 400 million of its citizens live on less than $1.25 a day.[1] With a per capita GDP of $1,200, it is still far behind the United States ($46,000) and the United Kingdom ($35,000).[2] At the same time, the image of India as a poor country is misleading, for three reasons.

First, India is rapidly becoming wealthier. The Indian economy has grown at an annual average above seven percent over the past decade.[3] At present rates, India will surpass the United Kingdom as the fifth largest economy in the world by 2020.[4] By 2030, it will overtake Germany and Japan to become the world's third largest economy behind the United States and China.[5]

Second, India is already much wealthier than it appears. It is inaccurate to compare India's GDP per capita to that of developed economies on a like-for-like basis; an Indian's quality of life is determined by the goods and services he can procure locally, and these are much cheaper in India than in developed economies. It is more appropriate to compare India's GDP with other nations' in purchasing power parity terms; by that measure the per capita wealth advantage of the United States over India shrinks from a factor of 38 to a factor of 14.[6]

Third, and most importantly, India was not always poor relative to the West. Four centuries ago India was a 'developed' nation and England was a 'developing' nation. Seventeenth century India had wealth, and the power that comes with it. Moreover, at that time India had been rich and powerful for most of human history. Most Westerners today, however, are not aware of India's history of wealth and power. That is because the winners write history.

Agra and London in 1605

By the time of his death in 1605, Akbar, the greatest of the Mughal emperors, had ruled for nearly fifty years. He had taken the throne as a boy of thirteen. By the end of his life, he could look back with satisfaction on what he had achieved. Under him, the Mughal Empire became one of the most powerful in the world. Its territory stretched from Kabul and Baluchistan in the west to present day Bangladesh in the east; and from the foothills of the Himalayas in the north to parts of Maharashtra and Orissa in the south.[7]

Mughal per capita GDP under Akbar was a bit over half of England's at the time.[8] The ruling Mughal class, however, enjoyed an even higher standard of living than European aristocracy, thanks to the Mughals' exploitation of the lower classes. Given the relative size of the Mughal Empire (twenty-five times the population of contemporary England),[9] the scale of wealth that accrued to Akbar, his court and to Mughal nobility was far beyond anything a British monarch could command.

Captain William Hawkins was the first Englishman to visit the Mughal court, and stayed in Agra from 1608-11. What he saw amazed him. Hawkins estimated the annual income of the Mughal Emperor Jehangir (Akbar's son and successor) to be fifty million sterling.[10] This compared to one million sterling income for the English and Scottish crowns at the time, and about five million sterling for France's Court of Louis the XIV.[11]

The Mughals' wealth produced massive military power. According to Hawkins, the Mughal emperor could, through his nobles, summon 300,000 horsemen within a week. Italian traveller Gemelli Careri (1651-1725), who visited India during his round-the-world voyage (1693-99), described the Mughal court as 'a moving city containing five million souls and abounding not only in provisions but in all things that could be desired'.[12] Careri estimated the ready military strength of the Mughals at one million foot soldiers and sixty thousand horses. Baggage was carried by fifty thousand camels and three thousand elephants.

The wealth that funded Mughal might derived, in turn, from a highly sophisticated imperial administration under which commerce flourished, enabling the empire to raise substantial tax revenue. Akbar was the head of the governing structure and had absolute law-making powers. The empire was divided into fifteen provinces called subas. Each suba was further sub-divided into administrative sub-units. Local officials were entrusted with maintaining law and order, as well as tax collection.[13]

The system of imperial administration was but one of Akbar's many achievements. He also set new standards in religious tolerance, abolishing a special tax on Hindus (for not following Islam) that his predecessors had imposed. Under Akbar, the Mughal Empire saw stability, expansion and a flourishing of art and culture.

By 1605, Akbar had created an empire as powerful as any on earth, and he would have known so from his contacts with other courts. He formed ties with Portuguese merchants in Goa[14] and sent emissaries to the Ottoman Empire.[15] He certainly was aware of the great states of Europe, and had he lived a few years longer would have met Captain William Hawkins himself.

Akbar would hardly have seen England as a threat to the Mughal kingdom or even a credible rival to it in size or power. For England was only a sliver of India's size and wealth at the time of Akbar's reign. Mughal India encompassed 135 million people, about one quarter of the world's population, and nearly a quarter of its wealth. At the start of the seventeenth century, Mughal India was more comparable to Western Europe in size and wealth than to England or any individual European state.

Indeed, Akbar would have found London in 1605 little more than a bustling commercial city – one of many in Europe – and certainly not the future seat of a great empire that would rule the descendants of his people.

Two years before Akbar's death, England had lost its own great monarch, Queen Elizabeth I (1533-1603). Like Akbar, Elizabeth reigned for nearly half a century. Yet the empire she presided over was nowhere near as mighty as the Mughal empire. Her kingdom was one of many in Europe, and certainly not the most powerful. Throughout much of her reign she considered (but never accepted) various marriage proposals from other European monarchs, alliances that would have given the English Crown much needed strength. England only narrowly avoided invasion by Spain in 1588, when Queen Elizabeth's naval forces defeated the Spanish Armada. During her reign, England was constantly struggling to keep rival states at bay.

London in 1605 was a city of 200,000 people,[16] about the size of Agra under Akbar.[17] By then, London was in the middle of a population explosion that would make it, by 1680, a city of half a million people. But at the beginning of the century, London was still on a par with cities such as Naples and Antwerp, and not yet a major European capital.[18]

Knowing what England was to become, it is tempting to look back at the London of 1605 as a great city in-the-making. In the early years of the seventeenth century, William Shakespeare (1564-1616) was at the height of his creative powers. Inside London's Globe Theatre, plays that have become part of the canon of western culture were being performed: *King Lear* in 1605 and *Macbeth* in 1606.

Yet Shakespeare's audience was confronted with a different world on exiting the Globe. London at the time showed no signs of becoming the greatest city in the world. It was an unhealthy place, racked by outbreaks of tuberculosis, typhus, smallpox, scurvy, measles, and, above all, the plague. In 1603, London suffered a severe plague, which may have killed as many as twenty percent of the city's inhabitants.[19] This year was but one of nine years between 1563 and 1665 when plagues were bad enough to be considered epidemics.[20] London was so unhealthy to live in that, were it not for high levels of immigration, the population would have declined throughout the sixteenth and seventeenth centuries.[21] Seventeenth century Londoners never starved *en masse*, but food shortages were severe enough during some years to cause widespread malnutrition, making the city even more susceptible to outbreaks of disease.[22]

Crime rates were another cause of grave concern. London, an observer wrote in 1587, attracts 'all men whose maisters have cast them offe for somme offence...lustie rogues and common beggars'.[23] One London reform house recorded a steep rise in the number of offenders it dealt with each year.[24]

By the standards of Akbar's Agra, Elizabethan London was a poorly organised urban mess. To be sure, for the underclass in both places, life was pure misery. Yet Akbar achieved a level of organisation – expressed through efficient imperial administration – that Elizabeth (and her immediate successors) did not. Nor did seventeenth century English monarchs approach their Mughal contemporaries' achievements in tax collection, military conquests or religious harmony.

The Mughals have a better record of having upheld liberal values than contemporary European nations. Akbar believed in religious freedom, and created an environment of religious tolerance in his realm. Akbar kept non-Muslim thinkers and artists in his court, and also appointed a former Hindu king, Raja Man Singh (whom Akbar had defeated in battle), as commander of the Mughal army.[25] In 1592, he issued a firman, an imperial order, that 'no man should be interfered with on account of religion, and anyone is to be allowed to go over to a religion that pleases him'.[26] This stands in contrast to the see-saw battles between Protestants and Catholics that consumed the British monarchy during much of the sixteenth century. Henry VIII broke the Church of England away from Rome; his daughter, Mary I, restored Catholicism during her reign and persecuted Protestants; and her half-sister, Elizabeth I, re-established the independence of the Church of England.

Mercy/No Mercy: Conspirators Bairam Khan and Guy Fawkes

A few weeks after Akbar died in Agra, Elizabeth's successor, King James I, narrowly avoided a plot to assassinate him by blowing up the Houses of Parliament. The conspirators (led by Guy Fawkes) were discovered and found guilty of treason. The death sentence was explicit in the punishment it ordered: Each condemned man was to be drawn and quartered; his 'privy parts' were to be hacked off and burnt before him; his bowels and heart were to be cut out; his head 'which had imagined the mischief' was to be cut off; then the various pieces of each man were to be exposed in the public to become 'prey for the fowls of the air'.[27]

Akbar had his own insurrections to deal with, but handled the rebels with a good deal more mercy. In 1560, Akbar dismissed his army commander Bairam Khan after a dispute, and ordered him to make a pilgrimage to Mecca. Khan complied, and left Agra. Along the way Khan decided to raise an army against Akbar, but was defeated. Akbar brought Khan back to Agra, forgave him, and gave him the choice of remaining in the emperor's court or resuming his pilgrimage. Khan headed back to Mecca, no doubt grateful for his reprieve.[28]

From the vantage point of today, it is all too easy to look back in history and assume that 'the West' was consistently more advanced, wealthier, more powerful and more tolerant than 'the East'. Evidence suggests otherwise. While random traveller accounts and single incidents cannot characterise an entire empire or society, they nonetheless demonstrate that the Agra of 1605 bears a closer resemblance to present day 'Western' society than does London of 1605. Just four centuries ago, England was 'backwards' and India was 'advanced' by today's standards.

Akbar would have had a hard time believing that these labels were to be reversed in coming centuries. To him India's position of relative wealth and power in 1605 was not a new thing: it was the continuation of the norm that had prevailed for much of the last two millennia.

All the Riches of India

As the discipline of economics is a relatively recent invention – dating, some argue, to Adam Smith's *Wealth of Nations* (1776) – students of economic history have had to rely on writers from other fields to form a picture of past economies. Fortunately, as long as mankind has been writing things down, it has been concerned with goods, trading and wealth.

Although ample evidence is available to economic historians, it tends to be scattered across a wide range of primary (and secondary) sources. Marshalling the required evidence to draw firm conclusions about economic activities in the past requires the ingenuity and persistence of a detective. Even so, frequently the data are sufficient to evince only broad economic trends, rather than a detailed picture of past economies.

When studying comparative economic history, it is that much harder for the economic historian to justify relative conclusions about one region (or time) versus another. The late British economic historian Angus Maddison (1926-2010) painstakingly constructed a picture of world economic growth, by region and by nation, all the way back to AD 1. Thanks to his work, the economic historian does not have to piece together disparate bits of evidence to draw conclusions about where wealth lay in the world and when; Maddison has already done that. The result is a comprehensive picture of the contours of the world's economy for the last two millennia.

Before the Second World War (1939-45) only ten countries kept systematic estimates of national incomes, and these national incomes were measured on different bases, making comparative use of the data impossible.[29] Maddison relies instead on population figures (for which there is some evidence) and on per capita income (which he estimates based on demographic changes) to compute national income figures. The demographic changes he uses to estimate per capita income include increases in life expectancy, changes in average age, labour force changes and, above all, the urbanisation ratio. Maddison considers a growing urbanisation ratio to be a key determinant of higher per capita income, as increasing urbanisation means that an economy is generating an agricultural surplus and that more people are employed in non-agricultural (and, he presumes, higher income) activities.[30] In extending his study back to the year AD 1, Maddison admits that for periods before 1820 the data is weaker and therefore, conjecture plays a larger role in his estimates.[31]

Maddison's methodology leaves him open to charges of using guesswork or circular reasoning (as urbanisation leads to greater wealth, and yet greater urbanisation). Certainly no one could claim that Maddison's work has replaced missing historical statistics with accuracy. Nonetheless, his numbers for national income are a useful basis for broad conclusions about the relative wealth of nations throughout history. For India,[32] the insights offered by Maddison's work may be general, but they are also illuminating.

India's recent centuries of poverty are an exception in its history of wealth. For most of the past two millennia, India accounted for one quarter or more of world GDP. It was the single largest contributor to world GDP until around 1500, when it relinquished that position to China (which in turn gave it up to the United States by the early twentieth century).[33]

India's share of world GDP, which was close to thirty percent for much of the first millennium, began a long term decline thereafter. The drop was interrupted only by a small recovery during the Mughal era, when efficient administration helped India to outgrow the West and thereby regain, ever so briefly, a greater share of the world's wealth.

The nineteenth century Industrial Revolution in Europe and the United States brought no such riches to India. India's share of global wealth dropped especially sharply during the peak years of the Industrial Revolution, beginning in 1820, and fell to under five percent by the twentieth century. The decline moderated somewhat in the years after Indian independence, as the West's rapid growth due to the Industrial Revolution slowed down.

Finally, after nearly two millennia of decline, there was an uptick in India's fortunes in the beginning of the late twentieth century. Its share of global wealth has continued to grow since then. The period from 2001-10 showed an even steeper increase than the 1990s, given the relative economic growth of India versus the United States and Europe in the past decade. India has finally begun to inch its way back to prominence in the global economy.

Looking at India's per capita income over time, compared to that of the United Kingdom and the United States, it is clear just how far behind India has fallen. All three nations were close to each other in terms of income through the first half of the second millennium. Around 1500, the United Kingdom began its upward climb, which became ever steeper after 1820. The United States was a bit slower than the United Kingdom to stimulate growth, but it did so with vigour beginning in the late 1800s, overtaking the United Kingdom and never looking back.

India's trend line, by contrast, is nearly flat until the late twentieth century, when a modest but noticeable growth emerges. If the United Kingdom's and United States' historical experience is any indication, India could well be at the early stages of a dramatic and sustained rise in national income levels; India will need precisely that to make up the ground lost over recent centuries.

The Winners Write History

How the winners see history has shaped the world's perceptions of India's past, present and future. The winners in recent history are easy to identify: Western Europe and its offshoots, principally the United States. For the past 500 years the Western powers have had a stunning run of success. They developed the science to discover the new world, and then colonised that world with overwhelming force. Having taken control of global commerce, they went on to cement their advantage with the industrial revolution, allowing them to achieve a concentration of wealth and power unprecedented in the history of mankind.

Europe represents less than seven percent of the world's landmass. Yet this small corner of the earth, first by its own hand and later through its American offshoot, has been able to dominate global economic activity for centuries.

Individual European states have risen and fallen in supremacy over this period. Spain and Portugal, once great powers, faded over time, to be replaced by the Netherlands, France and Britain. Gradually, all these European powers were eclipsed by the United States. Yet, whichever particular state held sway at the time, the last half millennium has belonged to what has come to be known as 'the West'. As a winner, the West could write its own history, and the history of the world. In fact, under the pen of Western writers the history of the world became largely synonymous with Western history.

The West's Historical Narrative

Over the course of the centuries, Western thinkers have collectively composed a historical narrative to tell the story of the West in simple, yet dramatic terms. It goes something like this:

Civilisation for mankind began in Ancient Greece, followed by Ancient Rome. For the better part of a millennium, Greece and Rome made great contributions to science, philosophy, art and literature. Along the way they invented, and perfected, self-government.

In the middle of all of this came Jesus Christ. (He was from the East, but the West took him as its own.) His teachings were the source of a powerful new Western 'super-state', the Church. His life became the focal point of Western culture, and his birth year the basis for its dating system.

Suddenly disaster struck: 'Barbarians' from the North (the Huns) and the East (the Muslims) destroyed what Greece and Rome had built. There followed a period of decline and the 'Dark Ages'. The light nearly went out on Western civilisation.

Then, a glorious rebirth. In the Renaissance, Europeans rediscovered learning and culture, inspired by their ancient Greek and Roman forebears. The superiority of Western society was again evident, as its scientists explained the ways of the universe and its explorers took to the high seas. The result was the West's inevitable, and much-deserved, half millennium of global domination.

Largely absent from this narrative of course, are other (non-Western) states and actors. In the generalised Western view, much of the world was a blank slate when the Europeans arrived: Africa, Australasia and the Americas. The Europeans understood Asia to have had civilisations of long standing such as China and India, but the products of these civilisations – be they artistic, administrative or scientific – get little more than a polite nod from Western thinkers and historians, even today.

In the case of India, the winner's view of its history is exemplified by James Mill's *The History of British India*, published in 1817.[34] Mill spent twelve years on the three-volume work, and his diligence was rewarded with a lucrative appointment to the British East India Company.

Mill's extensive research, however, did not include a visit to India. That Mill could write his book, and that his work could be taken seriously by both British scholars and the British public, without his ever having set foot in India demonstrates how little regard nineteenth century United Kingdom had for Indian society, culture and history.

Mill must have sensed his audience's hunger for negative judgments about India, and he did not disappoint. His general criticism of India ('[it has] in reality made but a few of the earliest steps in the progress to civilisation') is supplemented with specific dismissals of Indian achievements in math and the sciences. He gives no credence to the claim that Indian mathematicians invented the decimal system, and mocks the notion that Indian astronomers (including Aryabhata and Brahmagupta) once postulated the existence of gravity and a rotating earth. Of course, Mill would see no reason to believe that such ideas could have originated in India, as he had roundly dismissed native (Indian) scholars as having 'a general disposition to deceit and perfidy'.

Mill's work was a big commercial success in the United Kingdom, and also had a strong influence on British imperial policy towards India: In the case of United Kingdom and India, the winners were not only writing history, but also dictating the course of future events.

Many Indians themselves imbibed colonial biases. As subjects of the British Crown, Indians came to lack self-confidence and, as a people, looked for a way to distinguish themselves in areas where their colonial masters were not strong. Spirituality and religion became India's niche, but at the expense of neglect (by Indians and Britons alike) of India's real achievements in areas such as math, science and reasoning.[35] The British view of India could allow distinction in matters of the spirit, but not in the hard sciences, where contributions remained the exclusive province of the United Kingdom and Europe.

The British narrative of India – materially poor, yet spiritually rich – was to be the dominant image of the nation for the next two centuries. India's flat economic growth curve reinforced this image, and the world's view of India as a poor nation took on a permanence.

Even after the non-violent struggle for Independence won India the respect of the world, its growth curve remained flat and the prevailing narrative remained in place.

It was only in the 1990s that India's growth began to accelerate and the West began to take notice of it as a rising economic and political power. But before India could rise again it had to hit rock bottom. That happened in 1991, when a confluence of two crises forced India to change itself.

Conscious of the friendship between our two countries stretching over two millennia and more, and recognizing the importance of nurturing this traditional friendship, it is imperative that both Sri Lanka and India reaffirm the decision not to allow our respective territories to be used for activities prejudicial to each other's unity, territorial integrity and security.

– Letter from Rajiv Gandhi, prime minister of India, to J.R. Jayawardene, president of Sri Lanka, 29 July 1987

As we enter the last decade of the twentieth century, India stands at the (sic) cross-roads. The decisions we take and do not take, at this juncture, will determine the shape of things to come for quite some time.

– Manmohan Singh, as finance minister, in his Budget Speech, 24 July 1991

2

1991: ANNUS HORRIBILIS

Independent India's Slow Crawl

By the time of India's independence in 1947, its former wealth and power had become a lost artefact of history. In 1950, India's share of global wealth was just over four percent, having dropped from sixteen percent in 1820.[1]

Meanwhile, the West, thanks to the Industrial Revolution, had sprinted ahead, with the United States alone accounting for over one quarter of the world's wealth by 1950.[2]

The erosion of India's relative wealth continued after Independence. The United States and Europe were experiencing post-Second World War economic booms, while India's rapidly expanding population meant its growth rates were sufficient only barely to nudge up average income levels. The rich became richer and the poor only a bit less poor.

In the first four decades of its independence, India had its crises: wars with China and Pakistan, the 1975-77 state of emergency, and the communal violence that followed Indira Gandhi's assassination in 1984. Things, however, never got bad enough, either economically or politically, to force India to adopt radically new economic policies.

That is, until 1991. By mid-year, a former Indian prime minister was dead, the victim of a suicide bomber; and India's economy was on the verge of default, the victim of external shocks and years of mismanagement.

Clouds on the Horizon

The year 1991 began much like many other years in India, with political and economic uncertainty. Two months before, Chandra Shekhar – the leader of a small breakaway faction of the Janata Party – had taken office as prime minister, with the support of the powerful Congress party, led by Rajiv Gandhi. Despite this support, Chandra Shekhar was no friend of the Gandhi family. He had been a vocal critic of Indira Gandhi from the Congress back benches in the early 1970s, and one of the few members of the Congress to be imprisoned when she imposed a state of emergency in 1975.

As the year 1991 began, it was unclear how long Congress's support of Chandra Shekhar would last, as Rajiv Gandhi was clearly biding his time for a return to power as prime minister. Most observers anticipated that there would be fresh elections sometime during the year. On new year's day, a front-page headline from *The Hindu* asked: 'India enters an election year?'[3]

Even with political uncertainty, which was not particularly concerning to most Indians, there were no indications that 1991 would be an unusual year. A new year's day editorial in the *Indian Express* noted that few will mourn the passing of the 'ghastly year' 1990. Little did that paper's editors know that 1991 was to be far more ghastly.

India, of course, was not problem-free as 1991 began. Communal tensions were high in the Punjab, and the previous year had seen fresh violence in Kashmir. But there were no major national security clouds on the horizon. In fact, less than a year before, in March 1990, India had removed the last of its troops from Sri Lanka, thereby disbanding the Indian Peace Keeping Force (IPKF). Over one thousand Indian troops had been killed during the IPKF's deployment, and the departure of the IPKF from the island was greeted with relief by many Indians. With the IPKF troops back home, Indians could have reasonably assumed that the conflict in Sri Lanka was not to consume any more Indian lives.

Indian policy makers viewed their nation's own economic situation with much greater concern than they viewed the civil war across the Palk Strait. Economic trouble had been brewing for years, and the problems were beginning to be felt. On new year's day 1991, *The Hindu* noted, in an article entitled 'Economy puts up mixed performance', the 'critical situation in terms of foreign exchange reserves'.[4] Four months later, however, an editorial predicted confidently that 'the crucial phase of the [balance of payments] crisis has in any case been overcome'.[5]

That prediction was premature. By May, India's financial troubles were more acute than ever.

Economic Shocks

Throughout most of the 1980s, India was putting up respectable GDP growth numbers in the range of three to five percent per annum.[6] Growth hit 9.6 percent in 1988, followed by figures above five percent in both 1989 and 1990.[7] This growth, however, was not strong enough to avert a major economic crisis when a global recession struck in 1991.

The seeds for a 1991 balance of payments crisis in India were sown years before. As the International Monetary Fund (IMF) points out in its study of the causes of India's 1991 economic crisis,[8] India's current account deficit widened in the second half of the 1980s. The country financed these deficits through sharply increased overseas borrowings, as external debt nearly doubled to $69 billion between 1984/85 and 1990/91. Worse for India, short term foreign debt grew sharply to $6 billion. The growing current account deficit and increased reliance on overseas borrowing, particularly short-term financing, left India susceptible to shocks as it entered the 1990s.

Those shocks came quickly. The 1990-91 Gulf War had the twin effects of increasing India's import bill dramatically (higher oil prices drove oil imports from $2 billion to $5.7 billion in 1990-91) and decreasing India's remittance earnings from workers in the Gulf (who returned home in the run up to the war). In addition, a weakening global economy in the late 1980s had decreased India's export earnings, particularly from the United States, its biggest export market. By 1990-91, India's export growth had slowed to four percent.

The cumulative effect of these shocks was nearly fatal to India's ability to pay its bills. By late 1990, India had to cope with steep oil import costs and high interest payments on overseas debt. An unstable union government, led by Prime Minister V.P. Singh with support from the outside by the BJP, added to the country's woes. A long-time senior figure in the Congress, in the mid 1980s V.P. Singh had served as both finance and defence minister in Rajiv Gandhi's Cabinet. After Rajiv Gandhi removed him from his post as defence minister in 1987, V.P. Singh helped cobble together a group of smaller parties, the National Front, to defeat Rajiv Gandhi's Congress in the 1989 elections, and emerged as prime minister of the new government.

V.P. Singh's term as prime minister, however, was to be a short one. In October 1990, the BJP withdrew its support, after the arrest of its then-leader L.K. Advani as he led a procession of Hindu nationalists headed for the Babri Masjid in the town of Ayodhya in the state of Uttar Pradesh. (Advani had been agitating for the construction of a Hindu temple on the site, considered sacred by Hindus.[9]) The collapse of the V.P. Singh government, not even a year into its term, shook investor confidence. As 1991 began, India was nearly broke, and borrowing was getting harder.

Indians were well aware that the economic outlook for the country was grim. They were also accustomed to the political uncertainty that ushered in the new year. They could not have expected, however, that in a matter of months, the economic crisis and an unforeseen political crisis would together bring the nation to the brink of disaster.

Twin Crises Brewing

The twin crises that were to plague India in 1991 unfolded in opposite corners of the country. In Delhi, economic policy makers worked to diffuse a BoP time bomb that threatened to be fatal for the Indian economy. In Chennai (formerly Madras), 2000 kilometres to the south of Delhi, a group of assassins was working on a bomb of their own, designed to kill a former Indian prime minister.[10]

The two operations were conducted over a period of months, one meant to save India, the other to destroy it. One group was motivated by love for their country, and a desire for economic stability. The other group was motivated by hatred for their enemy, and a thirst for revenge.

For years, Indian economic officials had known a balance of payment crisis was possible, and worked hard to avoid such an outcome. Discussions with the IMF for assistance to plug the BoP gap took place as early as September 1989.[11] In July 1990, India had begun to draw from its IMF reserve tranche, and took out a total of $660 million over the next three months.[12] By the end of the year, India had an agreement with the IMF on an emergency funding (Compensatory and Contingency Financing Facility, or CCFF) of $1.8 billion, and a standby arrangement on top of that.[13]

Deep in the jungles of northern Sri Lanka, Vellupilai Prabhakaran had his own worries. The leader of the Liberation Tigers of Tamil Eelam (LTTE) had been fighting for an independent state for Sri Lanka's minority Tamil people since 1983. Prabhakaran had just been through the most difficult period of his armed struggle: the presence of the IPKF in Sri Lanka. He was confident of defeating the Sri Lankan army in a one-on-one battle, but the Indians were another matter. The LTTE leader had been relieved to see the IPKF leave the island in disgrace, and would stop at nothing to ensure that the IPKF stayed out.

The fall of the government of V.P. Singh in India in November 1990 forced Prabhakaran to acknowledge the possibility of his worst fear coming true: the return of Rajiv Gandhi to power. Prabhakaran knew that Rajiv Gandhi would certainly crack down on LTTE sympathisers in Tamil Nadu, and worried that he might also send the IPKF back to Sri Lanka. A return of the IPKF almost certainly would mean an end to Prabhakaran's dream of an independent Tamil nation. It was a chance he was not prepared to take; he resolved to prevent Rajiv Gandhi's return to power by any means necessary.

By early December, Prabhakaran had decided to assassinate Rajiv Gandhi. He knew Rajiv Gandhi would be a more difficult target if he became prime minister. The best time to do it, Prabhakaran reasoned, would be during elections, ideally during a campaign swing through Tamil Nadu. As a candidate, he would still have protection, but far less than that of a prime minister. Furthermore, the 'man of the people' image Rajiv Gandhi had crafted would require him to mix with the electorate. Yes, Prabhakaran figured, it would be possible to put an assassin within striking distance of Rajiv Gandhi.

But there was no time to waste; Indian elections were around the corner, and Prabhakaran knew he had to put his plan in motion immediately. He assembled a team of four trusted senior LTTE operatives to lead the operation, and briefed them in the Wanni, a densely forested area of northern Sri Lanka where the LTTE was holed up. By January 1991, two of the operation's leaders were in Chennai, putting together a team to provide logistical support in the run up to the planned assassination.

The Reckoning Nears

Meanwhile, in Delhi, the early months of 1991 saw government officials working hard to bridge India's yawning foreign exchange gap. With war all but certain to come to the Persian Gulf, they knew that India's oil import bills were not going to get any smaller. The only solution was to arrange new loans before India's coffers were completely empty. Yet India's credit rating had been downgraded in October 1990, raising the cost of borrowing.[14] With the country's political situation uncertain, commercial loans were becoming harder to come by, even at high rates.

India got loans from Japan ($300 million) and Germany ($60 million).[15] It was not enough to last for long, and India's BoP situation was worsening by the day. By March 1991, when it was time for the annual budget, there was no denying the predicament India was in. Yashwant Sinha, finance minister in the caretaker government, described in his budget speech a BoP situation that had reached 'crisis proportions'.[16] India's finance officials, feverishly trying to avoid a default, developed a ten-point strategy for keeping the country solvent, including accelerating receipts from the multilateral aid agencies such as the World Bank and Asian Development Bank (ADB).[17] The Reserve Bank of India (RBI) also kept a close watch on all foreign exchange transactions, to avoid any large transfers depleting what little reserves remained.[18] This measure was necessary, because India at the time was using BoP data that was three years out of date.[19] The government did not have a clear picture of the nation's true BoP; they only knew it was dire, and that cash could run out at any time.

While Delhi's policymakers were making up economic policy as they went, the LTTE was conducting what was proving itself to be a methodical and well-planned operation. They had selected both the assassin, Dhanu, and the backup, Shubha. Both were members of the LTTE's female Tigers. The LTTE had chosen its lead assassin well. Armed resistance was in Dhanu's blood: Long before the LTTE existed, her father A. Rajaratnam had been part of a 1960s militant group called the Tigers Army, organised to oppose the Sinhalese government in Colombo.[20]

At the time of their selection, Dhanu and Shubha had never been out of the Wanni, much less Sri Lanka. By March 1991, they were in Chennai, where the local team was already assembled. Prabhakaran had appointed one of his key lieutenants, Sivarasan, as leader of the operation. The key support person in Chennai was S. Nalini, a company secretary whom the LTTE had recruited when it set her brother up with a printing press to disseminate anti-IPKF material in Tamil Nadu.

The assassination team was a five-member squad: Sivarasan, Nalini, Dhanu, Shubha, and Haribabu, a photographer. Nalini was to house Dhanu and Shubha at her apartment close to the Chennai High Court and wait for instructions from Sivarasan.

Prabhakaran had ordered the team to conduct dry runs so that when the time came, the assassination itself would go off smoothly. By April, Sivarasan began to look for opportunities for the team to go to an election rally, learn the security measures and see what would be required to get close to a politician. The first opportunity presented itself on 18 April, when Rajiv Gandhi made a public appearance at Chennai's Marina Beach.[21] The assassin team attended the event but failed to get close to Rajiv Gandhi. The next dry run took place on 8 May at an election rally for V.P. Singh; this time Dhanu was able to bend to touch V.P. Singh's feet, as she would, thirteen days later, Rajiv Gandhi's.[22] It was valuable experience that gave the team the confidence to believe they could complete their mission.

While the would-be Rajiv Gandhi assassins were doing their dry runs in Chennai, Finance Minister Yashwant Sinha was travelling the world seeking accelerated aid. He led the Indian delegation to Washington in April for the spring World Bank-IMF meetings. Later, he went to Tokyo to ask the Japanese for the early release of aid. Sinha wrote that he was able to secure commitments for the early release of about $500 million each from Washington and Tokyo.[23] Whether this claim is valid or not, Sinha's efforts did not improve India's financing situation in the near term, as its exchange reserves continued to deplete throughout April and May.

In Chennai, the assassins found the opportunity they were looking for. On 19 May the newspapers carried an announcement of Rajiv Gandhi's election rally two days later that would take place in Sriperumbudur, about forty kilometres from Chennai.

There was only one problem. The day before, Dhanu had fallen down the stairs outside Nalini's apartment and twisted her ankle; now it had swollen up badly and Dhanu was limping. Sivarasan was worried: Would his human bomb be fit enough to detonate herself in front of Rajiv Gandhi in just two days' time? Dhanu assured him that she would be ready.[24] Sivarasan gave the go ahead: The assassination attempt would take place as planned on 21 May.

The next day Nalini, Dhanu and Shubha went to watch a movie in the evening. Dhanu had become a fan of Tamil cinema during her stay in Chennai, seeing on average of two or three films a week.[25] The LTTE spared no expense to keep her happy, buying her clothes and make-up as she desired, as well as her favourite food, chicken biryani.[26] Sivarasan had brought with him sufficient gold from Jaffna to cover the team's expenses.[27]

While the LTTE was spending some of its gold to keep its human bomb happy, India was preparing to mortgage some of its gold to avert a default. By May, it was election time, and Sinha spent much of the month campaigning in his constituency in Patna, the capital of the state of Bihar. He made regular visits to Delhi to tend to Finance Ministry business. During one visit, his staff told him that the government's foreign exchange reserves needed urgent replenishment, and there was only one option: mortgaging India's gold to secure immediate cash financing. Sinha agreed, and allowed the Finance Ministry to begin negotiating with foreign parties for a loan against the gold.[28]

Day of Horror...

On 21 May 1991, the five-member squad decided to take an early evening bus to Sriperumbudur, in order to be there well in advance of Rajiv Gandhi's scheduled arrival. Haribabu was sent ahead to buy a garland for Dhanu to present to Rajiv Gandhi. Late in the afternoon, he met with the rest of the squad at the main bus stop in Chennai.

The photographer Haribabu filled two roles. As Sivarasan was posing as a journalist, a companion with a camera was useful for the cover. He was also the squad's official photographer; Prabhakaran had requested pictures of the assassination.

The five rode the bus to Kancheepuram and got off after two hours at Sriperumbudur. They arrived at around 8:00 p.m., only to learn that Rajiv Gandhi's arrival was delayed. They had dinner at a local restaurant, bought some flowers and reached the venue by 9:45 p.m., about twenty-five minutes before Rajiv Gandhi's arrival. Dhanu positioned herself near the stage where Rajiv Gandhi was to speak. In her hands she had a garland and around her waist an explosive belt. The bomb, well concealed under her green salwar and mustard-coloured kameez, was packed with gelatine sticks, and full of metal pellets to make the explosion that much more deadly.

Rajiv Gandhi's motorcade arrived, and India's former prime minister made his way to the stage. Dhanu had no trouble getting close to him. She approached him with the garland, her finger ready on the detonator switch. Witnesses reported seeing her bend to touch Rajiv Gandhi's feet, and Gandhi bending to lift her up, just before the explosion. The time was 10:18 p.m.

In addition to Rajiv Gandhi, the assassin and several bystanders, Haribabu was also killed in the blast. His camera, though, survived intact, and the photographs he took of the assassins just before the blast later helped Indian investigators crack the case.

Late on the evening of 21 May, the Indian authorities intercepted a coded radio message sent from Chennai to Prabhakaran's base in Sri Lanka: 'the job is done'.

...And Day of Shame

Sinha spent the days prior to 21 May campaigning in Patna.[29] It was hot, with daytime temperatures reaching forty degrees Celsius.

Around the middle of the month, one day Sinha had returned to his office, exhausted from a series of election speeches, to find a senior official waiting for him with a file. Sinha knew it must be an urgent matter, as he had left instructions for only the most pressing Finance Ministry matters to be brought to him in Patna.

The file contained a proposal to sell twenty tonnes of Indian gold for about $400 million.[30] The only good news in the file was that the gold was not part of India's official reserves, but rather was on deposit with the State Bank of India (SBI). The bad news was that, despite the best efforts of India's negotiators, the buyer of the gold would not consent to it remaining in India; it would have to be sent to Europe, or there was no deal. Sinha signed the file and sent it on for Prime Minister Chandra Shekhar's approval.

On the evening of 21 May, a chartered plane left Mumbai (then Bombay), loaded with twenty tonnes of gold and the lost pride of a nation.[31] Word of the charter leaked to a reporter who arrived at the airport in time to take a few photographs of the plane.[32] When the story broke, it sparked national outrage. India had done what was a last resort for any Indian family, even one facing a severe financial crisis: It sold its gold to pay its bills.

The twenty-first of May turned out to have been only the beginning of the fire sale. Six months later the Indian public learned what really happened with the nation's gold. By then there was a new finance minister, Dr Manmohan Singh. On 22 November 1991, Manmohan Singh rose in Parliament to tell the story of India's gold shipments overseas. His tone was contrite:

> I had spelt out in detail that the previous Government, (sic) had taken a decision to send abroad 20 tonnes of gold out of Government stocks with an option to repurchase it at the end of six months. The actual export of this gold took place between 21st and 31st May, 1991. I had also mentioned that the previous Government had agreed with the decision of the Reserve Bank of India to send abroad up to 15 percent of its gold to be kept in safe custody with a Central Bank, with the intention to seek a short term loan against the pledge of gold. Because of the crisis situation on the Balance of Payments, our government endorsed this decision and RBI sent abroad the gold out of its reserves...between the 4th July, 1991 and 18th July, 1991. These two transactions put together enabled us to raise about $600 million an (sic) help tide over the serious liquidity problem we were facing.[33]

Note Manmohan Singh's careful use of language, bordering on the misleading, when describing the gold sales India made. India entered into two transactions. The first, in May, involved the sale of twenty tonnes of gold to Union Bank of Switzerland. When describing this transaction, Manmohan Singh avoids the usage of words like 'sell' or 'sale'; he finds the words 'send abroad' and 'export' more to his liking.

India's second transaction, in July, involved using forty-seven tonnes of its gold to secure a loan with a bank in the United Kingdom. This time

India decided, in Manmohan Singh's terminology, to 'send abroad...its gold to be kept in safe custody with a Central Bank, with the intention to seek a short term loan against the pledge of gold'. Manmohan Singh gives the impression that India decided to send the gold in order to facilitate its application for a loan. The reality was that India tried to secure the loan without moving the gold. The British bankers, however, insisted that India transport the actual gold to the Bank of England, just as the Swiss had insisted India send its gold to Switzerland. Neither party was ready to trust India to give up the gold voluntarily in case of a default on the loan payments.

The money raised from the sale and pledging of the gold did not last for long. Soon, India was drawing money from the multilateral agencies left and right. India withdrew $221 million from its IMF facility in July 1991, and a further $637 million in September.[34] In December 1991, the World Bank granted India a structural adjustment package of $500 million, followed by another $1.4 billion to support social safety nets and further liberalisation.[35]

Singh called the gold transactions a 'painful necessity'.[36] Whatever the terminology, the effect was the same: shame for the nation.

The Aftermath

The events of 21 May 1991 represented a low point in the history of modern India. In Chennai, a foreign terrorist group had assassinated a former Indian prime minister on Indian soil. In Mumbai, a plane full of Indian gold had flown to Europe to secure much-needed cash.

India, it would seem, had not achieved full independence after all: Europe still held the purse strings. At the same time, India was under attack from a rebel group holed up in the thick jungles of a small island nation off its coast, a nation India's armed forces had withdrawn from in defeat the year before. It is difficult to imagine two greater disgraces for a proud nation of nearly 900 million people.

Rajiv Gandhi's killing had several immediate consequences. An investigation into the assassination sparked a nationwide manhunt for those involved in the conspiracy. The three members of the hit squad who survived the blast – Sivarasan, Nalini and Shubha – were all brought to justice. Nalini was arrested in June 1991.[37] Sivarasan and Shubha killed themselves in a hideout in Bengaluru (then Bangalore) two months later, while under siege by the Indian police.[38]

A total of twenty-six people faced trial for playing a part in the assassination.[39] On 28 January 1998, they were convicted and sentenced to death. These sentences were later commuted to life in prison, after an appeal by Rajiv Gandhi's widow, Sonia.

Prabhakaran, Pottu Amman (chief of the LTTE's intelligence wing) and Akhila (deputy leader of the LTTE's women's intelligence wing)[40] were among those convicted for their roles in the killing. Since they were in Sri Lanka, and since Indian law does not allow trials *in absentia*, they were categorised by the court as 'absconding'.[41]

In subsequent years, India formally and repeatedly requested Sri Lanka to extradite Prabhakaran.[42] He nonetheless eluded capture and justice for nearly two decades after Rajiv Gandhi's assassination. Prabhakaran was finally killed in May 2009 by advancing Sri Lankan troops, under orders from President Mahinda Rajapakse to end the nation's quarter century civil war.

The LTTE inasmuch admitted its involvement in Rajiv Gandhi's killing in 2006, with then-spokesman Anton Balasingham calling it 'a monumental historical tragedy…which we deeply regret'.[43] In one respect at least the LTTE had good reason to regret the killing. Prabhakaran's strategy of eliminating Rajiv Gandhi backfired on the LTTE: After the killing, the terrorist group lost the support of the vast majority of Indian Tamils. Yet in a larger sense the strategy was successful, as eliminating Rajiv Gandhi prevented a return of the IPKF to Sri Lanka.

India took a much more activist approach to overcoming its other crisis of 1991. Thanks to the gold transactions and the subsequent funding tranches from the IMF, India was able to avert a full-blown financial crisis, but only by the narrowest of margins. By November 1991, Manmohan Singh was able to announce to Parliament that 'all the loans taken through pledging the RBI gold of forty-seven tonnes stand repaid and the gold now has become unencumbered'. In addition, he said that India had decided to exercise the repurchase option on the twenty tonnes of gold, and that the repurchase would be complete by 4 December 1991.[44]

Still, the damage was done. The gold transactions reinforced the image of poverty that had plagued the country for centuries, and added to it an impression of Third World-style economic mismanagement. The assassination of Rajiv Gandhi, following as it did that of his mother Indira Gandhi seven years before in 1984, also associated India with political violence and ethnic strife. Fair or unfair to India, the world could not dismiss the killing of a sitting prime minister and a former prime minister, a mother and her son, by ethnic minorities.

While the two crises of May 1991 were damaging to India's reputation, they also offered the country an opportunity to learn from its mistakes. As the intervening years have shown, India has learned from one crisis, but has not yet learned from the other.

On the Road to Wealth

Finance Minister Manmohan Singh delivered his budget speech on 24 July 1991, just three days after taking office.[45] His dedication of the budget to the memory of Rajiv Gandhi was more than Congress sentimentality, or a perfunctory homage to a fallen leader. In Manmohan Singh's view, Rajiv Gandhi's memory and the need for economic reform were inter-related.

Manmohan Singh praised Rajiv Gandhi's economic policies in the speech, particularly the late prime minister's commitment to rural development, technological advances, and stimulating growth through well-regulated financial markets. Manmohan Singh saw further economic reform as critical to upholding Rajiv Gandhi's 'dream of a strong, united, technologically sophisticated but humane India' ready for the twenty-first century.[46]

In addition, Manmohan Singh's invocation of Rajiv Gandhi in the budget speech was recognition of a political reality: The events of that year, both Gandhi's assassination and the economic crisis, as awful as they were, offered an opportunity for real change. Although the election did not give the new prime minister P.V. Narasimha Rao an outright majority in Parliament, Manmohan Singh knew his boss had a clear mandate from an electorate both mourning Rajiv Gandhi's death and frightened by the prospect of further economic deterioration. Manmohan Singh sensed that India had reached a watershed in its development, and he intended to make full use of that opportunity. 'We must act fast and act boldly,' he said. 'There is no time to lose.'[47]

Manmohan Singh indeed acted fast. That same day, the Ministry of Industry issued its Statement on Industrial Policy. It is a remarkable document. Viewed today from the perspective of the two decades of strong growth since 1991, it is an example of that rare occurrence in government: just the right policy at the right time.

The Statement began by paying deliberate homage to India's previous Industrial Policy Statements and Resolutions, including that of Jawaharlal Nehru in 1948. It billed its stated policy as 'continuity with change'.[48]

Fortunately for India, there was far more of the latter. In 6,000 words the Statement laid the foundation for a complete transformation of the Indian economy: dismantling of a suffocating system of business licenses (the so-called 'license Raj'), liberalisation of foreign investment, and reduction in state-owned enterprises. The new economic policy's goal was no less than 'to unshackle the Indian industrial economy from the cobwebs of unnecessary bureaucratic control'.[49]

Industrial policy was only one part of India's new approach to managing the economy, as Manmohan Singh's statement itself acknowledged: 'These measures complement the other series of measures being taken by Government in the areas of trade policy, exchange rate management, fiscal policy, financial sector reform and overall macro-economic management'.[50]

The Unsung Hero of India's Economic Reforms

Manmohan Singh deserves great credit for India's 1991 economic reforms, as he was their architect. With Singh's elevation fourteen years later to the office of prime minister – at a time when India was enjoying the economic growth that his earlier policies begot – his name became nearly synonymous with the 1991 reforms. But there is another hero of the summer of 1991: Manmohan Singh's boss at the time, Prime Minister P.V. Narasimha Rao.

Rao entered active politics after Independence in 1947, and was an elder statesman of the Congress party by the time the LTTE's suicide bomber cut down Rajiv Gandhi. He had been a Member of Parliament, chief minister of Andhra Pradesh, as well as Union Minister of External Affairs, Home Affairs and Defence.[51] When he took the leadership of Congress in June 1991, and – with his party's election victory weeks later – the post of prime minister, there was nothing in his background to indicate that he would have been especially attuned to the need for economic reform. Yet on assuming office he saw clearly that India's economy needed a radical break with the policies of the past, if the nation was to avert economic catastrophe.

Another prime minister might have argued for an incremental approach, but Rao gave Manmohan Singh the political cover to design, legislate and implement the far-reaching reforms that India so desperately needed. Manmohan Singh himself is quick to credit Rao with a key role in India's reforms, saying that 'without [Rao's] active support and help, I could do nothing'.[52] In addition, Rao and Manmohan Singh both benefitted from Rajiv Gandhi's 1991 Congress party election manifesto, which declared the need for economic reform, and made it possible for the new prime minister and new finance minister to take bold action without recrimination from those members of the Congress party resistant to change. Manmohan Singh has called the manifesto a 'legacy left to us by Rajiv Gandhi';[53] both Rao and Singh honoured that legacy with their vision and courage.

India's new policies worked, and the economic crisis of 1991 proved in time to be a lesson worth its weight in gold. By the end of the fiscal year 1991-92 the current account deficit had fallen to 0.7 percent of GDP (from 3.5 percent the previous year) and foreign exchange reserves had increased to $6 billion (from a low of $1 billion, or two weeks' worth of imports, in 1991).[54] India's economic crisis was intense, and serious, but short-lived.

Since 1992, India has achieved a strong and consistent pattern of GDP growth, a yearly average of 6.7 percent with its worst years at around four percent growth (1997, 2000 and 2002).[55] This performance is all the more impressive, as it has remained relatively steady in the face of multiple global recessions.

India has achieved this growth with little social disruption. Manmohan Singh made good on the promise in his July 1991 budget speech to minimise the effect of the reforms on the poor, to achieve as he put it 'adjustment with a human face'.[56] India's 1991 reforms constituted a revolution, but a peaceful one.

The reforms and the growth they produced led to a dramatic expansion of India's corporate sector. The market capitalisation of listed Indian companies increased twenty-five fold from 1992 to 2010.[57] In addition to the rise in the values of listed companies, the months and years following July 1991 were a fertile period for start-ups. Some of India's most successful companies were founded in the wake of 1991's liberalisation, including leading telecom player Bharti-Airtel. India had ushered in a new age of entrepreneurship that continues to this day.

Had the nation not come so close to economic ruin in 1991, it is doubtful that its leadership would have had the will or political leverage to implement the reforms that spawned a future of growth. With courage and speed of action, India's leaders managed to turn a crisis into a triumph.

Off the Road to Power

As great as India's economic triumph since 1991 has been, its foreign policy since then has been equally tragic.

By assassinating Rajiv Gandhi the LTTE wanted to avenge his decision to send the IPKF to Sri Lanka. The LTTE also had another objective: to send a clear message to India not to interfere in the Sri Lankan ethnic conflict. The assassination was successful on both counts.[58] India had withdrawn the IPKF in 1990, but with Rajiv Gandhi's killing, India's retreat from Sri Lanka became irrevocable. Prabhakaran had figured he could scare India, and he was right.

India's decision to avoid future involvement in Sri Lanka's conflict was a miscalculation. By withdrawing from Sri Lanka, India ignored the fact that the two nations share both a common heritage and common destiny. Their common heritage dates to prehistoric times, when the first settlers from India crossed the Palk Strait to Sri Lanka. Their common destiny is ensured by their close proximity and India's emerging economic might.

The killing of Rajiv Gandhi was a tragedy and shame for India. An equal shame was India's response to the killing, or lack of response. India's allowing Prabhakaran to orchestrate the killing of a former prime minister with impunity is one of the greatest displays of weakness by a sovereign state in the twentieth century. It is indefensible that India allowed itself to be intimidated by a rag-tag group of rebels hiding in the jungles of northern Sri Lanka.

Paying the Price

What should India have done in response to the assassination of Rajiv Gandhi? Send its troops back to Sri Lanka to kill or capture Prabhakaran and the LTTE leadership? Yes, that is precisely what India should have done. There is no doubt that with a commitment of sufficient troops and equipment, including air power, India would have been successful. Had India captured Prabhakaran in 1991, the LTTE, stripped of its senior leadership, would have ceased to exist as a rebel force. As it was, the Sri Lankan civil war lasted a further eighteen years, with untold suffering for the Sri Lankan people, especially the island's Tamils.

India could have avoided all this misery if it had been willing to act as forcefully against foreign enemies as it had against economic instability. Rajiv Gandhi's killing was an attack on India's status as a regional power. Forcibly bringing Prabhakaran to India to face trial would have sent a clear message to the region, and the world, that India would defend its political leaders from attack, defend its political system from intimidation, and defend its primacy in South Asia against any challengers.

The assassination of Rajiv Gandhi did more than cause India to retreat from active involvement in Sri Lankan affairs; it also caused India to avoid a prominent role in world affairs. A frightened India became content with being a passive regional power, rather than an active global power.

Now Prabhakaran is dead and the Sri Lankan civil war has ended, without any additional bloodshed for India. But at what price? India's window of opportunity to influence Sri Lanka will never be as wide open as it was in 1991 after Rajiv Gandhi's killing. Two decades later, China is building a major port on the southern coast of the island. As we will see in Chapter Seven, this foothold in Sri Lanka represents a dangerous incursion by China into India's backyard.

China has no such timidity in its foreign affairs. In addition to the port in Sri Lanka, it is also helping expand the Pakistani port of Gwadar and Chittagong port in Bangladesh. China has also requested Burma to allow its warships to dock at Burmese ports, which, if approved, would give China ready naval access to the Indian Ocean.[59]

India should note the vociferousness with which China responds to any potential foreign power intervening in its neighbourhood. China was infuriated in June 1995 when the United States granted Taiwan's then President Lee Teng-hui a visitor's visa. Teng-hui was doing nothing more than deliver a lecture at his *alma mater* Cornell University, yet China responded one month later with missile tests off the coast of Taiwan. India would do well to adopt a similar protective attitude towards its backyard.

India cannot ignore the island nation on its doorstep. Sri Lanka is central to India's national security, and not only because both nations share an ethnic Tamil minority. The island, a mere fifty kilometres from Rameshwaram, represents the Achilles' heel of Indian national security: Any instability in Sri Lanka, not to mention influence by another power, is a threat to India.

India's craven inaction in Sri Lanka after Rajiv Gandhi's assassination cost it valuable years in its quest to become a global power. Two decades later, India is still struggling to emerge from its shell.

If India is to be a regional power – let alone a global power – it will have to secure Sri Lanka and bring it firmly into India's orbit. India has to be willing to pay the price to do so. Rajiv Gandhi understood this; his successors have not.

The events of 1991 were a low point in the history of modern India. Fortunately for India, and for the world, it recovered relatively quickly. Seven years after India's *annus horribilis,* the nation was able to make its first crucial step towards true power. The move stunned the world, and earned India virtually universal approbation. But history has proven India's 1998 nuclear test to have been a wise choice.

He had always been quiet, speaking little, but always gentle, always reasonable, which was extraordinary in a young Sicilian male. What [his wife] was seeing was the shedding of his protective coloration of a harmless nobody now that he was ready to start on his destiny. He had started late...but he was to start with a flourish.

– Mario Puzo, *The Godfather*

3

NUCLEAR INDIA: THE END OF IRRELEVANCE

Change in the Air

Even as India's economy recovered quickly from the crisis of 1991, its foreign policy remained stuck in the same kind of thinking that had characterised most of the post-Independence years. Based on its self-proclaimed identity as 'the world's largest democracy', India continually stepped forward to claim its due as a global power. The world took little notice.

An observer of India in the mid-1990s could not have been faulted for thinking that the country would continue as it was for decades, confident of its right to great power status, but unwilling to take any action to convince the world. There was, however, change in the air. In the years after 1991, as its economy strengthened and as India integrated more with the world, a greater sense of assertiveness started creeping into Indian policy-making.

By 1998, that assertiveness found full expression. Over the next decade, India transformed itself from a global non-entity to a future superpower. The story of how India accomplished this feat is a triumph of two great qualities of modern India: patience and restraint.

Visa Capital of the South

10 May 1998

All was tranquil at the United States Consulate General in Chennai, a small post in a large country that did not cause Washington too much concern. The one dozen American staff at the Consulate busied themselves with what seemed to be their primary mission: granting (or refusing) visas to the hundreds of applicants who came daily from all over South India to the well-fortified building at the junction of Anna Salai and Cathedral Road.

The Visa Queue: Out of Chaos, Order

For a time in late 1996 and early 1997, there was a tremendous queue outside the United States Consulate in Chennai. The queue built up due to a Consulate policy of restricting the number of applicants who could apply for a visa on a given day. Aware that entry to the Consulate's Visa Office had become a scarce resource, would-be applicants rushed to secure their place in the queue. At the peak hundreds of people were virtually living outside the Consulate at any given time, some of whom would have to wait for days to actually enter the Consulate and apply for their visa.

As with any queue there were people who tried to jump to the front and there were people holding places for others. An industry of professional 'waiters' developed – people who would stand in the queue for a time and then sell their place to the highest bidder.

The queue became chaotic, and Consulate guards had trouble policing the growing and increasingly restless crowd.

Meanwhile, the presence of hundreds of people outside the gates, all day and night, became a security concern and cause for embarrassment at the Consulate. Some hard-working and innovative visa officers cleared the backlog and made the queue disappear.[1] But not before those waiting outside the Consulate, in an inspiring act of self-government, had made the queue into a reasonably well-functioning society.

With standing in the queue becoming a major investment of time, and with the United States visa critical in some way to everyone there, one's place in the queue was valuable. Everyone had a common interest in maintaining some order; even those at the back of the queue knew that they would move forward, and wanted to know that their improved position in the queue would be secure. Over time the queue developed its own system to impose order on this new society, and especially to handle the inevitable disputes that arose among queue-dwellers. Was it permissible to leave the line and retain one's place? Under what circumstances? The queue-dwellers formed a tribunal to establish broad rules and adjudicate the more difficult cases. Death in the family while waiting in the queue? The tribunal would tell you how long you could be absent for. The genius in the 'judiciary branch' of the queue's government was in its composition: to safeguard the interests of all queue-dwellers the tribunal was composed of representatives from the front, middle and end of the queue. The episode was a testament to Indians' ability to fashion a degree of order out of chaos.

Inside the Consulate there were queues, often long ones, before each of the visa windows. The American visa officers used to marvel at how close to one another the applicants would stand. Mere millimetres would separate the back of one applicant's trousers from the front of the next applicant's belt buckle; sometimes they would appear to be touching. It was an invasion of personal space that no American would tolerate for a second, much less hours on end.

Normally, the officers did all the interviews in the morning. In the afternoon they handled other work while the local staff processed the approved visas. One day, the computers crashed late in the morning and the officers had to stop interviewing candidates and issuing visas for a few hours. The doors to the Consulate's visa office were long-since closed for the day, but there were around twenty remaining applicants already inside the building, standing in a queue waiting to be interviewed. The Consulate staff offered them a number with their place in the queue, and suggested they sit down in the waiting room for a couple of hours; the queue was to re-form, in the same order as before, once the computers start working.

No one would sit down; they were all afraid of losing their place. They knew the Consulate accepted no applications after the appointed hour, and that no new applicants could appear that day. Still they refused to move. One officer went out to make a personal appeal to the last person in the queue: 'Sir, you are last in the queue, have a seat and relax; it cannot get any worse for you'. The applicant would not budge. He and everyone in front of him held their ground until the computers started working again.

On normal days the guards would manage traffic to ensure a smooth flow of applicants to the interview windows. One female visa officer at the time was a tough interviewer. Her visa rejection rate would have likely been the highest among the officers in Chennai. Apparently, word had gotten around South India about this woman. She had other duties besides interviewing, so she was not often at the window. But when she was interviewing, the queue in front of her window was always the shortest. The guards would direct applicants from other queues to hers to even out the waiting time. Some went willingly and apparently unaware; some had to be prodded and pushed into her queue; and others flatly refused to move. Such dramas played out regularly, the course of applicants' lives determined by whether they were interviewed at Window 1 or 2.

A Window on Indian Culture

Standing on the other side of the visa window interviewing applicants offered a fascinating view on South Indian culture. It was not a comprehensive view – most South Indians, the urban poor and those living in villages, would never even contemplate a trip to the United States Consulate. Those who did come were mostly part of the educated elite.

For a visa officer new to India, after a few weeks most of the applicants began to fit into certain categories, and those categories in turn offered glimpses into the work lives and family lives of South Indians.

The proto-typical Chennai visa applicant of the late 1990s was the young male technology professional. Most were applying for H-1B visas to do computer programming work in the United States. (Some were applying for business visas, hopeful of going to the United States, landing a programming job, and then returning to the Consulate to apply for the H-1B.) Studying had been this applicant's life until only recently; now work was to be his life. He was an endearing mixture of earnestness and nervousness, and gave the impression of having the weight of an entire family's expectations on his shoulders. Above all, there was a certain bookish quality to him that only years of studying electrical engineering can impart.

In a few years he would be back at the Consulate with his new bride, the H-4 dependent visa applicant. Sometimes he would not be there at all, having rushed back to the United States to rejoin at his work place. (The standard two weeks' annual vacation at American companies is hardly enough to go to India to get married, much less accompany one's bride afterwards to the Consulate.) If he was not there in person, he was there in the wedding photos the bride showed to prove she was in fact entitled to the spousal visa. The photo showed that his once-bookish qualities had been softened by the extra pounds he had put on, and the new-found confidence he had acquired in the United States.

Not all the young H-1B applicants were male. Every so often a recently married woman would appear for an H visa. But she was not an H-4; she was an H-1B holder in her own right, who had recently married another H-1B holder. She and her husband made up the arranged marriage dream couple of India in the 1990s: a double dollar income.

Finally there were the parents, she in a sari, he in his Western clothes. They had worked hard their entire lives to give their son the best education possible. They had instilled in him the ambition that propelled him along the golden path: from an Indian Institute of Technology (IIT) to an American graduate program in engineering (on a full scholarship) to an H-1B visa. Then came marriage, the green cards, the children and finally United States citizenship for all. Now, in their old age, the parents enjoyed visiting their son, daughter-in-law and grandchildren for a few months every year. A ten-year visa was just the answer, enough for them to 'go and come' as many times as they pleased.

Fraudsters were interspersed among the legitimate applicants. Committing fraud was a young person's game; no one bothered to pose as aged parents of United States citizens. But fraudsters posed as nearly every other category of visa applicants. The most daring of them were those who had not bothered to procure any fake documents at all. They showed up at the Consulate ready to take their chances. The tell-tale mark of this species was found on their application form under 'Purpose of Your Visit': 'Busnes'.

Those were the so-called 'non-immigrants'. It was technically the correct term according to United States visa law, because they were not immigrating at that time. Most of them would in fact immigrate to the United States sooner or later; they knew that and so did the visa officers. That was alright; the United States was fortunate to have the vast majority of them.

Those coming for immigrant visas (green cards) were an entirely different sort of South Indian. A disproportionate number of them, it seemed, were Keralite families sponsored for green cards by American relatives who owned small businesses in the United States. The naming rituals of the Keralite clans were endlessly fascinating, ranging from the unbelievably common (an astounding number of George Varghese-s) to the outright strange (Tity Baby Varghese, the youngest daughter of one Abraham Varghese).

A Quiet Post

Chennai in February 1997 was still a sleepy place. The name had formally changed the previous year, but most people still called it Madras. Ford, the motorcar company, had recently opened a factory outside town; so there were a few other non-Indians around, but not many. All the Westerners knew each other.

Visiting Bangalore from Chennai in early 1997 was like entering another world. People wore jeans in Bangalore, and there was a Pizza Hut. Chennai was as yet untouched by these Western influences. There were no cafes in Chennai, and non-Indian fast food was in its infancy. There was a Mexican restaurant where the food tasted liked Indian food, but the Americans were happy to have it. There was also a pizza place that delivered, and the pizza was pretty good. The owners had taken the trouble to import real pepperoni from the United States; the topping itself cost more than the pizza. Plain pizza – 300 rupees; pizza with real pepperoni – 750 rupees.

For an American diplomat intent on building his career, the right assignments are essential. The vast majority of Foreign Service officers are dedicated and do outstanding work; and so, challenging postings are critical for an officer who wishes to stand out from his peers in the annual evaluation and promotion process. For today's diplomats, those challenges inevitably involve postings to Iraq, Afghanistan or both. In the mid-1990s, in the absence of large scale American-led military conflicts, the ambitious diplomat had to seek other venues to test and display his talents.

Going to an extreme hardship post was one way. The hardship postings were graded on a scale based on the salary premium an officer received by going there – the tougher the living conditions, the higher the premium. The most difficult posts carried a twenty-five percent premium: places that were remote, poor, or unsafe, or some combination of the above. (This was before re-opened United States missions in Iraq and Afghanistan introduced a new tier of hardship postings.) Many posts in sub-Saharan Africa rated twenty-five percent. Posts that were slightly difficult to live in might offer five percent or ten percent, like the Balkan countries and some places in South America. Places that had living standards comparable to the United States (like Western Europe, Australia and Canada) carried no premium at all.

India was somewhere in the middle of the hardship scale. Chennai at that time carried a fifteen percent premium. So on that metric India was considered a moderate hardship post.

The other metric that ambitious Foreign Service officers considered in choosing posts was the significance of the host country to American interests. The idea was that working hard and doing well in a 'significant' country was better for one's career than working hard and doing well at a post in a 'less significant' country. There was no grading scale for this more subjective judgement, and significance was to some extent in the eye of the beholder. There was a cadre of officers who argued that Western Europe was still the key to advancing American foreign policy; some genuinely believed this, and others just liked to make their careers in London, Paris and Rome (a collection of postings that some on hardship duty derided as the 'Pierre Cardin circuit'). Other areas were considered to be sure 'front line' postings of the day, like the capitals of major powers (Moscow, Beijing), key allies (Tel Aviv) or of constant irritants (Havana).[2] Many countries, including quite a few extreme hardship posts, were seemingly doomed to insignificance; going there won hardship points but nothing else. Of course insignificant posts sometimes did become significant overnight. Some officers made great career leaps by being in sleepy posts that suddenly became trouble-spots, like the Balkans when Yugoslavia broke up in 1991.

On this scale too, India was somewhere in the middle: not a backwater, but not a high profile assignment either. India was a large nation, but not on the highest tier of American diplomatic relationships in 1997. As morning broke in Washington on 11 May 1998, that was about to change. India had started late on the path to power, but it was to start with a flourish.

Outrage

When news of India's nuclear test reached the American government, Washington reacted with shock and outrage. India had learned from its experience two-and-a-half years before, when it had been caught red-handed in its test preparations by Washington's satellites. This time it was Washington that was caught by surprise. The State Department heard the news on CNN, and the CIA heard it from the State Department.[3]

The shock and outrage of American diplomats in the field in India was no less great. One of the core principles of American foreign policy – which the typical Foreign Service officer also believed in – was that the United States must halt any further spread of nuclear weapons. The United States had used nuclear weapons against Japan in the Second World War, and the world must never experience death on that scale again. Since the end of the Cold War the nuclear world had been stable, and American diplomats were committed to maintaining that stability. The United States and the other declared nuclear powers had shown since then that they understood the responsibility that came with nuclear weapons.

How could India think that it belonged in that category of nations? An India that could not even take care of its own people, much less a stockpile of weapons that could kill millions. A nation whose political system was characterised by constant instability, with six different prime ministers so far in the decade. A nation whose most storied political party seemed to spend all of its time courting an Italian widow to be its saviour. Such was the bewilderment of a 1998 vintage American diplomat at his host country's decision to test.

A Post Pokhran Conversation

Pokhran changed India overnight into a 'front-line' post in the United States Foreign Service. It also made India a much more interesting assignment for an American diplomat. Suddenly there was something to talk about with Indians in Chennai other than visas and the weather, neither of which topics offered much variety.

'You (the American government) are punishing us for the nuclear test.'

'The test was a big mistake. The United States takes non-proliferation very seriously, and we cannot accept what India has done.'

'Why the United States can have nuclear weapons, and India cannot?'

'We have shown that we can act responsibly with nuclear weapons.'

'What nonsense this is. You do not think that India can act responsibly with nuclear weapons?'

'Well...'

[Awkward silence. Change in topic or conversation ends.]

In the weeks after Pokhran, the United States announced and implemented a range of sanctions against India: halting economic aid (except food aid and other humanitarian aid), voting against assistance from multilateral agencies such as the World Bank and International Monetary Fund, and a bar on arms sales.[4] The sanctions also prohibited or limited scientific and technical collaboration between the United States and India. The United States blacklisted around 250 Indian laboratories and companies, preventing them from undertaking collaborative initiatives with American counterparts. The sanctions included a prohibition on the selling and sharing of 'dual-use' technologies fit for both industrial and military purposes.[5]

Though the sanctions did not affect the issuance of visas to Indian tourists and businessmen, they had a direct impact on issuance of visas to Indian scientists. The United States Consulate in Chennai, for example, had to refuse some visas for Indian scientists to travel to the United States for conferences, visas that would have been granted as a matter of routine before the test.

The truth is that the sanctions, while in part mandated by American law, were also fit of pique. Bill Clinton was angry, and wanted to come down on India 'like a ton of bricks'.[6] Inside the wider American government apparatus, the test embarrassed those whose job it was to predict these kinds of things, such as the State Department and the CIA.

The United States need not have been surprised by Pokhran, as the signals were clear that India intended to test. First there was India's aborted nuclear test in late 1995. Second, the BJP's 1998 election manifesto inasmuch declared that a BJP government would make India a declared nuclear power. Though the manifesto did not specifically commit to a nuclear test, it did promise to 're-evaluate the country's nuclear policy and exercise the option to induct nuclear weapons'.[7] Years earlier, in April 1995, the BJP, then in the opposition, had criticised Rao's Congress government for 'giving up' on the nuclear option under pressure from the United States.[8] After all these indications, the American government should have expected BJP leader Atal Bihari Vajpayee to take the first opportunity he had to test, once he himself assumed power with a firm majority.[9] India had all but said it would go nuclear; the United States simply did not listen.

The Rise of the BJP

The premiership of Narasimha Rao was a decisive one in the history of modern India. Rao was the first prime minister to serve a full five-year term after Rajiv Gandhi left office in 1989, and the first one ever outside the Nehru-Gandhi family. While Rao and his party were enjoying unbroken power, however, Congress's political opponents were gathering strength. By the time Rao's tenure ended in 1996, there was a new force in Indian politics: the BJP.

The rise of the BJP and its precursors had been slow and episodic until the early 1990s. The destruction of the Babri Masjid in December 1992 by Hindu nationalists, and the ensuing intra-communal violence, brought the issue of Hindu nationalism to the fore in Indian politics. Though the BJP came under widespread criticism for inciting the destruction of the mosque (and the violence that followed), the episode helped more than it hurt the BJP. Babri made religious identity (Hindu identity in particular) a major factor for the first time in Indian politics at the national level.

India's integration into the global economy, which began with Rao's 1991 reforms, helped give the BJP its signature issue: greater international assertiveness for India. It was an issue that resonated with a broader portion of the electorate than Hindu nationalism, and an issue with which the BJP was ultimately able to ride to power. By the time Rao aborted India's planned nuclear test in 1995, the BJP had gained an advantage over Congress as the party of an increasingly assertive Indian foreign policy. One year later, the BJP was in power (for a short time), and returned in 1998 for an unbroken five-year term of its own. Rao's tenure witnessed, along with the entry of India into the global economy, the maturation of the BJP as a political force, and the ebb of secularism in national politics.

American outrage over Pokhran was only partly due to concerns that it would hurt nuclear non-proliferation efforts. The United States was also concerned – rightly, it turned out – that the test would inflame tensions between India and Pakistan. Most of all, however, the United States was angry because India had so openly defied it. After the fall of the Soviet Union, the United States had quickly gotten used to being the sole superpower; it expected to be able to dictate the policies of other nations.

The United States felt it had to do something, and imposed sanctions because it wanted to teach India and other would-be nuclear testers a lesson. In the years that followed, the United States did indeed make an example of India, but not in the way that Bill Clinton had envisaged during the dark days of 1998.

Nuclear Winter

Indo-American relations hit rock bottom in June 1998. While Bill Clinton was upset with India immediately after Pokhran, his anger only seemed to increase in the following weeks. On 3 June, he called the tests (both India's and Pakistan's) 'self-defeating, wasteful and dangerous' and said they would make the people of both countries 'poorer and less secure'.[10] Later that month on 27 June, the United States hurled one of the greatest possible indignities upon India: the notion that China would be America's partner in reforming a wayward India. In a joint statement, the United States and China promised to 'jointly and individually contribute to the achievement of a peaceful, prosperous, and secure South Asia'.[11] The joint statement gave the impression of an Indo-American relationship in free fall.[12]

Against the backdrop of government-to-government estrangement, bilateral business ties had become stronger than ever. The flood of H1-Bs and business visitors (many employed by large Indian companies like Infosys and Wipro) continued unabated. More importantly, the worldwide technology boom was in full swing in 1998, and large American technology companies had discovered India in general, and South India in particular. American companies like Motorola and Cisco had fast-growing local offices and were selling products to Indian customers.

The United States Commercial Service office at the Consulate was caught in the middle. Its job was to help American business, specifically to increase American exports. Yet it also had to follow American law while doing so. American and Indian businessmen, each keen to tap the potential in the other's market, were befuddled at the legal roadblocks the United States government had suddenly thrown up in the form of sanctions. The policy-making level of government seemed to be moving the Indo-American relationship backwards when business leaders from both countries saw so much reason for moving it forward.

India's test had exposed a gulf between the way the United States perceived India and the way India saw itself. Before the test, the United States saw India as significant mostly as a potential trouble spot, should tensions with Pakistan lead to another war. Though India spoke of global ambitions, there was little in India's actions then to indicate to the United States that India was serious about amassing, and then wielding, power. The United States did not have large business interests in India (exports to India in 1998 were only $3.5 billion),[13] nor did it see much future potential for commerce. Within the State Department, India would rarely have been mentioned in the same breath with China back in early 1998.

India's view of itself was very different. In fact, India saw itself much the same way the United States saw itself. While few Indians would have claimed superpower status back in 1998, most believed in an Indian version of American exceptionalism – that theirs was a unique nation. A typical American visitor to India then would understandably have been surprised that so many Indians were proud of their country. In his blinkered 'the United States-only' arrogance he might have found Indians' national pride misguided albeit somewhat charming. He might not have stopped to consider then that the Indians might in fact have much to be proud of. He certainly would not have believed that estrangement between the United States and India was harmful to his nation, nor that within a matter of years the American government would encourage India's nuclear ambitions.

Thaw

By any measure the 1998 American sanctions on India were a failure. Withdrawn in stages, and completely by 2001,[14] the sanctions achieved little other than to make the United States feel that it was taking action against India's nuclear test.

Like most nations, however, the United States is slow to reverse any policy it has announced. Part of this is the inevitable saving of face. Equally important is the bureaucratic inertia which sets in once Congress and the Executive Branch have agreed on a given policy; the work required to reverse that policy is great, and there are many other issues on the agenda competing for the time and attention of senior officials.

In the case of sanctions against India, the complete reversal of the policy in a matter of three years amounts to a nano-second in American policy-making terms. It could only have happened faster if World War III had broken out with the United States and India fighting side-by-side. As it was, policy makers came to their senses as quickly as they could in a time of peace. That they did so is due to the hard work and vision of two men: Strobe Talbott and Jaswant Singh.

In June 1998, the month after India's test, Jaswant Singh floated, through a back channel, the idea of a series of meetings between India and the United States to rebuild ties. State Department officials, Talbott included, thought it was a good idea. But the diplomatic details still had to be worked out. The United States proposed Talbott as Jaswant Singh's negotiating counterpart. Talbott, as deputy secretary of state, and Jaswant Singh, as minister of external affairs, were not, strictly speaking, equivalents in rank for the purposes of diplomatic protocol. If India had wanted to be difficult, it would have insisted on Jaswant Singh meeting his true counterpart, Secretary of State Madeline Albright. To India's credit, it did not insist on strict protocol, and accepted the American proposal.

Diplomatic Montage Sequence

Film-makers often use montage sequences in their storytelling to show the rapid passage of time and to transition to the film's conclusion. In a montage sequence, for example, the director might show the hero, having been bested by the villain earlier in the film, and then training hard in a rapid succession of short clips, in preparation for his final battle with the villain. The montage allows the audience to get to the juicy part of the story faster: the resolution of the film's central story line.

If the story of Indo-American relations were a film, then Talbott and Jaswant Singh provided the montage sequence. The director might have shown the two meeting, as they did, at various points around the globe over a period of two-and-a-half years. The director might have shown the two arguing, as they did, their respective nations' positions forcefully, whilst also listening to their counterpart attentively.

At the time of the Talbott-Singh dialogue, one could not be faulted for concluding that the two diplomats achieved little: In the end, both nations stuck largely to their pre-dialogue positions and did no more than agree to disagree about a nuclear India. In retrospect, however, there would have been no Indo-American nuclear deal in 2008, had there been no Talbott and Jaswant Singh dialogue a decade earlier. Without their intensive discussions it would have taken years longer for the United States and India to understand each other. Talbott and Jaswant Singh sped up the story line, and the audience of international relations reached the juicy part faster: the repair of the rupture in Indo-American relations.

The two men got to work immediately. They followed their initial June 1998 Washington meeting with two in July (Frankfurt and Delhi), and three more (Washington, New York and Rome) before the year was over. They met a total of fourteen times during their 'dialogue' on bilateral relations. They finished without convincing each other of the justness of each other's position. But something more significant had happened: Both Talbott and Jaswant Singh understood each other's position, and both also felt understood by the other.

Their discussions were important in three respects. First, the amount of senior-level time and attention that the United States and India each devoted to the dialogue demonstrated to the other party that the bilateral relationship was important. The result was a level of mutual trust that had previously been absent.

This trust was reinforced in July 1999 during the Kargil crisis, when Pakistani troops crossed the Line of Control (LoC) to invade the town of Kargil in the Indian state of Jammu and Kashmir. The crisis was defused after Bill Clinton – who saw the Pakistani invasion as an attempt at 'nuclear blackmail'[15] – convinced Pakistani Prime Minister Nawaz Sharif to pull back his forces and restore the previous LoC. Talbott, thanks to his dialogue with Jaswant Singh, felt that Clinton had to take a hard-line with the Pakistanis, if a larger conflict was to be avoided. He was right, and the American approach to Kargil earned the gratitude of the Indians, especially Jaswant Singh and Vajpayee.[16]

The second reason the Talbott-Singh dialogue was important was that it helped the United States understand India's reasons for testing. The United States could not yet be happy with a nuclear India, but nor could it deny that India faced legitimate security threats from its nuclear neighbours, China and Pakistan.

Third, the dialogue allowed Clinton to proceed with a visit to India in March 2000. The visit had been under consideration well before Pokhran, but the nuclear test had put it on indefinite hold. Following Talbott and Jaswant Singh's discussions, enough diplomatic 'work' had been done to justify Clinton's going ahead with his trip. That visit, in turn, further strengthened bilateral ties, and broadened them beyond nuclear matters.

Thanks to Talbott and Jaswant Singh the tide had turned, and an improvement in bilateral relations could now take place. By the time the decade ended, the United States had become resigned to a nuclear India. But it would take two devastating acts of terrorism the following year to convince the United States that a nuclear India was not just acceptable but perhaps desirable.

Alone

Nine months after his visit to India, Clinton was out of office, and George W. Bush was the new American president. Strobe Talbott was also gone, replaced by Richard Armitage, Bush's pick for deputy secretary of state. Jaswant Singh, meanwhile, was still in office but would have to get to know a new team in Washington. The Indo-American relationship, which had come so far in a short time since the nuclear test, would also have to adjust if it was to continue to develop. Jaswant Singh could not have known that the Bush administration, led by the president himself, would do more to advance Indo-American relations than any previous American administration.

When morning broke on 13 December 2001, Bush had been president for less than a year and the United States was barely three months into its post 9/11 world. The invasion of Iraq was more than a year away, but the United States had already launched the war on terror: a war that was to define the first decade of the twenty-first century for the United States and much of the world. American attacks on Afghanistan, which had begun in October 2001, were in full swing. The United States was bombing Tora-Bora in Eastern Afghanistan in the hopes of killing Osama bin Laden, the man who planned 9/11 and previous attacks against the United States. Bin Laden narrowly escaped, and was to live for nearly another decade until the United States troops finally found and killed him in Abbottabad, Pakistan in May 2011.

In India, meanwhile, little had changed after 9/11. If the 9/11 attacks awakened the American people and their government to the dangers of terrorism inspired by Islamic fundamentalism, Indians and the Indian government had long been aware of those same dangers. Genuine Indian sympathy for the victims of 9/11 was mixed with equally genuine satisfaction that the United States could no longer deny the Islamic-terror nexus, and by extension, could no longer deny Pakistan's threat to India. After 9/11 Indians could be excused for feeling as Winston Churchill did after the Japanese bombing of Pearl Harbor brought the United States into the Second World War – a degree of relief at no longer being alone in their fight.

9/11's Victim of 'Mistaken Identity'

9/11 claimed the lives of 118 Indians.[17] All but one of them died on 11 September itself. Balbir Singh Sodhi perished on 15 September 2001 in front of his gas station in Mesa, Arizona, the victim of five gunshot wounds by an American angry over the attacks of 9/11.[18] In a press release after Sodhi's death, the Indian Embassy in Washington referred to it as a case of 'mistaken identity'.[19] It is a phrase that may have attracted little attention in the days after 9/11; today it looks bizarre and misplaced. Whom in the eyes of the Indian Embassy was Sodhi mistaken for? A terrorist, or a Muslim?

Two days earlier, the Indian Embassy used the same term in connection with other reported attacks against Sikhs, emphasising that Sikhs are 'adherents of a modern, open and democratic faith'.[20] If Sikhism were not such a faith, would attacks on its adherents be any more permissible? Would attacks on a gas station owner whose faith was not modern, open nor democratic be permissible? The language of the Indian Embassy leaves the reader wondering whether it is a not-so-subtle swipe at the Islamic faith. If so, it is out of step with India's tradition of tolerance and secularism.

When a car bomb exploded outside the Jammu and Kashmir Assembly less than three weeks after 9/11, India confidently cited the democratic world's 'broad and determined coalition against international terrorism'. The statement ended on an ominous note: 'There is a limit to India's patience'.[21]

India felt emboldened to threaten a reprisal for the Assembly attack, because it believed the world, and the United States, was on its side, finally paying attention to Islamic terrorism. If the United States could pursue terrorists half a world away in Afghanistan, India's policy makers reasoned, it could hardly deny India's right to pursue terrorists living right across the border in Pakistan.

India was only partly right; the United States was focused on Islamic terrorism, but consumed with its own Islamic terrorist enemies. The United States had not yet associated the planners of 9/11 with those instigating terrorism from Pakistan. So, as the white Ambassador, with a flashing red light on top and forged Home Ministry sticker on the windshield, drove up to the Parliament building in New Delhi at around 11:30 a.m. on 13 December 2001, India was actually still alone. But not for long.

9/11 and 13/12

Had 9/11 never taken place, the attack on India's Parliament would have yielded little more than the usual condemnations from the American government. Yet a post 9/11 United States was ready to look at India and its cross-border terrorism affliction in a new way. The United States ambassador in New Delhi on 13/12, Robert Blackwill, realised this. Thanks largely to Blackwill's efforts, 9/11 and 13/12 added up to a new level of understanding in Indo-American relations.[22]

In the American view of the world there are two types of countries: those that truly matter to American interests and those that do not. Being an American diplomat in each place carries its own bureaucratic frustrations and limitations. The United States has a simple way of defining which countries are important: those that have a large impact on either its national security or economy. American policy towards such countries is largely developed in Washington, and executed in the field. Often American diplomats, even ambassadors, to such countries are relegated to delivering the post.

For other countries (those where there are no vital American interests at stake), policy is developed largely in the field, but often falls on deaf ears back in Washington. American diplomats to such nations have autonomy to think the big thoughts and craft new initiatives towards the host country. Insofar as these ideas do not require funds or political support in Washington, diplomats can also implement them. If Washington's support is needed, however, initiatives towards these nations often wither and die for lack of interest back home.

Ever since the 1998 nuclear test, India was definitely a country that mattered, and Washington took a firm hand in guiding policy. This meant Blackwill, sitting half a world away from the power centre, had to persuade Washington, as well as India, of his vision for an enhanced relationship. The events of 13/12 offered him the ideal impetus.

The morning after the attack, the Indian government held a memorial service at Parliament for those who had died. When Blackwill showed up at the event, he surprised his hosts and won the gratitude of the Indian government at the highest levels. 'We really didn't expect anybody,' said Jaswant Singh later. 'For years – decades, in fact – we had been ploughing this field alone.'[23]

After the memorial service Blackwill told reporters that 'United States and India are as one in this outrage,' and added that 13/12 was no different in its objective than 9/11.[24] The Indians saw that Blackwill could be an ally in persuading Washington to believe that Delhi had the moral high ground in its conflict with Pakistan. Now Blackwill focused on convincing his own government. In the days after 13/12, he unleashed a diplomatic offensive against Washington, peppering the State Department with cable after cable outlining Pakistan's support for cross-border terrorism.[25] This whirlwind of activity, combined with fast-moving events on the ground in South Asia post 13/12, helped Blackwill seize a degree of policy-making authority from Washington.

Increasingly, Washington began to sing his tune. Before the month of December was over, the United States had officially designated two anti-Indian terror groups, Lashkar-e-Tayyeba (LeT) and Ummah Tameer-e-Nau (UTN), as terrorist organisations under American law.[26]

'Client-itus' is State Department slang for a condition some diplomats suffer from: Far from home, and identifying closely with their host country, they begin to spend most of their time representing their host country's interests to Washington, instead of doing their job, which is to represent American interests to their host country. As the 2001-02 tensions between India and Pakistan escalated, American diplomats in both nations developed cases of 'client-itus'. Diplomats in Delhi were sympathetic to Indian arguments about Pakistan's support for cross-border terrorism, while those in Islamabad were sympathetic to their hosts' complaints about Indian efforts to destabilise Pakistan.[27] Both embassies made their cases to Washington with vigour.

The Indo-Pak proxy war by diplomatic cable played out over several months. On 14 May 2002, an attack on a bus of Indian tourists near the town of Kaluchak in Jammu and Kashmir, which left thirty-one dead, further inflamed tensions. By June, the countries seemed to be readying for a real war. South Asia had Washington's attention.

Based on its own first-hand knowledge of the events surrounding 13/12, the American government was certainly sympathetic to Indian claims that Pakistan was behind the attack. When, for example, news broke of the attack, the American Ambassador to Pakistan Wendy Chamberlain happened to be in a meeting with a Pakistani two-star general. There was a television on in the room, and the news from Delhi suddenly flashed across the screen. Chamberlain asked the general for his reaction. His reply: 'Oops.'[28]

Yet the Americans were not out to assign blame; they simply wanted to protect American interests. The two key policy considerations at stake for the United States were avoiding an Indo-Pak war (which could go nuclear) and not undermining its own war on terror in Afghanistan (for which Pakistan's active involvement was needed, especially in the tribal areas along its border with Afghanistan). Both aims were achieved by active and discreet mediation by the United States, which succeeded in getting India and Pakistan to ratchet down their military postures. In a critical moment, then Deputy Secretary of State Richard Armitage convinced India to recall some warships from the Arabian Sea off the Pakistani coast, based on a commitment from Pakistan's President Pervez Musharraf to crack down on jihadi infiltration across the LoC. It was the beginning of the end of the crisis, and tensions abated from then onwards.[29]

India felt duped by Washington's mediation. In India's view, Pakistan never upheld its promise to halt cross-border terrorism. As Jaswant Singh later recalled, he learned a lesson from 2002: 'Hereafter, I really will never ask the United States for anything as far as Pakistan is concerned'.[30] Yet there is an irony in Singh's lament: The events of 13/12, and India's restraint thereafter, sparked a decade of ever-closer relations between the United States and India.

Decade of Bust, Decade of Boom

India's actions after 13/12 stood in direct contrast to American actions after 9/11. Those post-9/11 and post-13/12 actions had a profound and lasting impact on both the United States and India, as the different responses to terrorism were a major factor in the different courses the nations took during the first decade of the twenty-first century.

The American economy is still suffering from the effects of 9/11. Osama bin Laden wanted nothing more than to kill Americans on that day, and did not have a grand plan to inflict lasting economic damage on the United States. Nonetheless the attacks of 9/11 helped set in motion a series of events that led to Wall Street's collapse in September 2008, the ensuing financial crisis, and crippling level of debt for generations of Americans to come.

While the United States was already headed towards recession on 9/11, the attacks took further steam out of the economy. To pull the United States out of recession, the government incentivised Americans to binge on debt. The Federal Reserve lowered interest rates by a total of two-and-a-half percent in the two years after 9/11 (reaching a low of one percent by June 2003). Interest rates stayed below three percent for almost four years after 9/11, until May 2005.[31] The Fed's cheap money inflated a housing bubble that encouraged Americans to borrow more and spend more. United States housing values rose by fifty-six percent between the beginning of 2002 and the end of 2006.[32] Richer feeling Americans took over $500 billion out of their 'more valuable' homes in home equity loans and so-called 'cash-out refinancings', nearly twice the amount of just three years before.[33]

Little of this money was saved: On the eve of 9/11, the American personal savings rate stood at 4.7 percent; by 2007, it had dropped below two percent.[34] From 2002 until 2007, when the global recession began, the American economy lived in a dream world of ever increasing house prices fuelling ever higher consumption.

One cause of the United States' current financial trouble pre-dates 9/11. In 1999, the American government repealed the Glass-Steagall Act, which prohibited commercial banks from being involved in investment banking and vice-versa. The Act dated from 1933, and had been passed to prevent a repeat of the speculation that led to the Great Depression. Its repeal came just in time to enable commercial banks to bet their depositors' savings on any number of investments, however risky. Wall Street had become Las Vegas, with American savings on the betting table as the roulette wheel spun.

Bank speculation, a housing bubble and easy credit – this was a toxic combination that brought the American economy to the edge of collapse in September 2008. The wars in Afghanistan and Iraq – a direct and indirect consequence, respectively, of 9/11 – were an additional drain on American government finances throughout the first decade of the twenty-first century, together claiming over 6,000 American lives and costing over $1.2 trillion.[35] By late 2011, the United States was still struggling to return to 2007 output levels, suffering unemployment above nine percent and carrying $15 trillion in gross external debt (nearly one one hundred percent of American GDP).[36]

The first decade of the century worked out very differently for India. There was a steady rise in both GDP growth and the Indian stock market, in spite of repeated terrorist attacks. 13/12 and the ensuing tension with Pakistan had put the Sensex into an eleven month slump, but it recovered to pre-13/12 levels by the end of 2002.

On 26 November 2008, terrorists from Pakistan attacked downtown Mumbai, killing over 150 people and injuring many more. Even 26/11, a direct attack on India's financial centre in the midst of a global financial crisis, was unable to interrupt share price rises for more than four months. By the end of the decade, the Sensex was three times higher than it was at the decade's start. If the LeT and Pakistan's Inter-Services Intelligence (ISI) intended to goad India into a conflict that would derail its economic growth, they failed. The Indian people proved as resilient to attack as the Indian economy.

By the end of 2010, the United States' Dow Jones Industrial Average,[37] by contrast, had not returned to the levels where it started the decade. Of course there are numerous other factors at play in the varying performance of the American and Indian markets over the decade. Most importantly, while the United States entered the century as a mature economy, India entered with substantial upside growth potential having suffered centuries of low productivity. It would be wrong to ascribe the difference in performance to the nations' response to terrorism alone. Yet it would also be wrong to ignore that both nations responded in different ways to the attacks they suffered within three months of each other in 2001. It is impossible to quantify how much of the United States' economic troubles stemmed from its response to 9/11. What is clear is that India did not take the same actions as the United States, and prospered.

Another Mumbai?

A terrifying sequel to 26/11 played out in Mumbai on 13 July 2011, when bombs exploded in three areas of the city, killing 17 and injuring over one hundred. The only consolation was that the loss of life from the latest attack on Mumbai was not as high as from 26/11. Yet the prospect of another 26/11 scale attack, or worse, in

India is all too real, and the domestic pressure on India's leaders to retaliate in that event would be enormous. There may well come a time when India is unable or unwilling to continue restraining itself in the face of attacks from across the border in Pakistan. If India were to respond militarily to a future terrorist attack, what scale and form would that response take? One possible scenario: India would launch a strike against terrorist camps in Pakistan, sparking a counter-counter-strike from Pakistan.[38] While such an exchange is unlikely to lead to a nuclear war between India and Pakistan, a conventional military confrontation on a scale larger than any previous Indo-Pak conflicts is possible, even probable.[39] India's best option to prevent such an outcome is to ensure that Pakistan has as much to lose economically from a conflict as India does. This will require shrinking the growing prosperity gap between India and its troublesome neighbour.

Hyper Growth Nation and De-Hyphenation

By mid-2002, when post 13/12 tensions between India and Pakistan had abated, the Indo-American relationship was well on its way to transformation. The United States' view of India had gone from indifference (in the 1990s) to mistrust (after India's 1998 nuclear test) to common purpose (after 9/11 and 13/12).

Yet a common struggle against terrorism does not make for a broad strategic partnership. There was still a major impediment to closer Indo-American relations: the Indo-Pak hyphenation.

Since Independence, India's foreign policy has been obsessed with Pakistan. The decades-long result of this obsession, to Pakistan's delight and India's dismay, was the virtual equation in the eyes of the world of a democracy of 1.2 billion people and a quasi-failed state of 170 million people. Little Pakistan succeeded in holding India's global ambitions hostage.

On the face of it, the population imbalance alone makes the Indo-Pak equation absurd. Yet the 1998 nuclear tests by both nations reinforced it.[40] Suddenly the world had two new declared nuclear powers in the space of a week. The two nations' nuclear capabilities added a new and dangerous ingredient to their long-standing dispute over Kashmir. This meant that each nation's greatest significance to the world was its hostility towards the other. 'Indo-Pak' had become a short-hand for that danger. Bill Clinton called Kashmir, on the eve of his March 2000 visit to India, 'the most dangerous place in the world'.[41]

India felt, rightly so, that until 2005 American policy makers looked at it only through the 'prism' of Indo-Pak. Although Indian leaders routinely rejected the hyphenation, it was a problem of their own making. India's obsession with Pakistan continued to strengthen the image of two nuclear Siamese twins, joined at the hip in Kashmir. Even the sense of common purpose the United States and India felt in the struggle against Islamic terrorism post 13/12 and 9/11 was unable to supplant the Indo-Pak prism.

It was only after 2002 that India began to break the pattern. It did so by using its greatest weapon against Pakistan and others who wish to harm it: prosperity.

India's increasing economic output in the first decade of the century provided the missing link to a true strategic partnership with the United States. The United States saw pre-nuclear India as large and largely inconsequential; and nuclear India as large and bothersome. But a nuclear India with one of the fastest growing major economies in the world? That sounded to American policy makers like a future strategic ally.

Had India attacked Pakistan (or groups within Pakistan) in the years after 13/12, it would have been pulled back into the Indo-Pak hyphenation. By not doing so, even in the face of multiple provocations since 13/12, India was able to best Pakistan economically instead of militarily. From 2002 to 2009 India outgrew Pakistan by an average of 2.8 percent a year.[42] This growth gap ended the Indo-Pak equation in the eyes of the United States and the world.

The irony is that, even as the United States was engaged in two wars sparked by 9/11, it successfully persuaded India not to avenge 13/12: The United States wanted India to do as it said, not as it did, and India complied. By rejecting the American example of an aggressive military response to terrorism, India was able to keep its own economic growth on track and grow closer to the United States.

This strengthening of Indo-American ties took place against the backdrop of the continued rise of China. India's own growth combined with the values India and the United States share – democracy, pluralism, respect for both the rule of law and free market principles – proved an irresistible combination to American policy makers who were concerned with the prospect of an Asia dominated by China.

In mid-March 2005, then United States Secretary of State Condoleezza Rice argued for de-hyphenation as she tried to justify the sale of United States F-16 fighter aircraft to Pakistan: 'What we are trying to do is break out of the notion that this is a hyphenated relationship...that anything that happens that is good for Pakistan is bad for India and vice versa'.[43] Within three years India and the United States would sign an agreement on civilian nuclear cooperation. In a mere decade India had transformed itself from a nuclear outcast to a member of the nuclear club. Cross-border terrorism would remain a threat to India, as 26/11 showed. But the world would come to view attacks such as 26/11 not as an element of the Indo-Pak equation, but as a weak neighbour taking pot shots at an emerging world power. Hyphenation was dead, killed by Indian patience and restraint.

British India's Bad Bank

The 1947 partition of India was the source of enormous human suffering. As many as a million people died in the chaos and violence of the two-way mass migrations (Pakistani Hindus to India, and Indian Muslims to Pakistan) sparked by the split.[44] Families were torn apart, children went missing never to be seen again, and some people lost everything, arriving in their new nation with little more than the clothes on their backs. Since Partition the two nations have been virtually constant foes, an enmity that has until recently prevented both nations from reaching their true economic potential.

Nonetheless, more than six decades on and considering the current instability facing Pakistan near its Western border with Afghanistan, perhaps it is time to look at Partition in a different light. While not minimising the suffering that Partition brought, it is possible to argue that, over the long run, Partition has been a benefit to India, and that India would not have the stability and rising prosperity it enjoys today had Partition not taken place.

Banks, during times of crisis, face a stark choice: split up or fail. The splitting up sometimes involves creating a 'bad bank' where all of the bank's bad assets (e.g. loans that are unlikely to be repaid, poor investments) are concentrated. The 'bad bank' is sold off for little or no cash, and what is left over (the 'good bank') gets much-needed stability and the opportunity to grow again, freed of burdensome assets.

Think of India on the eve of Partition as a bank in financial trouble, with some good assets and some bad assets. Partition effectively created a bad bank, where the bad assets (tribal areas bordering Afghanistan) went off India's balance sheet and onto Pakistan's. Of course, some good assets (Lahore and the Punjab, for example) went with them, but India was left with many more good assets than it gave up. With the exception of its short military conflicts with China and Pakistan, as well as the occasional outbreak of cross-border terrorism, Partition left India largely in peace to develop into the pluralistic secular democracy that it is today. It worked, and India now is, after China, the fastest growing major economy in the world. Pakistan meanwhile has suffered six decades of strife and instability fighting internal battles that India has been spared, and is left with an economic future far less bright than its neighbour's. The bad bank, alas, is still in trouble.

With de-hyphenation complete, India must now turn its attention to greater economic integration with Pakistan. Extrapolating from current population growth and economic growth trends, by 2020 India will reach a GDP twenty times Pakistan's.[45] While India can outgrow Pakistan, and must continue to do so, it also has an interest in a stable Pakistan. An India vastly richer than its neighbour is not a recipe for cross-border harmony, as an impoverished Pakistan has less to lose in a conflict than a prosperous Pakistan.

Trade between nations has been shown to be the single biggest deterrent to armed conflict. Empirical analysis of militarised disputes between rival states since the 1945 period shows that economic integration, defined by two-way trade, helps prevent conflict.[46] When the two states are next-door neighbours, the trade relationship is especially critical to reinforcing both friendship and wealth.

Canadian-American trade is an example of the wealth that a close trading relationship between neighbours can create. Two-way trade in 2010 for the North American nations was over $500 billion,[47] which is equivalent to over three percent of American GDP and over thirty percent of Canadian GDP.[48]

The current level of Indo-Pakistani trade is paltry in comparison: Two-way trade accounts for one percent of Pakistani GDP, and one-tenth of a percent of Indian GDP.[49] If India were to trade proportionally as much with Pakistan as the United States trades with Canada, Indian trade with Pakistan would increase by a factor of thirty (from one-tenth of a percent to three percent of Indian GDP). For Indian business this trade shortfall represents an annual commercial opportunity in excess of forty billion dollars. For India as a nation it represents the only way to achieve lasting national security.

Nuclear Two-Step

India's nuclear diplomacy has been brilliant. It weathered the world's criticism for the 1998 test, confident that it had done the right thing and the world would come to accept it as a nuclear power. When the world did, India accepted membership in the nuclear club with grace rather than triumphalism. By the time Prime Minister Manmohan Singh was feted in November 2009 at a White House State Visit, his host, President Barack Obama called India 'indispensible' to a global future of security and prosperity.[50]

Today there is only one missing element for India to become a full-fledged nuclear power: signing of the Nuclear Non-Proliferation Treaty (NPT) as a nuclear weapons state. The treaty was conceived by the five declared nuclear powers in 1968 – the United States, the United Kingdom, France, Russia and China – in an attempt to prevent the further spread of nuclear weapons. The NPT defined a nuclear weapons state as one which 'has manufactured and exploded a nuclear weapon or other nuclear explosive device prior to 1 January 1967'.[51] The nuclear club's members had declared, in effect, that they were not accepting new applications.

For years India derided the treaty as 'discriminatory and flawed'.[52] In 1998, a few months after the Pokhran tests, then Indian Foreign Minister Jaswant Singh wrote about the 'closed club' of nuclear powers practicing 'nuclear apartheid'.[53] Indian Prime Minister Manmohan Singh, for his part, complained that the NPT had failed to prevent nuclear proliferation.[54]

Much had changed in the thirteen years since Pokhran. During Prime Minister Manmohan Singh's November 2009 visit to the United States, he made it known that India would like to sign the NPT as a nuclear weapons state.[55] It seems the NPT 'closed club' would be far less objectionable to India from the inside looking out than it was from the outside looking in.

For India, signing the NPT would be the second step of a nice dance move. First say the treaty is discriminatory and you will never sign it. Then, once you have an exemption to trade in nuclear technology, sign the NPT anyway.

Signing the NPT as a declared nuclear power would enable India to achieve what no nation has since the NPT came into effect over four decades ago: strong-arming its way into the closed nuclear club. Like many delicate dance moves, the second step is the hardest. India should devote its diplomatic resources to making it happen. Doing so will require the same tough foreign policy mindset which guided the 1998 test and subsequent nuclear diplomacy – a toughness that, apart from the nuclear field, has been notably absent from India's international relations.

Poised for Global Power

The bomb alone did not make India a global power. Nor did the patience and restraint India showed in the aftermath of 13/12; those qualities earned India the world's respect, but no more. Neither did the triumphant admission to the club of nuclear nations in 2008 confer global power status on India. All those actions have merely put India within striking distance of becoming a global power.

The world is no longer responding to India with indifference. India has the world's attention and respect. Now India must reach out and claim global power status. Doing so will require a transformation of India's economy far greater than that which followed the reforms of 1991, and a foreign policy far more assertive than that of the past decade.

Fortunately, India is starting the second decade of the twenty-first century in a demographic-economic situation that would be the envy of almost any nation on earth: A sweet spot that can set the stage for further economic transformation and geopolitical assertiveness.

PART TWO

The Making of a Superpower

There is a tide in the affairs of men.
Which, taken at the flood, leads on to fortune;
Omitted, all the voyage of their life
Is bound in shallows and in miseries.
On such a full sea are we now afloat,
And we must take the current when it serves,
Or lose our ventures.

– Brutus, in William Shakespeare's *Julius Caesar*

4

THE SWEET SPOT

Money and Power

When the Non-Aligned Movement (NAM) was formed in 1961 the United States had a per capita GDP of $2935.[1] India and its fellow NAM members, meanwhile, were lagging far behind in wealth. Leading NAM founders such as India, Egypt and Indonesia hovered in the range of $55 to $150 GDP per capita.[2]

Founding NAM members shared common goals of 'resisting the pressures of the major powers, maintaining their independence and opposing colonialism and neo-colonialism, specially (sic) western domination'.[3] Yet

NAM was more than an attempt by former colonies to retain independence; they wanted to pool their influence into a power bloc. It did not work, but the attempt and its failure are nonetheless instructive.

NAM was (and is) doomed as a movement for many reasons. Foremost among them: It was a collection of impoverished countries. NAM's fifty-year record of impotence underlines a simple fact of geopolitics: Money means power. No union of poor countries, however well-coordinated, could ever exercise power or influence on a par with a single wealthy state. NAM was destined from its founding to be a spectator, not an actor, in the global power struggle of the second half of the twentieth century.

Today, fifty years after co-founding NAM, the age of Indian irrelevance has passed, and India is now finally credible as a future global power. Yet great power status will not simply come to India because of its size. As we will see in the following chapters, there are several actions India will need to take in order to become a global power. Its economy will have to make a transition from outsourcing to innovation-intensive industries. Its multinationals will have to become truly global companies, with more business outside India than within. Finally, India must develop and implement a more assertive foreign policy, one that backs talk of great power status with military might and a willingness to use it.

A muscular foreign policy will only be possible if India concurrently becomes a major economic power. Throughout history there has been no such thing as a nation that could exercise political power abroad without commensurate economic power at home. Only a nation that creates wealth on a large scale can create the requisite military strength to project power overseas. Only a nation that creates wealth on a large scale will fund the innovation and attract the global capital needed to create a sustainable economic advantage over other nations. When a nation achieves this level of wealth creation, as the United States did in the twentieth century and as China aims to do now, political power can accrue rapidly. Economic strength and geopolitical strength are mutually reinforcing in a virtuous cycle: Money begets power, which begets more money, power and so on.

India, in its first fifty years of independence, tried its best to be a global power. India's arguments ('world's largest democracy') and tactics (NAM), however, were ineffective.

Today, as the second decade of the twenty-first century begins, India is a responsible nuclear power, and one of the fastest growing major economies in the world. Yet India cannot take its emergence as a global power for granted. Building wealth, and converting that wealth into power takes time. The United States learned that during its own rise to power in the late nineteenth and early twentieth century.

In 1865, the United States emerged from its civil war with the South virtually destroyed in defeat, and with much of what is today the Western United States still in the hands of other powers. The young nation worked hard to bind its war wounds and build its economy. It took decades of sustained economic performance before the United States was able to project its influence overseas. Only America's entry into the First World War (1914-18) – which proved decisive for the Allied cause – cemented the nation's position as a global power.

America's emergence as a world power might never have taken place. After the North won the civil war, economic mis-steps could have put off America's emergence as a world power temporarily or even permanently. If the South had won, the nation would have been divided into two hostile parts. It is easy to imagine these two nations being consumed with fears of each other rather than being motivated by ambitions for their roles in the world, the same trap that has bedevilled India and Pakistan post-partition.

Today India has but one decade of consistent growth behind it. If the United States' example a century ago is instructive, India will need several decades more of rapid growth before it is capable of projecting power on a global scale.

India's domestic market will be the most important source of this growth. But it alone will not be sufficient. To achieve 'great power' growth, India's private sector enterprises will have to make their businesses global. Only by tapping the world's markets fully can India's companies create the wealth that will be needed for India to catch up with China and, ultimately, the United States. Yet going global is fraught with as many risks as opportunities for India's companies. How India's companies navigate these risks will mean the difference between success and failure for them, and between great power status and the status quo for India.

The 'tide in the affairs of men' that Shakespeare wrote of is in India's favour today. Now India must deliver the growth needed to reinforce its emerging strength, or risk losing the opportunity. If India does act today, a century from now historians will talk of the first quarter of the twenty-first century as India's *debut* as a world power. But first India will have to tune out the 'Free Trade' advice that the United States and other developed economies are continuously chanting in its ear.

Beware Free (Trade) Advice

The American government would have Indians believe that the key to their prosperity lies in freer and freer trade. As Barack Obama told the Indian Parliament during his November 2010 visit: 'The United States remains – and will continue to remain – one of the most open economies in the world. And by opening markets and reducing barriers to foreign investment, India can realize its full economic potential as well.'[4] Secretary of State Hillary Clinton struck the same theme during a July 2011 visit to Chennai with her assertion that 'the opening of India's markets to the world will produce a more prosperous India'.[5]

The Free Trade Mantra

Every American diplomat learns a free trade mantra, and is sent forth to chant it throughout the world, to rich and poor nations alike. The American emissaries extol the virtues of open markets in stimulating growth and creating jobs, citing the United States as the prime example. They warn against the dangers of economic protectionism. Nations, they say, must avoid protecting domestic companies through import tariffs or other trade barriers. Such actions, American diplomats argue, shield inefficient domestic producers from competition and keep prices high for consumers. Let each nation focus on what it does best, the mantra goes, and the world benefits from efficient use of labour and capital, leading to rising prosperity for all.

Applying this viewpoint to India's recent history yields the following analysis: *India began its life as an independent nation no poorer than many other Asian countries. However, Nehru's misguided policy of import substitution cut India off from the benefits of world trade, while his affinity for socialism saddled India with inefficient domestic producers. The result was more than four decades of sub-par growth ('the Hindu growth rate'). Only when India finally opened up its economy in 1991 did things begin to change. Since 1991, greater integration with world markets has helped India create wealth, reduce poverty and establish itself as a future global economic power. Now, in order to continue and accelerate its growth India must increase further its integration with global markets by reducing trade barriers yet further. The more India opens its markets, the richer it will become.*

This analysis is accepted as conventional wisdom in American policymaking circles, as well as in many American corporations doing business with India. Yet this narrative misses an important point: India may find it can grow faster in the coming year if it mixes free trade with liberal doses of protectionism.

The United States has a clear interest in preaching a free trade doctrine, to India and other nations. American policy makers have made an 'all in' bet on open markets. Having removed nearly all barriers to foreign trade in the United States, their only option now is to cajole other countries to do the same. Furthermore, the United States – as a mature economy with its major demographic led growth behind it – cannot increase its standard of living dramatically without cracking new export markets that are growing faster than it is. India, as one of the largest growth markets in the world, is a prime target market for American exporters – and a prime target audience for American officials preaching free trade.

In spite of what the United States says, the case for India to open up even more to trade is not clear cut. Of course the Indian economy underperformed until 1991, and of course India has benefitted from freer trade since. Yet this conventional analysis neglects three important points. First, import substitution was not a wholesale economic loss for India; indeed, it serves as the foundation for India's current and future growth. Second, wealth creation is not a relentless and linear march towards open markets; some nations find protectionist policies a useful approach to building economic strength. Third, India is at a point in its development where it needs free trade less than it used to, and less than other countries now do. Much to America's dismay, India may find that some protectionist policies accelerate its development as a global economic power.

Growth Runway

In 1951, Nehru made a decision to follow an import substitution approach to industrialisation, whereby government policy supported the development of domestic industry and protected this industry with a shield of tariffs and trade barriers. Economists and policy makers have since criticised import substitution for holding back India's development.[6] These criticisms are justified, as India's economy certainly grew slower than its peers' in the years following its independence.

In 1960, South Korea had a GDP per capita of $155, compared to $84 in India.[7] Little did the world then know that South Korea, having emerged from a civil war less than a decade earlier, was poised for rapid economic growth. The export-led growth strategy South Korea followed paid off: Today it has a GDP per capita of $17,000, or fourteen times that of India.[8]

There is no doubt that import substitution cost India growth for the first four decades of its independence. But this period was not an economic dark age for India. Far from it. Import substitution was a dynamic and fruitful period when the birth and development of some of India's leading corporations took place. Today these companies are serving as a runway for India's growth.

The breadth and depth of corporate India is one reason India's economy has been able to grow so fast since liberalisation, especially in manufacturing. Without import substitution, and the companies it generated, India's corporate landscape would be much less diversified and strong than it is. Import substitution worked, albeit slowly, and India today is reaping the benefits.

During the first decade after liberalisation, India's manufacturing sector had yet to take off. The 1990s saw erratic performance in manufacturing, with growth of two percent in 1992 accelerating to fifteen percent by 1995, before dropping to zero in 1997; 1998 and 1999 saw growth of only three percent.[9] Import substitution and post 1991 liberalisation, however, eventually proved a potent combination. By 2003, manufacturing growth began to accelerate, averaging nine percent a year through the end of the decade.[10] Along the way India turned import substitution on its head, and became a substantial exporter of manufactured goods. In 2010, India exported $46.3 billion of goods to Europe, up by forty-three percent from 2006;[11] Indian export of goods to the United States grew by thirty-five percent over the same period.[12] It was due in part to import substitution that India had the corporations in place to ramp up its post-liberalisation manufacturing so quickly.

In India there is a company to meet virtually every industrial need. A comparison of India with other Asian nations shows just how diversified India's corporate landscape is. There are over 5,000 listed companies on the Bombay Stock Exchange (BSE), more than twice the number in China (Shanghai and Shenzhen stock exchanges combined) as well as in Japan, the world's second and third largest economies.[13]

Compared to India, other Asian nations have concentrated a much higher portion of their economic activity in a few firms. India has its corporate giants, to be sure, but they are far less influential in India than in other nations. India is a nation of small- and medium-sized companies. Even listed companies in India are small by global standards: Over sixty percent of the companies listed on the BSE have an annual turnover of less than $70 million.[14]

Along with its corporate diversity, India's advanced capital markets are another strength, and an indirect legacy of import substitution, which helped ensure India's capital market had a corps of substantial companies post-Independence. Over 3000 small- and medium-sized corporations are listed, and many of these have been listed for years. Today young firms continue to find the capital they need to continue to grow. In 2010, there were a total of 194 initial public offerings (IPOs) on the BSE and National Stock Exchange (NSE).[15] India's efficient capital markets help its fuel its corporate diversity and vice versa.

Rapidly developing economies can often concentrate wealth in the hands of a few firms, as their dominant market power, political influence and control of capital trump competitive forces. The 'License Raj' – whereby the Indian government effectively gave companies permits to control certain industries – had the near-term effect of propping up a small number of Indian firms. The system ensured that the recipients of government licenses prospered and grew at the expense of would-be competitors, and at the expense of efficient use of labour and capital. Still, over the longer term, the propping up of the licensee firms also had a beneficial effect. When the License Raj was dismantled after 1991, India enjoyed the best of both worlds: A large number of healthy companies that had grown to critical mass under government largesse, mixed with an open system that fostered free competition and allowed dynamic new entrants.

India's diverse manufacturing base offers the country another advantage: efficient allocation of capital. Consider China's manufacturing sector, which grew up in a different way than India's. China turned itself into a manufacturing powerhouse over the course of twenty years, beginning with Deng Xiaoping's decision to liberalise the economy in the late 1970s. In this period China went from an economy based about forty percent on agriculture to an economy based about forty percent on manufacturing. It did this primarily by keeping its currency weak to stimulate export demand. While this policy attracted foreign investment, created jobs and stimulated GDP growth, it did not necessarily foster the most efficient allocation of capital. China's has been a risky approach to building a manufacturing sector in a short time; if demand for Chinese goods in the West dries up, or evolves to different sectors, the dislocation for Chinese manufacturers and their workers could be painful.

India did not have to backfill a manufacturing sector the way China did; India's grew slowly under the nurturing care of import substitution over the course of four decades. By the time India was ready to open up its economy, its manufacturing sector was broad, deep and capitalised largely according to market demand (notwithstanding the distortions of the License Raj). The result was a growth runway that is capable of propelling India's development for decades to come.

Demographics and Protectionism

The past fifty years have seen a dramatic reduction in the world's average tariff rates for manufactured goods, from fifty percent to four percent.[16] Through successive rounds of multilateral trade discussions, the world has moved towards ever freer trade. Some countries, of course, are freer than others, and many nations, developed and developing alike, maintain formal and informal trade barriers.

Bangladesh is the greatest holdout against international trade, maintaining tariff rates as high as 463 percent for certain goods.[17] Singapore is the world's most open economy, with a trade-to-GDP ratio exceeding two times. India is somewhere in the middle, with average tariff rates of around thirty percent,[18] higher sales tax rates for imported goods in some states, and substantial non-tariff barriers such as licensing, packaging and testing requirements.[19]

Looking at the last half century it would be tempting to conclude that the world is on an irreversible march towards free trade; and that trade links among nations are too strong to be broken by any resurgence of protectionist sentiment. It would be equally tempting to conclude that India, though less open than many more developed nations, is on the same irreversible path towards freer and freer trade, eager to export its goods and services to other nations and willing, in exchange, to expose fully its domestic manufacturers to foreign competition.

We have been through all this before. The world goes through cycles of free trade and protectionism, and neither side has ever won the debate conclusively. There have been periods where either was the dominant view; the last thirty years may be regarded by historians simply as a period when the free traders held sway. It is entirely possible that we are now entering into a period when protectionism will gain ground as an acceptable policy, and eventually become the dominant view once again. As for India, import substitution was its first major experiment in protectionism, and it will certainly not be the last.

India will be under tremendous pressure to create employment as its demographic wave crests. India's workforce will grow by at least 80 million in the coming decade.[20] If more Indian women come into the workforce, the number of new workers could grow to 110 million, or thirty percent of all new workers in the world.[21] The notion that India will reduce trade barriers further just as its economy begins to reach its maximum growth potential – and when its need for employment is greatest – flies in the face of historical evidence and India's rational self-interest. More likely is that India, like most developing countries before it, will see protectionism as a viable economic strategy. If so, it will be making the same choice the United States, the United Kingdom and other now-developed countries have made at similar points in their evolutions.

The developed countries that preach free trade do so out of a professed interest in creating a system that fosters global growth, for developed and developing countries alike. In reality they are preaching a system that is clearly in their interests, but not so clearly in the interests of developing countries.

Friedrich List was a nineteenth century German economist and early proponent of the 'infant industry' case for protectionism. List argued that a nation in an early stage of its industrial development should protect its young industries from foreign competition through tariffs, until they grow large enough to compete effectively.

Who was one of List's inspirations? America's first treasury secretary, Alexander Hamilton, whose 1791 'Report on Manufactures' argued for industrialisation by protection of infant industries in the newly independent United States.[22]

List believed that free trade is only beneficial among countries at similar stages of development.[23] Far from being a boon to less developed nations, free trade can harm their development, particularly in manufacturing. Not that developed countries care. Just the opposite: Stunting the growth of industry in developing nations is, in List's view, exactly what many developed countries want to achieve with 'free trade'.

Kicking away the Ladder

If Friedrich List were here to listen to American and European admonitions today to complete the Doha Round[24] of free trade negotiations, he would recognise the same developed country hypocrisy that he noted in his 1841 work 'The National System of Political Economy'. List wrote that preaching free trade was an act of self-interest by developed countries. A developed nation, once it has achieved growth and prosperity through protection of its own industries, then 'kicks away the ladder' of industrial development 'in order to deprive others of the means of climbing up after him'.[25] Convincing developing countries not to protect their own industries, if successful, would have a double benefit for developed nations: The developing markets remain open to goods, and would-be industrial competitors from these new markets do not materialise.

Great economic powers have risen through protectionism, and then tried to kick away the ladder before other nations could ascend it. One day India, having ascended to wealth, may preach the virtues of free trade to places like Africa, eager to at once open new growth markets and stifle the next generation of industrial competition. But first it will likely go through its own phase of protectionism.

Britain was the first country to use infant industry protection, which it did to great effect in the seventeenth century, eventually surpassing the continental powers in manufacturing.[26] Once its manufacturing power was secure, the United Kingdom tried to stop its former colonies in the United States from attaining the same strength. 'It is well worthwhile,' Lord Henry Brougham, MP, told Parliament in 1816, 'to incur a loss upon the first exportation, in order by the glut, to stifle in the cradle, those rising manufactures, in the United States'.[27] The young United States resisted the United Kingdom's attempts to under-price its manufacturing sector into oblivion. In fact, over the next century the United States became the leading proponent of protectionism, and its manufacturing sector prospered behind a shield of tariffs.[28]

Protectionism continued to be a mainstream economic tactic (and political philosophy) in the United States well into the twentieth century.[29] The United States, in fact, continued to be protectionist until it no longer needed to be. At the end of the Second World War, with Europe and Japan in ruins, the United States was far and away the dominant manufacturing economy in the world. The United States then embarked on a concerted effort – enthusiastically joined by Europe – to reduce tariff rates worldwide. Having ascended the ladder of wealth, they were not about to let developing countries climb up so easily after them. Such is the progression of national development: protectionism, followed by growing industrial strength, then wealth and – suddenly – a conversion to the free trade religion.

Today India may well be in the midst of a century-long protectionist swing that began with import substitution. In such a scenario, the liberalisations since 1991 would be a temporary retreat from protectionism. By any standard, India is still a protected economy. Average tariff rates on manufactured goods in India are double those in the United States.[30] Moreover, India's non-tariff barriers decrease competitiveness of imports and favour domestic manufacturers.

As we move into the twenty-first century, India could determine that a reversion to protectionism is in its interest, especially if the economic crisis that began in 2008 continues to dampen GDP growth in the United States and Western Europe. A prolonged slump in the developed world would widen the looming growth gap between India and the West. In that case India could conclude that – like Britain in the eighteenth century and the United States in the nineteenth – it has more to gain from shutting out foreign players at home than it has to lose by being shut out of foreign markets. The coming decades could well see India continue to grow between eight to ten percent, and the rest of the world, in the most optimistic scenario, at two to three percent. Protectionism is a strategy worth considering for any nation outgrowing its trading partners by a factor of four or five.

The Sweet Spot

For years the world's dominant image of India was one of swarms of humanity living in poverty. Those who did not know the country, and many who did, felt it was condemned to permanent impoverishment, as runaway population growth ate away at whatever meagre economic growth it was able to manage.

Today India's curse has become its blessing. It has what every nation wants: demographic-led growth. China does not have it, though it used to. The United States has a bit of it, thanks to immigration. For Japan and Western Europe, it is a distant memory.

India is in a demographic-economic sweet spot, with large numbers of young people coming into the work force, and an economy growing fast enough to employ them. Nearly one-third of the Indian population is fourteen years of age or younger. Until the 1990s, India's growth was too anaemic to make use of its rapidly growing population, and GDP per capita grew only slightly. Now, however, India's turbo-charged economy has not only absorbed its growing population, but also turned them into consumers that fuel additional growth. India's demographics have become one of its great advantages.

If India is able to get its urban infrastructure in place, it will be able to make productive use of an even greater portion of its population: city dwellers. Indian cities are under-invested, though they hold the key to future job creation. Seventy percent of Indian jobs are expected to be created in cities by 2030.[31] Yet India currently spends just $17 per capita on urban infrastructure, one-seventh the level of China.[32] There is additional GDP growth to be unlocked if India can create urban environments that can foster job creation and absorb additional migrants from rural areas. If India is able to supply the infrastructure to allow its cities to grow more rapidly, it can add as much as 170 million workers to its urban workforce.[33]

All the rich countries of the world have had their time in the demographic sweet spot. Europe was there in the eighteenth century. The United States in the nineteenth. Japan in the early twentieth. China in the 1980s. Now it is India's turn.

Japan today is the anti-India. Twenty-two percent of the country's population is sixty-five or older (versus five percent in India).[34] The birth rate has dropped to 1.37 per woman.[35] Immigration is low, with international migrant stock less than two percent of the population.[36] All of this, against a backdrop of two 'lost decades' of economic growth, has put the country into a demographic-economic sour spot. The earthquake and tsunami that hit the country in March 2011 was a human and economic catastrophe that demographically-challenged Japan could ill afford.

Europe is slightly better off, partly due to the macabre circumstance that its people do not live as long as the Japanese. European birth rates are far below replacement level, with Germany, Italy and Spain all producing only around 1.4 births per woman.[37] While Europe is helped by higher immigration rates than Japan, it is having a hard time integrating immigrants, with abundant social and religious tensions between native Europeans and the new arrivals.

The United States is fortunate, unlike Europe, to have a tradition of assimilating new cultures. Were it not for immigration, the United States might well share Europe's fate as an ageing society unable to replenish its own population, much less grow. The overall United States population has similar birth rates as France (which, at two births per woman, is among the highest of major European nations).[38] International migrant stock in the United States however, remains high among developed nations,[39] and these new arrivals to the United States are having more children on average than native born Americans. While the United States will never again see the population growth it enjoyed when immigration was at its peak (in 1890, one in seven Americans was foreign born),[40] the nation today depends on the positive demographics of its immigrant groups. Immigrants bring a much-needed infusion of developing country growth to American demographics.

Yet immigration has become a contentious political issue in the United States, particularly since the global recession that began in 2008. Hard economic times have increased mainstream American society's suspicion of immigrants. American policy makers, however, must not abandon the policy of immigration that has made the nation strong and continues to strengthen it. Of course, the United States must halt illegal immigration; but it must not do so at the expense of legal immigration.

The United States greatly benefits from legal immigrants such as highly skilled H-1Bs from India and elsewhere. The United States also benefits from lower-skilled immigrants, albeit in different ways. The unskilled come to pursue their version of the American dream: a better life for them and their children. In doing so, they help keep the entire nation dynamic and growing. This steady flow of new arrivals hungry for success is one key to America's continued competitiveness. If American critics wonder what the economy would look like without immigration, they need look no further than Europe or Japan, where low GDP growth has reigned for decades.

Americans need not worry about overcrowding. There is still plenty of room to expand; the population density in the United States is 34 people per square kilometre, well below that of countries such as France (114) and Germany (235).[41] The United States could swell to three billion people and still have a population density lower than the Netherlands (490 people per square kilometre) has today.[42]

The Big Prize

The United States, Europe, and Japan – all have advanced industrialised economies that have grown up in boom times. Their populations are used to an escalating standard of living. They have companies with established brands, proven technologies and talented management teams. Now that growth at home has trailed off, these mature economies have only one choice if they are to increase, or even maintain, their standards of living: They must export to where the growth is today.

Number one on their list of markets will be India. The United States is already pushing India hard to open its markets.[43] The United States' motive for preaching free trade to India is clear: It sees the Indian market as vital to the future of American businesses. Forget India as an outsourcing destination. The big prize of the next fifty years will be the Indian customer, not the Indian supplier.

China will also be a big market, but it will be second on the American multinationals' lists, not first. Of course, China is already an enormous economy. It is already three times the size of India's, and could well overtake the United States as the world's largest by 2027.[44]

The relative attractiveness of India as a future export market for the United States is evident in recent trade statistics. American exports to India have grown five-fold in the past decade.[45] While American exports to China are still more than four times those to India, the gap is closing quickly.

Behind these numbers are two facts that make India more attractive than China as a market for American goods over the long term.

First, India has better demographics. Indiaʼs birth rate is fifty percent higher than Chinaʼs (2.68 versus 1.77 births per female).[46] Over thirty-one percent of the Indian population is under the age of fifteen; China has only twenty percent.[47] The gap is the legacy of Chinaʼs one-child policy, the 1978 decree to limit most families to one child. Recent research shows that the policy was short-sighted in the extreme.

Chinaʼs Great Leap Backwards

In the 1960s and 1970s, China appeared to enjoy the kind of demographic tailwinds that India has today: strong population growth and a steady supply of new workers as far as the eye could see. The problem was that China was not confident of employing all of these new Chinese; it saw population growth as a liability instead of an asset. So it introduced the one-child policy in 1978.

In retrospect, China forsook population growth at precisely the wrong time. Five years after the one-child policy, Chinaʼs economic growth began to take off: From 1983 to 1988, China achieved double digit GDP growth in all but one year (1986, at 8.8 percent); in 1984, growth hit an astounding fifteen percent. Had China not put the brakes on population growth, its rapidly growing economy would have had a steady supply of new workers, rather than worries about labourʼs declining supply and rising cost.

Research by a Chinese think thank has shown that China over-estimated its fertility rate (live births per woman) at the time of the introduction of the one-child act.[48] While fertility increased throughout the 1960s, reaching a peak of nearly six live births per woman late in the decade, it dropped sharply throughout the 1970s. By the time the policy was introduced in 1980, fertility rates had already settled at around 2.5. The one-child policy drove fertility below the replacement level of 2.1.

It turns out Chinaʼs population growth problem was in the midst of solving itself when China intervened. Had China not interfered with its population growth, its self-moderating population increases and new economic growth would have solved any perceived population problem. Moreover, the combination of economic growth and positive demographics would have put it into the demographic-economic sweet spot.

As it is, China will face increasing social costs over the coming decades, and lower GDP growth, as members of its working age population retire with fewer young people to replace them. By the second quarter of the century, twenty-eight percent of China's population will be fifty-five or older versus just sixteen percent in India.[49] China's one-child policy may well go down in history, along with communism and the Cultural Revolution, as one of the nation's greatest blunders.

Compared to China, India has engineered a more gradual transition to lower birth rates. Rather than decree a procreation policy, India has used incentives and social programmes to persuade families to have fewer children voluntarily. The government has run sterilisation programmes, and promoted the use of contraceptives in the media and elsewhere.[50] More recently, it has also offered cash incentives to couples to delay having their first child.[51]

Whereas China's population growth fell off a cliff after its one-child policy, India's has declined slowly, from 4.7 births per woman in 1980 to 2.7 in 2009.[52] The result is that today India is enjoying the demographic dividend that China is missing. Today India looks like China of the 1980s, while China is starting to look increasingly like present-day Japan and Europe.

China's second weakness relative to India is its over-dependence on exports to generate economic growth. In 2007, thirty-eight percent of Chinese GDP was due to exports, versus just twenty percent for India.[53] When Chinese exports dropped to twenty-seven percent of GDP by 2009, GDP fell as well, by five percentage points (from 14.2 percent in 2007 to 9.1 percent in 2009).[54]

China's growth has not only been export-led, it has been export dependent: China has yet to demonstrate that it can achieve GDP growth in excess of ten percent without extraordinarily high levels of exports. While exports are attractive for any country, in order to create sustainable wealth the exports must be based on a sustainable competitive advantage. China's exports have been dependent on a weak national currency to make its products cheaper to foreign buyers. This approach has driven GDP growth for years, but it does not count as a sustainable competitive advantage.

Indeed, there is evidence that China's vaunted export industry creates little value for the nation. In the case of China's exports to the United States, the dependence of Chinese exporters on foreign components (from the United States and elsewhere) means that as little as thirty percent of the value of China's 'exports' actually accrues to China.[55]

China's artificially low currency will be harder to maintain as China's economy grows. Moreover, stimulating export demand through a weak currency has hidden costs. China's consumers suffer higher costs for imports. In addition, capital allocation may be inefficient, as capital flows to a broad range of export-oriented industries, rather than to those industries where China has the greatest competitive advantage.

The question is whether China's strategy to drive GDP growth through an export sector turbo-charged by a weak currency will, over time, prove to be wise or foolish. The answer will come only over a period of decades, as China gradually ceases its currency interventions and begins to compete on an even basis with other nations. If the allocation of capital in China has not been efficient, China's export industries will suffer, and GDP growth will lag as the economy transitions capital to new, more efficient uses tied to natural competitive advantages.

India's economy, by contrast, is driven by domestic consumption rather than exports. Indian businesses make most of their money selling to Indian customers. With a domestic market buoyed by favourable demographics, India's consumption-led model constitutes a major advantage over China's export-led model. Moreover, India does not carry the risks associated with export-led growth; a global trade war would hurt India's growth, particularly in the IT services sector, but India would suffer far less than China.

With India in the demographic-economic sweet spot, and sporting a better long-term economic model than China, it is ideally positioned to become a global economic power in the next three decades. Domestic-driven demand is a great foundation on which to build, but that alone is insufficient to develop true economic might. To build the kind of economic power India needs – economic power that will breed and reinforce political power – India will have to move beyond outsourcing to the innovation that produces better technology and stronger brands.

The ministers of George I in 1721 openly declared, on the occasion of the prohibition of the importation of the manufactures of India, that it was clear that a nation could only become wealthy and powerful if she imported raw materials and exported manufactured goods.

– Friedrich List, *The National System of Political Economy*, 1841[1]

5

FROM BACK OFFICE TO FRONT

Colonialism 2.0

In the previous chapter, we saw how countries experiencing rapid growth and development have sought to limit foreign goods in order to protect domestic manufacturing; and how, having achieved technology and scale in manufacturing, those same countries then preach free trade in order to maintain their advantage over other, up-and-coming nations.

As an empire, England took this one step further. Imperial England's economic strategy was simple: Import raw materials from the colonies, and export manufactured goods from England. It was a trap the British Empire sought to force all of its colonies into. In the eighteenth century, for example, it was England's official stated policy that not a single horseshoe nail should be allowed to be produced in North America.[2] Similarly England prohibited import of manufactured goods from India.

Today India is falling into the colonial trap all over again, except this time it is doing so willingly. Of course, today India has a thriving manufacturing industry and exports where it pleases. Nonetheless, a large portion of India's economy is still stuck producing 'raw materials' that help other nations become rich and powerful. These 'raw materials' are low-margin for India, but confer great margins to the countries, including the United States, that import them.

Worse yet, India's political and business leaders are genuinely excited about these 'raw material' exports. They do not see that, by focusing its efforts on low value 'raw materials' rather than high value finished products, India is subjecting itself to colonial economic policies all over again.

The difference today: India's 'raw materials' are services, not goods. The export of these services – outsourcing – represents the single greatest limitation on India's future growth.

Two centuries ago, the United Kingdom used Indian cotton as raw material to run its textile mills and strengthen its industrial base. Today, the United States uses Indian IT services to run its software products and strengthen its technology base. The effect is the same: a colonial style enrichment of other nations, at India's expense.

Innovate or Die

Companies – and countries – that innovate, backed up by intellectual property and packaged into brands, will grow rich and powerful. They will generate the profits to fund yet more innovation in a virtuous cycle.

Companies – and countries – that do not innovate will be condemned to see others pass them by in wealth and power. They may soldier on, eking out an existence; but they will never truly ascend the prosperity curve. Eventually they will either change their ways or disappear. Change comes when a visionary leader, tired of living on the margin of survival, embraces innovation and dares to invest in the future. Once the investments bear fruit, the patience of the people is rewarded with rising incomes and the security of a more sustainable approach for the long term. This is the path of courage and action.

But few choose action, or fail somewhere in the execution of action. Most companies or countries that suffer from a lack of innovation become weaker and weaker, eventually falling prey to a larger rival. In the case of companies the end game is often a takeover by another firm, sometimes hostile, sometimes friendly. Where there is still some value left in the enterprise, the selling shareholders get cash, or shares in the buyer's more successful enterprise, as compensation; sometimes the shares are worthless, and the sellers must content themselves with having part of all of their liabilities taken over with the shares.

In the case of countries, the penalty for not innovating is harsher: Takeover is at the hands of a foreign power, and anything but friendly. Men are slaughtered, women raped, children enslaved, and a cultural heritage extinguished. That is the steep price a people must pay for leaders who fail to foster innovation.

Looking at a map of the world, it is all too easy to forget the names of nations and civilisations that have perished at the hands of neighbours. In the ancient world there were the Babylonians, the Phoenicians and the Minoans; later the Mongols, the Mughals and several civilisations in sub-Saharan Africa. More recently noble and ignoble experiments in government alike have fallen apart after decades of neglecting innovation: the Austro-Hungarian Empire, Yugoslavia and the Soviet Union, to name a few.

The native inhabitants of North and South America were also victims of a lack of innovation. European settlers arrived in the new world in the seventeenth century with superior weaponry and new diseases, and began a drive to take over the entire North American continent. Within three centuries, millions of Native Americans were wiped out. With them went most of their cultural heritage. In the United States today, there are only the scattered descendants of those who survived the arrival of Europeans, remnants of a lost civilisation.

Around eighty thousand years ago, Europe and North America were both hunter-gatherer societies, sparsely populated and without formal political structures.[3] The people of Europe adopted organised farming and livestock rearing around three thousand years ago. They ordered themselves into city states, and later kingdoms and nations, where people had the time to write, read and think how to make better ploughs and better weapons. Great empires sprang up – Rome, Byzantium, the Holy Roman Empire, and the Ottomans. Governments sponsored centres of learning – in Bologna and Oxford in the eleventh century, and in Heidelberg three centuries later.[4]

All the while native Americans continued living off the land in a largely nomadic lifestyle. In South America, the Mayan and Inca civilisations achieved a certain degree of organisation, with effective imperial administration and organised armies. But it was nothing next to what was going on in Europe. By the time Old World's ships reached the New World's shores, the battle of innovation had already been fought and won; the Native Americans never had a chance.

Of course one cannot blame the Native Americans for being conquered by the European settlers. Such is the merciless nature of human competition and conflict as Adam Smith (*The Wealth of Nations*) meets Charles Darwin ('survival of the fittest'). Today the struggle continues to play out on battlefields worldwide, and in corporate boardrooms. Capitalist societies have set up their own free market 'battlefields' where corporations fight daily for customers and their cash, in the hope that the sum total of these skirmishes will strengthen their nations and prepare them to be the victor – not the vanquished – when they must do battle with another state, as the irrefutable record of human history says they must.

Thinking too Small

Indian industry, led by its outsourcers, is thinking too small. In order to build a sustainable competitive advantage at the national level – in order to be the victor, not the vanquished – India must not be satisfied with being a leader in outsourcing. Just as, a century ago, India chafed at enriching England with the export of raw materials, today it should chafe at enriching the United States through outsourcing.

India should aspire to be the global leader in technology products, not in technology services. India has the domestic talent to do so; its technological raw materials already power many of America's high technology products. There is no colonial power restricting India to the provision of technology services. The only restriction in India is a lack of ambition. To build true wealth, India must leave technology *services* behind and focus on developing, owning and marketing its own finished technology *products*.

Technology products can, and should be, what India takes to the world. Like glass was for Venice, silk was for China and – once upon a time – spices were for India, technology can be the product that defines India of the twenty-first century. For technology products to become India's leading industry, its technology companies must move beyond outsourcing: They must move from back office to front.

Outsourcing[5] was a $64 billion industry for India in 2010, expected to grow to $76 billion in 2011.[6] The industry employs over 2.2 million Indians directly and accounts for around six percent of GDP.[7] The industry is expected to grow to $225 billion in turnover by 2020.[8] It has been described as India's 'golden goose of the moment'.[9]

Yes, outsourcing has generated income and employment for India. Yes, outsourcing is a new phenomenon made possible by the ability to deliver services remotely. But outsourcing is neither good for India, nor the wave of the future.

As an industry, outsourcing depends on an Indian labour cost advantage for its very existence. Outsourcing firms argue that the services they offer are becoming more sophisticated, and more tied to value-addition instead of cost. This much is true. Still, were India's labour cost advantage to disappear, outsourcing would shrink to a fraction of its current size, if it could survive at all.

India's interest as a nation is in a rising standard of living that will ultimately undermine outsourcing's viability as an industry. Outsourcing's interests as an industry – a labour cost advantage – are therefore at cross-purposes with India's: Outsourcing can only thrive as long as India is poor. Faced between the choice of a vibrant outsourcing industry and broad-based wealth creation, there is only one path that India (or any other nation) would follow: wealth.

Building this wealth, and continuing to employ Indians as they get richer, will require moving beyond cost-based outsourcing to innovation-based industries that can thrive despite higher labour costs. Only with such industries leading the way can India reach its true economic potential.

Table Scraps of Global Commerce

Today India, sitting on a gold mine of talent, is uniquely well positioned to succeed in the global battle of innovation.

It produces 750,000 engineers a year.[10] The IIT entrance requirements – one in fifty students is admitted – are among the toughest in the world; some who cannot get into an IIT must settle for a place at an Ivy League university in the United States.

The pressing question for India is whether it is taking full advantage of its talent. For years many of India's brightest minds left the country to study or work overseas. In the past decade, a gradual reversal of this trend has begun to take hold, with more talented Indians staying put (and returning home) to take advantage of improving career opportunities offered by corporate India.

Although this is a positive trend for India's long-term competitiveness, India is still falling far short of fully utilising its talent base. Outsourcing is the main culprit: It consumes too much of India's talent and deploys this talent in pursuits that add too little economic value. Offshore services create more long term value for the client than they do for the outsourcing firm, and more value for the West than they do for India.

India's outsourcing industry hires some 225,000 employees a year.[11] The top three outsourcing majors – Infosys, Wipro and Tata Consultancy Services – alone hire 130,000 engineering graduates, on whom they spend some $450 million to train.[12] A full ninety percent of India's outsourcing revenue comes from exports,[13] of which the United States accounts for sixty percent.[14] So over half of this year's new outsourcing hires will be working for American clients. The work they will be doing will vary from basic invoice processing to software testing to advanced computer chip design. Many of them will toil all day long so that their work can be ready when their clients open for business in the United States. It is brain drain all over again. While this time the brains are physically remaining in India, the talent is being drained abroad via satellite link and high speed data lines.

Outsourcing might look like a great deal for India. But outsourcing is an even better deal for India's customers, first and foremost the United States. American companies have benefitted from India's talent to build their own businesses, with no upfront investment and no risk beyond the terms of the outsourcing contract. American technology firms are dining like kings, as Indian outsourcers scrounge for the table scraps of global commerce.

Some will argue that outsourcing is a free-market transaction where both the American client and the Indian outsourcing firm benefit. While this is certainly true, it is also a narrow view of the picture. India's larger strategic goal must be to develop the long-term competitiveness of both its employees and its companies. Outsourcing does little to accomplish either objective. In fact, there is a clear opportunity cost for India in the outsourcing industry that outweighs any near-term benefits that the industry provides: Lakhs of outsourcing employees are innovating for American clients, when they could be innovating for domestic consumers.

India has become the world's white label provider of IT services. The United States buys these services from India wholesale and then puts them into a product which it brands and markets at a huge mark-up.

The global value chain for smart phones, for example, demonstrates that most of the profit lies in the branding and distribution. Smart phones that retail for $500 or more in the United States often contain less than $200 in components. The balance consists of costs in designing, marketing and distributing the product – and for profit margin along the way.[15]

Apple is particularly good at lowering its component costs to drive profit margins up. An analysis of one of Apple's digital music players indicated components only account for twenty-eight percent of the retail price.[16] This is why Apple has a market capitalisation of over $300 billion and earned a net profit of $6 billion in the second quarter of 2011 alone.[17] Its offshore suppliers of components and manufacturing services, meanwhile, are struggling with razor-thin margins.[18]

It is the same for Indian outsourcers doing research and development (R&D), and engineering work for American clients. Infosys boasts that its Product Engineering Division can reduce engineering costs and time for its clients by thirty percent. The value proposition from Infosys is clear: India bears the 'rapid scale "up" and "tear down" costs' so that 'you can do more with the same and gain the leadership of your product'.[19] The net result of such projects is that Indian minds do the upfront work, and most of the long-term benefits accrue to the American client.

The Indian outsourcer's costs are largely variable, since to earn more money it has to hire more employees. When outsourced services are used by the American client to produce a product, as they often are, the American firm can benefit from economies of scale in marketing this product to customers globally. India is stuck with variable costs and thin margins, while the United States enjoys economies of scale without the upfront investment (and risk) that such economies would normally demand.

Outsourcing's dilemma is that its revenue follows a largely linear pattern in proportion to its costs. Outsourcers have been able to achieve modest economies of scale by pricing more of their projects at a fixed price, allowing them to wring higher margins out of greater operational efficiencies. Infosys increased the percentage of its total engagements that have a fixed price from 31 percent in FY 2008 to 35.4 percent in FY 2009.[20] This reflects a trend in the industry overall towards more fixed price contracts.[21] It is a testament to the industry's management ability that it has been able to achieve any scalability at all in a service business that is largely dominated by a 'cost plus' pricing model, whereby the profit margin is effectively fixed.

The industry's search for scalability has led it to focus on what Infosys CFO V. Balakrishnan calls 'the non-linearity of revenue'.[22] In this search, Infosys and its fellow outsourcers would do well to look at their customers and other American companies as models.

MSFT vs. INFY

The opportunity cost of outsourcing for India is illustrated by comparing two technology giants, Microsoft and Infosys. Both companies were founded on a shoestring a few years apart (Microsoft in 1975, and Infosys six years later). Both have grown to become global enterprises employing roughly similar numbers of employees.

The similarities end there. Microsoft and Infosys are in completely different arms of the technology business, with completely different results to show for it.

While Microsoft has twelve times the sales of Infosys, and over seven times the market value, this is not the entire story. The eye-popping numbers are the turnover per employee and R&D expenses. Microsoft produces over fifteen times the turnover per employee that Infosys does. Not coincidentally, Microsoft also spends nearly twice the annual turnover of Infosys on R&D alone. Infosys spent a paltry $59 million on R&D in 2009, and it still outspent its rivals TCS and Wipro.[23]

To a certain extent the comparison is unfair to Infosys. Microsoft is an extreme example of the favourable economics of the software industry, and one of the greatest business successes of the last century. Furthermore, both companies are a product of the environment they were founded in. United States GDP per capita was over eight times greater when Microsoft started than Indian GDP per capita was when Infosys started.[24] Even if Infosys's founders had conceived of writing software code and producing products (as Microsoft does), there would have been little or no domestic demand, and cracking overseas markets would have been next to impossible. Infosys could only have developed as it did, as a service business, and that alone has been a tremendous achievement.

Still, the comarison of Infosys with Microsoft highlights the inherent limitations in the outsourcing business model. Firms like Infosys that sell services are operating on thin margins, have mostly variable cost structures and have to invest in more people to grow. Product firms like Microsoft have higher margins, enjoy a higher proportion of fixed costs, and can increase their turnover faster than their costs. For successful R&D driven product companies, it is a virtuous cycle whereby high margin products funded by R&D can themselves fund the next wave of innovation. For service companies, it is a vicious cycle whereby the sale of services does not generate sufficient profit to fund serious innovations.

Infosys would find it hard to justify a steep increase in R&D spending to its investors and the wider market. While increased R&D investments might well pay off handsomely in the long run, they would mean a near term decrease in profitability with no certainty of future results. If Infosys were, like Microsoft, to devote fifteen percent of its turnover to R&D, its operating margin would drop by half and investors would flee.

Nonetheless, a massive increase in R&D is precisely what Infosys and other outsourcers need if they intend to maximise long-term value for their shareholders. India, for its part, must encourage the transformation of outsourcing to an innovation-led product business if the nation is to maximise the long-term value of its considerable base of talent.

An Innovation Index

The United States spends 2.8 percent of its overall GDP on R&D.[25] Over seventy percent of all R&D spending worldwide is by American corporations on American soil; a further fifteen percent is spent by foreign companies on American soil.[26] These investments have transformed America, over the course of the last century, into the most dynamic and innovative economy in the world. Thanks to this innovation, the American business environment is one of constant change and evolution, even at the top. Standard and Poors (S&P), a United States-based rating agency, keeps a list of the top American corporations. (Today it is called the S&P 500, though in earlier years it was smaller to reflect a smaller American corporate sector.) The list is a useful index for the pace of innovation in the United States, and how it has changed over time.

The companies on S&P's list in the 1920s could expect, on average, to remain on the list for another sixty-five years. By the end of the century, average tenure on the list had dropped to a decade.[27] In the dynamic United States economy, even large companies are prone to being unseated by smaller companies that are innovating faster, and therefore growing faster. The threat from these smaller companies in turn keeps the larger companies sharper than they would be otherwise, breeding a virtuous cycle of innovation.

India must propel itself on the same journey the United States took last century. It must evolve to become an economy where innovation is so rapid that it threatens even established players. Yet India need not take as long as the United States did to become an innovation-based economy. With the overall pace of technological change today, and India's own base of engineering and IT talent, India can do it much faster.

Today's world is different from the one in which Infosys was founded. India has matured into a burgeoning market in its own right, one where corporate and individual customers alike will pay for technology products that improve their efficiency or enhance their lives. There is no longer a need to build a business, as outsourcing has done, around developing intellectual property for others, especially for foreign companies. To do so sells India's talent short and, furthermore, strengthens the competition, from both foreign firms and other nations.

The Low Margin Services Trap

There are some early signs that India's outsourcers recognise the need to make a transition to higher margin product businesses. Infosys, Wipro and TCS have all increased their patent filings in recent years.[28] Many Indian outsourcing firms intend to increase their investments in R&D and develop more product-based business. This type of commitment to innovation will be necessary if India's outsourcers are to transition from developing intellectual property for others to developing intellectual property for themselves.

There is a long way to go. India currently spends less than one percent of GDP on R&D, and seventy-five percent of this is funded by the government. India lags behind other nations such as Singapore and South Korea in the amount of R&D funded by the private sector.[29] Private industry, led by outsourcing firms, will have to devote a greater percentage of its profits to R&D if India is to escape its low margin services trap.

More innovative work can also help the outsourcing industry address its persistent challenge of employee attrition. One outsourcing firm was awarded a contract by a financial services client both to manage its accounting systems as well as create a new derivatives platform from scratch. A recent study covering this firm and others, found that when thirty-to-forty percent of an outsourcing firm's work comprises creative tasks, employee attrition levels can drop by as much as half, compared to firms where more tedious work is the norm. The survey also found that outsourcing firms following fixed price contracts achieved higher client satisfaction rates than those operating on a cost plus model.[30]

Prudent employees in India know that working in an outsourcing position is short changing them in their long term career development. There is a difference between back office skills and front office skills. Back office skills tend to be highly specialised and repetitive; an employee may be a specialist in, for example, financial consolidation or processing insurance claims. These employees often miss out on developing 'front office' skills such as selling and client management. Of course there are positions at Indian outsourcing companies that require these skills, but comparatively fewer than those at Western firms that focus on innovation and product based businesses. Front office skills are particularly valuable later in an employee's career, when he will need to know how to sell to maximise his impact on the organisation, and therefore his income, during his peak earning years. Toiling anonymously in a cubicle in Bangalore may offer a good pay packet now, but it comes at a price: forgoing a chance to interact face-to-face with customers in a rapidly changing marketplace. If a young Indian graduate has a chance to work at a big outsourcing company in a back office role, or a small innovative Indian tech product company for half the pay in a front end role, he would be wise to opt for the front end role.

India's top outsourcing companies have all the tools to be the next great product innovators. Their employees have the technical skills: They can write code, engineer products, and redesign business processes as well or better than any of their clients. The leading outsourcers have a deep understanding of every conceivable industry vertical under the sun. They have a track record of innovating in services. Most of all, they are well managed by leaders who devote time and energy to understanding how the business world is developing globally. If these managers were able to become leaders in outsourcing, they may also have the wisdom to move beyond it.

Despite all these advantages India's outsourcers may well stumble in the transition to R&D-led innovation. There is a real possibility that

that they will miss the greatest business opportunity of the twenty-first century, an opportunity many times greater than outsourcing itself. It is an opportunity right under their noses: the rise of Asia as a market.

The risk Indian outsourcers face is that they will be so pre-occupied with Western customers and Western markets that they will not be able to see – even if they try – the needs of Asian customers and the Asian market. There is no certainty that the blockbuster products for Asia will resemble in any way what worked in the West. Developing products that are right for the Asian market will require a single-minded focus on the needs of Asian companies and consumers. Working for the West instead of the East could end up being a costly distraction.

The Battle Ahead

Today, in the second decade of the twenty-first century, India is in the middle of the second great economic transformation of our time. The first was the information revolution. We are now witnessing the second: a shift of consumption from developed economies to developing economies. In the coming decades, Asia will replace the United States as the primary source of global consumption. While other developing regions such as Latin America, Eastern Europe and Africa will also see consumption growth, these will be a fraction of Asia's contribution. The companies and countries that position themselves to serve Asian demand will be those that create greatest wealth in the first half of the twenty-first century.

Indian producers should be ideally positioned to benefit from this structural shift in demand. They are, after all, located where the customers of the future are. The danger is that they will be too focused on exports to see the opportunity at home.

Ironically, many Western companies are becoming more aggressive about innovating for Indian consumers than Indian companies themselves are. While Indian companies are busy with outsourced product design work for Western products, Western companies are locating their own R&D facilities in India, and telling their scientists to innovate for Indian consumers. Xerox, for instance, has located an innovation centre in Chennai, with a specific mission to develop document management solutions for emerging market customers.[31] Why does it take an American company to see this opportunity? The Indian outsourcers are too busy managing documents of their American customers to think about what next generation local demand will be.

A study of innovation in the Indian telecom sector found that one of the keys to successfully innovating for domestic customers in emerging markets is to develop modular product designs that are based on innovations in the architecture of the product itself.[32] In other words, rip up the design specifications and start over. Companies cannot build products for the Indian consumer using high cost Western platforms. Only innovations in architectures are likely to address the emerging market user's need for affordability. Global giants are beginning to realise the need to develop products locally for emerging market customers, and not just in technology-driven industries. The Swiss food giant Nestlé has planned to open, by 2012, a research centre in Manesar, south of New Delhi, to develop food specific to Indian tastes.[33]

General Electric (GE) is also investing in innovation for the Indian market. Its R&D centre in Bangalore used to develop, among other things, high-end diagnostic equipment for Western hospitals. Lately, GE has been intentionally discarding those designs in the search for products that will do the same or similar tasks for a much bigger, but much more price conscious, Indian medical sector. Once GE has developed a product for the Indian market, it can then migrate the design to developed markets at a small incremental cost. GE produced a 2.7 kg portable electrocardiogram (ECG) machine that created a huge new market for tests by making them accessible to a wider range of the Indian population. It then spent a few hundred thousand dollars to tailor the mini ECG to the United States market, and re-introduced it at a price point that shattered the competition there.[34] It is a good development approach: Tear up a Western design to produce a low cost Indian version, sell the new product to Indians at huge volumes, and then re-package it for the American market at many times the margin.

Most Indian tech companies, meanwhile, are perennially one step behind, chasing yesterday's growth markets instead of tomorrow's. By the time they turn their attention to domestic consumers, Western innovators will have had a crucial head start.

The further irony is that outsourcing to India has made many of these Western companies lean, profitable and nimble enough to react swiftly to the emergence of the Indian consumer. The Indian outsourcers are left with weighty fixed costs dedicated to low-growth Western markets, and Western modes of thinking.

It need not be this way. Indian companies should rightly capture the lion's share of domestic technology-driven market opportunities. They can do so, but it will require a radical new business model, one so radical that India's leading companies are unlikely to develop it themselves. More probable is that this route to market will be discovered by small Indian entrepreneurs that few people today have ever heard of.

A Cape Route for Tech

As long as Asia and Europe have known about each other, there has been trade between the two, and people have profited from that trade. The trade began with spices in the ancient world, carried overland from India through Western Asia to Byzantium, then by ship to Venice and onwards to the commercial centres of Europe.

From the fourteenth century until the seventeenth century, Venice had a virtual lock on trade between East and West. It supplemented its natural location with other advantages such as a strong administrative structure, able diplomacy and cunning ability to craft alliances and trade pacts with other regional powers. The result was a reliable channel, through a series of middlemen, for goods flowing from East to West.

Volume was good but the business model, even with near monopoly status, was precarious. Goods coming from Asia had to pass through many hands on land and at sea – along the Silk Route, in the Levant, in Byzantium – in order to reach Venice. The Venetians had cobbled together a series of agreements to create the links, and managed to keep them in place over the centuries.

With the advent of transcontinental ship travel, however, other powers had their sights on a piece of Venice's lucrative monopoly. When Columbus stumbled upon the Americas in 1492, he was after a sea route to the riches of Asia. His Spanish sponsors knew that whoever controlled that route could break the Venetian monopoly.

Portugal had the same goal, but a different approach. The tiny nation, perched at the Western edge of the European continent overlooking the Atlantic, needed a game-changing strategy to break Venice's stranglehold on trade. Its answer was a route to India around Africa's Cape of Good Hope. It is difficult today to grasp just how radical a plan that was at the time. Europeans had only the sketchiest of cartographic knowledge of the African continent. They knew India was on the other side, but great peril lay in between in the uncertain waters of the Cape.

Yet Portugal was uniquely well positioned to succeed in its plan. Like Venice, it supplemented its natural advantage in location with other, man-made advantages. Over the course of decades Portugal developed its knowledge of shipbuilding, navigation, and the Atlantic Ocean until it knew how to sail those waters better than any nation on earth.

Portugal's crown regarded maritime knowledge as the key to its power and wealth. It worked closely with its merchant class – in what today would be called a Public Private Partnership – to develop a mastery of the seas. During the fifteenth century, the Crown sponsored numerous expeditions far into unknown waters. The empire even had its own shipyard where skilled engineers, navigators, and builders worked together to perfect ship construction and navigation techniques, according to the demands of the Atlantic waters. Over a period of decades Portugal patiently yet doggedly developed its seafaring expertise.[35] All the while Portugal guarded these 'national secrets' as its own; the Crown did not permit export of ships to other nations.[36]

Finally in the late fifteenth century, the Portuguese were ready. In the 1480s and 1490s they conducted several expeditions to Africa, each time making further progress towards the Cape. In 1498, Vasco de Gama reached Calicut, and changed East-West trade forever. He returned from India in October 1503 with 1700 tonnes of spices, an amount Venice imported in a year.[37] The breakthrough allowed the Portuguese to shatter the Venetian business model by achieving the same result alone, without middlemen, at a lower cost and higher margin. Suddenly the notion of trading overland with Asia seemed archaic. Portugal held a virtual monopoly on the Cape Route until the last decade of the sixteenth century.[38] De Gama's breakthrough voyage was the end of Venice's golden age, and the beginning of Portugal's.

India's tech industry is the Venice of today. It has found a way to tap the riches of trade: outsourcing. It is a business model dependent on a powerful middleman – the United States corporation that takes the goods (India's technology services), packages them into a product, brands the product and offers it to Western customers at an enormous mark-up. Like Venice did, India's outsourcing industry is enjoying good business, and may not see the risk in its indirect approach. But also like Venice, outsourcing's business model is vulnerable.

The risk for India's outsourcers is that a Portugal will come along with a new approach that shatters their business model: a Cape Route for Tech. Tech's Portugal will be small, hungry, and innovative. It will have a single-minded focus on finding today's Cape Route: a direct route to bring the riches of India's talent to end consumers of technology products. It will not be content to rely on supplying white label services for others brands. Like Portugal, it will patiently develop its own intellectual property for as long as it takes until it is ready to pounce with a game-changing solution. When this happens, it can well mean the end of the Indian outsourcing industry as we know it.

The question for the outsourcing industry is not whether someone in India will find a direct route to trade in technology. The question is whether they themselves will find that route, or whether – like the Venetians – they will be too focused on their own business model to develop a new one.

In 1981, the founders of Infosys began a journey that upended established business practices, made them dollar billionaires, and created employment for lakhs of Indians. Now Infosys and its peer companies are the establishment, and without innovation aimed at scalable product businesses, they too will fall victim to new ideas. India's outsourcers would do well to question their own business model now, while they still enjoy the growth and profits that will help them fund new ideas. If they do not develop these ideas, someone else will. A new generation of Indian entrepreneurs is already busy innovating, and looking for the lucrative Cape Route for Tech. The Indian government, for its part, can give a boost to these entrepreneurs by creating innovation ecosystems where great ideas can form.

Building the Ecosystem

Corporate India alone cannot drive India's economy towards greater innovation; it is only one piece of the puzzle. A dynamic, innovation-intensive economy requires multiple participants and institutions that together form an innovation ecosystem. Entrepreneurs, start-up companies and established corporations hatch ideas, which angel investors and venture capitalists fund, with the help of service professionals like lawyers and investment bankers. Ideally there is a heavy dose of immigrants populating each of these categories, to bring fresh ideas and extra ambition. The final ingredient: universities, to train the workforce and incubate early technologies that are not yet ready for commercialisation.

This kind of ecosystem is rare and takes years to develop, but it can work magic for a region's economy. The participants in the ecosystem attract newcomers with similar talents, education levels, risk tolerance and ambitions. The region becomes a wealth creation machine, where an expanding tax base can also fund investment in additional infrastructure (good primary schools, cultural institutions) that makes the region even more attractive to residents. The result is a virtuous cycle of innovation feeding ever higher living standards.

California's Silicon Valley is the example the whole world aspires to, with an average annual income per capita of over $62,000.[39] Boston has become a similar type of ecosystem for the biotech industry, as have parts of Texas for the oil industry.

Without design or forethought Bangalore has developed as an outsourcing ecosystem in India. Bangalore, however, is an ecosystem short on true innovation. The innovation that has taken place has largely been built around outsourced and offshore services. The limitations of the outsourcing sector have meant that its new ideas have not produced the kind of outsized margins that can fund further R&D. The consequence has been a crowded, people intensive ecosystem that has put increasing strain on the city. Had Bangalore developed a true innovation ecosystem based on scalable, high margin products, it might still be the garden paradise that its long-time residents describe with nostalgia.

A far better approach for Bangalore is its nascent effort to develop into a biotech centre. It is still too early to determine if this effort will be successful or not. If this effort is concentrated around Indian companies developing their own intellectual property – rather than developing it for others on an outsourced basis – then biotech can do for Bangalore what an innovation ecosystem should do: provide exponential reduction in poverty, while improving the quality of life in the city.

Today nearly every city in India, not just Bangalore, has many of the ingredients to develop an innovation ecosystem. India could have dozens of Silicon Valleys, focused on technology, healthcare, alternative energy, financial services and practically any other sector it wants. India can have these ecosystems, and an innovation-based economy, if it concentrates its human development efforts in one critical area: building a world-class university system.

Society's First Venture Capitalist

Universities are a critical part of any innovation ecosystem. Silicon Valley has Stanford, Boston has both Harvard and MIT, and Oxford of course has Oxford. Universities fill in many of the gaps that the private sector cannot: They mould and train young minds, they foster knowledge sharing across disciplines, and they give professors the academic freedom (and job security, through tenure) to research and create. This third role is particularly important for any innovation-based economy: Some great ideas simply are not ready for commercialisation. They are ahead of their time, too narrow in their applications, or perhaps are too expensive to mass market. Such ideas would die, or maybe never be born, without universities; a private sector company would not be able to justify an investment in such an early stage idea if the return is too small or too distant in years.

The not-for-profit university system, whether funded through public or private money, is a critical part of any nation's economic infrastructure. By nurturing early stage ideas until they are ready for commercialisation, universities serve the greater good by spurring innovation and economic growth.

Once academic research proves the concept, the private sector becomes interested. Companies involved in cutting-edge research adopt and adapt ideas from universities, build business models around them, and take them to market. Frequently the private sector, aided by the passage of time and complementary technology, finds new uses for academic inventions. The laser, first invented in the 1950s as the 'maser', has developed a range of applications – such as eye surgery, precision welding and missile defence systems – that its inventors could never have envisaged.[40] A healthy innovation ecosystem profits from a symbiotic relationship between academia, which contributes the idea, and the private sector, which extracts business value; full innovation requires on-going contributions from both parties.

The relationship between business and academia is underscored by the close relationships many universities in the United States have with local companies. While universities must safeguard their independence by avoiding formal tie-ups with for-profit corporations, this restriction often does not apply to individual academics. Companies involved in cutting-edge research in any field often hire local engineering or science professors as consultants to get access to early stage ideas in the field. Universities, for their part, have found another way to commercialise their research work, by spinning out independent, for-profit companies from research labs. When spun-off from the university, the enterprise typically gets an injection of venture capital funding, the university gets a minority stake in the new enterprise, and academic freedom is maintained. Later the university can sell its stake to the public markets or a new investor, and put its 'profits' into its general fund to feed new research. In this way the university acts as a very early stage venture capitalist.

Even if the 'university spin off' corporation is a twentieth-century invention, European and American universities have been filling the role of venture capitalist of ideas for centuries. It is no coincidence that the richest parts of the world also have the oldest universities, nine centuries old in Europe and nearly four centuries old in the United States. Today's India must make do with University of Calcutta (1857), University of Bombay (1857) and of course the IITs (1950s onwards).

India's Missing Ingredient

India's problem in higher education is quantity, not quality. Many of the universities in India are good, and some are world class, but there are far too few to serve the needs of the country.

There is a strong correlation between average national income levels and gross university enrolment.[41] Those countries that educate most of their citizens are also the wealthiest. Furthermore, university enrolment is a leading indicator of economic development; nations are wealthy because they have increased university enrolment, not vice-versa.

Japan and Korea are examples of the return on investing in university education. In the 1970s, Japan increased the tertiary proportion of gross enrolment rates from 17 to 31 percent; the following decade it reaped the benefits, with average GDP growth of 4.4 percent. Korea's dramatic spike in tertiary education in the first half of the 1980s, from 13 to 32 percent of gross enrolment, was followed by even more dramatic average GDP growth of 9.7 percent in the second half of the decade.[42]

More recently, in the late 1990s, China knew it had to vastly increase university enrolment if it was to generate sustained economic growth on a par with what Japan and Korea had achieved earlier.[43] China's spending on higher education rose nearly three-fold between 1996 and 2006, to 1.5 percent of GDP.[44] What has China gotten for its investment? The fastest increase in university enrolment in the history of mankind.[45] It doubled the number of institutions of higher education (from 1022 to 2263), and increased enrolment more than five-fold (from one million to 5.5 million students).[46] Today China enrols more students in universities than any other nation.[47]

What have Indians received from their government over the same timeframe? Little more than talk. In 1996, only five percent of China's gross enrolment was in tertiary education, even lower than India's (six percent). By 2006, China had increased this figure to twenty-one percent, while India's had risen to only twelve percent.[48]

The Indian government has announced a goal of increasing both the quality and quantity of education. It aims to build fourteen new 'world-class' universities, and increase enrolment in post-secondary education from twelve percent to thirty percent by 2020.[49] This must not be yet another ambitious plan that the Indian government fails to realise; there is too much at stake.

In 1995, the Indian government introduced a bill to Parliament to open up the education sector to foreign universities. Sixteen years later the Foreign Education Providers Bill (a successor to the 1995 bill) has still not been signed into law, though the Cabinet approved it in 2010.[50] The bill must not remain in legislative limbo any longer. With post-secondary enrolment percentages a leading economic indicator, the future of India's economy hangs in the balance. Until it brings higher education to the masses India will be achieving far below its economic potential, even if it continues to record high single digit GDP growth rates for the coming decades.

The IIT Syndrome

The apathy of the Indian electorate on the current state of higher education in India is striking. Some bemoan having to send their children overseas for higher education; others complain about brain drain, and the loss of foreign exchange to India through the payment of school fees abroad. Still, not enough Indians are outraged by the inability of the government to provide higher education for the masses. The Indian electorate should be demanding from its government greater access to higher education. India simply needs more universities, and it needs them now; it matters little whether they are run by foreign or Indian institutions, or whether they are public or private.

India has been lulled into complacency by the success of its IITs. Tales abound of IIT-ans who have gone on to make fortunes in Silicon Valley and elsewhere. What about the ninety-eight percent of those who applied to IIT but were not admitted? The capacity of the IITs is laughably small, with an annual undergraduate intake of around ten thousand, a fraction of India's annual crop of undergraduates.[51]

Furthermore, the IITs excel in only one area of a university's mission: education. They have world class students but have not produced world class research.[52] If India is to become a centre for innovation, its IITs (and other universities) will have to increase their contribution to research. As it is the IITs have done more to promote innovation and economic growth in the United States than in India.

The United States has its world-famous Ivy League, which takes in about 15,000 undergraduates a year. But the Ivy League only accounts for less than one half of one percent of the United States' undergraduate enrolment of fourteen million.[53] A network of universities (public and private), liberal arts colleges and community colleges exists to provide almost any conceivable type of education to Americans. The United States has over 4,000 institutes of tertiary education for a country of 300 million people. India has around 430 for a nation four times the size.[54]

India's higher education system today looks like the United States' system did 150 years ago, with a small number of institutions failing to serve a rapidly growing population. In 1863, the Morrill Act, passed by Congress and signed by President Abraham Lincoln, vastly expanded the system of American higher education. Under the act the federal government granted to the states large tracts of land for the establishment of publicly-administered universities. Many of today's largest and most successful American state universities, including the University of Illinois and the University of California, began with such land grants; today they form the core of America's public education system.[55]

India will need to take an equivalent leap forward in education today, if it is to emerge as a global economic power, as the United States did in the late nineteenth and early twentieth century. This will mean building, at a minimum, one hundred new universities a year in India for the next decade. To do so, India will need dramatic increases in its higher education budget; the twenty-four percent increase provided for in the 2011 budget will not suffice.[56]

A New Model for Research

As the Second World War was ending, the United States faced a challenge similar to the one India faces today: tremendous potential for economic expansion and a university system under-equipped to provide the basic research needed to fuel that expansion.

Using a 1945 report commissioned by the Administration of President Harry Truman (1884-1972),[57] the United States developed a system of research funding that has helped it achieve and maintain its global leadership in innovation. The American research system is based on three principles: first, the government must fund basic science research; second, universities – not government run institutes or private companies – must conduct the research; third, allocation of funds must be based on project merit, which is judged through a competitive process of academic peer review. [58]

The system has helped the United States become the global leader in scientific research. Asia, by contrast, has directed most of its funding towards government-run research institutes, where inevitably money flows to the most senior scientists, not the best scientists.[59] In India the government-run institutes have not exactly turned the country into a centre of innovation. The problem is compounded by anaemic funding levels: The entire 2011-12 Indian government budget for the Department of Scientific and Industrial Research (part of the Ministry of Science and Technology) is under $500 million.[60] More money for India's universities (as opposed to research institutes) to conduct research would help boost India's research results, as well as bolster the entire higher education system. A robust system of peer review would ensure this money is directed towards those projects with most scientific merit.

Research funding will also attract quality scholars, but only if the facilities and pay are also up to Western standards. There are thousands of Indian-born academics doing research at universities in the United States and United Kingdom. How many of them would like to come back to work in Indian universities for a fraction of their current salary? By upgrading its facilities, China has had some success drawing some of its academic diaspora back from Western institutions.[61] India needs to make a concerted effort to do the same; success will require a massive improvement in facilities and professorial pay packets.

Minds Race

In parallel with its Asian arms race (discussed in Chapter Seven), China has also launched an Asian minds race. India is losing both.

Not only is China well ahead of India in expanding university enrolment, it is also building better facilities, funding more research and paying more to attract quality faculty.[62] One result of these investments is that China has surged ahead of India in scientific publishing. In 2008, China-based scholars published over 112,000 articles in peer-reviewed journals, nearly three times the number India produced, and second only to the United States.[63] Chinese works are also being cited more and more in other publications; at current rates they will be cited more often than American works by 2013.[64] China's growth in scientific publishing has outstripped that of every other major nation since 1990, and has accelerated since the late 1990s in particular.[65] India's pace of scientific publishing over the same periods has been relatively flat, with a small uptick in the past few years.[66] As the publications in question are peer reviewed, China's performance is a good barometer of its greater share of original contributions to the world's research base. Given the link between basic research and future commercial innovations, China's growth in scientific publishing also augurs well for its future innovation-driven growth prospects.

The world is beginning to recognise China's investments in research and education. In a recent ranking of Asian universities, eleven universities in China and Hong Kong made the top thirty. India's top entry: IIT Kanpur, at number thirty-six.[67]

China is not stopping with scientific research. Chinese education officials recognise that their students, though technically proficient, are less able than American students to think critically. In an effort to fill this gap, China has begun to introduce liberal arts colleges modelled after those in the United States. At Yuanpei Honours College, part of Peking University, China's brightest students learn not merely math and science but a variety of subjects, from literature to arts to the sciences.[68] After the end of their second year, as in most American universities and colleges, the Yuanpei students concentrate on one field of study.[69]

The number of students China sends to overseas universities peaked in 2007.[70] It has been declining since then due to two factors: the impact of China's one-child policy on the population of university-age Chinese; and the increasing quality of domestic universities.[71] Having attracted more domestic students to their campuses, Chinese institutions are now aiming to compete with their British and American counterparts for a share of the market in educating foreign students.[72]

While China is already a university powerhouse, and well on its way to becoming an innovation-driven economy, India is languishing as a back office powerhouse with also-ran universities. This situation represents a failure by the Indian state to make use of the country's own talent base. If the Indian government does not close the minds race gap with China soon, India may be condemned to being a low-value back office, rather than the high value innovator it is capable of being.

If India can build the universities, educate the masses and produce the research that drives commercial innovation, it will take a big step towards becoming a credible twenty-first century economic peer of the United States and China. But educating Indians and sending them forth to innovate is not enough to compete with the entrepreneurs of America. As it builds innovation ecosystems, India must multiply their effectiveness by attracting talent from around the world to its shores. True large-scale innovation, and the wealth it brings, will come to India only after the world's most innovative minds begin to call India home.

The Five Stages of Innovation

Being known to the world as a low-cost back office is no way to lift 400 million people out of poverty. Brand India can, and must, evolve to one of innovation. It can be cost-effective innovation, but it must be innovation.

For this to happen, India has to move beyond outsourcing to the next stage of its development. India's outsourcers must be more aggressive and capture more of the global value chain. This means moving into products that can be scaled up and brands that they themselves own. If they direct their innovation efforts at domestic Indian consumers, they can create products at a price point for the masses. No foreign company, especially one with a Western cost structure, will be able to compete with an Indian company that can develop a successful product for the masses. Such an Indian company can then take its products to the global market, subsidised by a large domestic customer base.

Looking back on India's modern commercial history, and considering its future, five distinct stages of innovation emerge. India's aspiration must be to become a Stage Five innovator. It is currently stuck at Stage Three.

Stage One: Copying (late 1940s to mid-1990s). Modern India began with the practice of import substitution. India sought to produce goods locally using technology that was largely of foreign origin. Some technology was licensed, some was stolen; little was developed at home in India by Indians. Reduced to copying, India suffered low GDP per capita.

Stage Two: Labour Arbitrage (mid-1990s to 2002). This was the dawn of outsourcing. It began with Indian IT companies doing basic programming work, some offshore, and some by 'body-shopping' employees to the United States. India benefitted from low wage rates in technology services, which helped it achieve modest improvements in GDP per capita.

Stage Three: Innovation…for others (2002 to present). This is India's current stage. Outsourcing is characterised by a level of skill and ingenuity, but this talent is directed at adding value to customers' products and brands. India creates wealth, but it leaves the majority of the value on the table for other nations. The GDP per capita increases sharply but is still at levels far below world averages.

Stage Four: Innovate…for yourself. India is on the verge of entering this stage. The innovation that is currently taking place in pockets of the Indian economy, such as biotechnology and agricultural/seed technology, must multiply and spread countrywide. Outsourcing firms must not only innovate in services and protect their intellectual property, but also develop high margin products that will fund further innovation. Indian production must be focused on building brands at home that Indian companies can take global. The United States reached this stage in the 1950s and 1960s, when its post-War investments in basic research began to pay off. When India achieves this stage, it will increase its GDP per capita to near world averages in purchasing power parity terms.

Stage Five: Talent Magnet. Only a handful of countries have reached this stage, including the United States, the United Kingdom and Singapore. These countries attract innovators and their ideas. The world's talent is drawn to the United States in particular, because it is a place where new ideas are commercialised and where great wealth is created. Innovation brings more talent, bringing yet more innovation and talent. This is the stage India must aspire to in the coming decade.

Transitioning from outsourcing to innovation-led technology; building a world-class, large-scale university system that can fuel constant innovation; and funding the research that will inspire the great commercial products of the future: These are all necessary steps on India's path to economic power. It is not enough, however, for India to use innovations to develop and sell new products at home. It will need companies that can take ideas and products to the world's markets. Corporate India can, and must, go global.

THE Government of the territories now in the possession or under the Government of the East India Company...shall cease to be vested in or exercised by the said Company; and all territories in the possession or under the government of the said Company...shall become vested in Her Majesty, and be exercised in her name....

– Government of India Act, 1858

On any measure, India's economy is on an upward trajectory. In Britain, we're waking up to a new reality....I have come to your country in a spirit of humility. I know that Britain cannot rely on sentiment and shared history for a place in India's future.

– United Kingdom Prime Minister David Cameron, 27 July 2010[1]

6

GOING GLOBAL

English: The Language of Success

Becoming a global economy does not mean simply exporting to the world, as China does. India needs to adopt a different approach, one that is based on unique features of its own history, economy, culture and base of human capital.

India's widespread use of the English language is often cited as an advantage over China. English indeed is an advantage for India, and cannot be overstated. History's most recent global powers – the United States and the United Kingdom – have both been English-speaking countries. English has become today's *lingua franca*, and shows no signs of relinquishing that status, for Chinese or any other language. Indians' familiarity with English will greatly smooth the entrance of Indian companies into positions of global market leadership, and thereby accelerate India's transition to a position of global economic leadership.

History shows that populations rarely, if ever, adopt new languages voluntarily; usually it happens through colonisation. English is a case in point. It spread from a small island off the coast of Europe initially through colonial domination of new territories. Only once one-third of humanity spoke English – from the United States to Australia to India and much of Africa – did other nations begin to adopt the language voluntarily. The same was true for Spanish and French. The idea that – absent Chinese colonisation – people would begin speaking Mandarin worldwide *en masse*, simply because China is an important economy, is one that is not supported by history.

The Multinational as Tool of State Power

With the dominance of English here to stay, India's head start over China in language is secure. India can use language to enhance another great advantage it has over China: its corporate sector.

Indian managers have proved themselves on the global stage. Famous India-born CEOs of multinationals like Indra Nooyi (PepsiCo), Vikram Pandit (Citigroup) and Ajay Banga (MasterCard) are only the most visible examples of a breed of managers that India excels in creating: highly educated, driven, ambitious and increasingly global. For every Indian who has excelled in the United States or the United Kingdom, there are thousands more back in India who are just as capable. Those managers who stayed in India have not become as globally-prominent as their developed-country counterparts, owing to corporate India having offered relatively fewer large companies to run in recent years. As India continues to outgrow Western markets, these once hidden stars will emerge with ever bigger achievements to their names.

American multinationals have, especially since India's liberalisation in 1991, become a fertile training ground for India's next generation of global managers. India's front offices and boardrooms are littered with alumni of American firms such as GE and McKinsey. In the outsourcing sector alone several founders and CEOs of fast-growing companies came out of McKinsey India.[2] These executives learned the trade of management from the best firms in America; now they are using those skills to build India's great companies.

India's cadre of global managers will form the most critical part of what will, in turn, be critical to India's economic success: the India-based multinational. No country can become a global economic power without its own multinationals leading the charge. History demonstrates that the power of nation states is closely linked with their ability to conduct – and control – commerce overseas.

Today the United States expands into new markets with Wal-Mart, GE and Pepsi. Well before there were for-profit corporations, nation states recognised that conquering new markets overseas was necessary to their consolidation of power. Without corporations to which they could 'outsource' economic expansion, nation states took on the role themselves. The great empires of the world, beginning with Rome, conquered territories and then unleashed an army of merchants and traders to solidify imperial power. This was the model for the next 1500 years: Conquer first with arms, then with commerce.

In the seventeenth century the British developed a new approach to imperial commerce. The British East India Company (EIC) was a hybrid between the modern for-profit corporation and the old Roman approach (Empire-as-business). It was a joint stock corporation, and also held privileges and protections from the British Crown. The EIC, of course, became the *de facto* ruler of India by virtue of its commercial hold on the country. When the British Crown assumed direct control of India in 1858, it formalised what was already clear: India had become a British colony, thanks to the EIC, the world's most successful commercial expeditionary force.

Today's successor to the EIC is the global multinational. Governments send them forth to conquer new markets as a means of exercising power beyond their borders. Some governments have ownership in multinationals (e.g., Indian Oil Corporation and China National Petroleum), using them to lock up resources overseas. Other nations, like the United States, have outsourced the commercial expansion function to the private sector.

Although there is no indication that the American government will nationalise any American companies' foreign business interests as the British did with the EIC, there are strong links between the government policy of the United States and the overseas activities of is major multinationals. On a basic level, the American government has an interest in promoting business interests of its companies, particularly exports, which create jobs in the United States. American corporations expect and receive their government's help in opening overseas markets to their products, and in keeping them open.

The United States government, for its part, expects more than just jobs and profits in return from its multinationals. Multinationals act as a tool of American foreign policy, to help the government achieve both political and economic objectives abroad. The American government tells its companies where they can, and cannot, do business. They cannot, for example, do business in states like Iran and North Korea, which Washington sees as hostile. For the past half century Washington has even succeeded in barring a large part of American trade with Cuba, an island ninety miles off the coast of Florida and once a major source of business for American companies.

A nation simply cannot become a global power without corporations (state-owned or not) that have substantial presences in overseas markets. One of the many flaws in communism was the absence of global scale for state-owned communist enterprises. Soviet firms sold goods to client states and other friendly nations, but their markets were limited by ideology. Meanwhile the capitalist countries were expanding their influence far and wide through the multinational, even to communist countries (where permitted). With narrower markets the Soviet companies never had a chance, and neither did communism.

Today there is an abiding correlation between national power and powerful multinationals. Of the world's largest ten corporations (the top of the 'Global Fortune 500'), China has three; the United States and Japan have two each; the United Kingdom, France and Holland have one each.[4] China's three top ten global enterprises – Sinopec, State Grid and China National Petroleum – are state-owned and have limited presences overseas; they are big companies, thanks to the state's backing, but do not signify global power. The same is true for India's top entry on the list: Indian Oil at 125th place.[5]

The interesting companies on the list are the private sector entities. The United States, today's number one global power, is represented by two private sector corporations (Wal-Mart and Exxon Mobil). Even the United Kingdom (BP), Holland (Royal Dutch Shell) and France (AXA), economic and imperial powers long past their prime, are still represented on the list. For India to become a global power it must send forth its private corporations to conquer the world through commerce as the United States and Europe have done.

India's Second Army

As India seeks status as a global power, its government resources alone will not be enough to project its power abroad. As we will see in Chapter Seven, both India's Armed Forces and its Foreign Service are underfunded and inadequate to the needs of a regional power, much less a global power. Even if India's government succeeds in enlarging its military and diplomatic presence, it will still need additional help to make India's power felt in every corner of the world. It will need a second army, staffed by the Indian multinationals of tomorrow.

More than half a century after the sun set on the British Empire, the United Kingdom's multinationals still carry weight around the world. In fact, big business in today's United Kingdom has little to do with earnings in the British Isles, and everything to do with earnings overseas. Among the largest listed companies in London, overseas earnings account for on average of about eighty percent of total corporate profits.[6] Many large American companies have a similar exposure to overseas business, such as

GE (sixty percent of total sales)[7] 3M (sixty-three percent)[8] and Coca-Cola (seventy-five percent).[9] Many of the United States' top 500 corporations earn about half of their sales overseas.[10] India's great companies must establish themselves as similar global forces.

General Electric currently has about 300,000 employees,[11] fifty-four percent of whom are overseas.[12] Tata already generates $46 billion in sales overseas (sixty-five percent of its total turnover).[13] It also employs more people in the United Kingdom than any other manufacturing company, domestic or foreign.[14] But a vast majority of Tata's 350,000 employees worldwide is still in India. Imagine a world where Tata has grown to the size of GE, with half of Tata employees located outside India. That is a true multinational.

Now imagine hundreds of other multi-billion dollar Indian companies with substantial operations overseas, and thousands of $100 million plus India companies also with a foothold overseas. Many of the larger Indian multinationals of tomorrow will have offices in the United States, Europe and China, as well as in smaller emerging markets in Africa, Asia and Latin America. Just by pursuing their own commercial interests alone they will bring tremendous power and prestige to India.

These Indian multinationals will, of course, employ primarily local people in their respective markets. Frequently, however, operations will be run by Indians with loyalties to India. These Indian executives will also, as American executives do, work closely with their own government on matters of national interest.

From the limited forays of Indian companies into overseas markets in the past decade alone, the nation has received great publicity. A handful of landmark acquisitions such as Tata-Jaguar/Land Rover and Tata Steel-Corus have catapulted India into the ranks of major economies. Ten years ago it would have been highly unusual, and frankly a bit embarrassing, for an American or European to say he is working for an Indian company. Today India's future growth is widely known, and its companies are seen as good employers, at least as attractive as American employers if not more so.

Multinational firms can have a disproportionately positive impact on their home country's economy. A recent study of data since 1990 shows that multinationals based in the United States have accounted for thirty-one percent of the nation's real GDP growth and forty-one percent of the growth in labour productivity over the period.[15] This is all the more impressive considering that multinationals represent just one percent of American firms.[16] American multinationals positively impact the economy in other ways too: by paying higher average wages and by carrying a more favourable trade balance (exports vs. imports) than the overall economy.[17]

India's multinationals can have a similar effect on India's economy. Multinationals' greater productivity and export-generation can accelerate India's growth. The large number of young people entering the labour force in India, along with high domestic consumption, will mean that the spending power of these new employees/consumers will be an important factor in the pace of India's economic growth. Yet overall labour productivity in India remains low, less than half of the world average.[18] Like their American counterparts have done, Indian multinationals can help improve domestic labour productivity, improve wage growth and therefore provide an additional boost to GDP growth above and beyond employment gains. A further boost will come if Indian multinationals are able to stimulate additional exports, as American multinationals have done.

India's future multinationals represent a huge advantage for the nation over China. China has its share of fast-growing companies, to be sure; it does not, however, have the talented, English-speaking management to take them global. China's state-owned enterprises will no doubt continue to expand in global markets. But their activities will be concentrated inevitably in a small number of firms, controlled by the government. India's activities will be more diversified, led by a patriotic yet independent private sector, and much more scalable.

Right now names such as Electrotherm, Glenmark Pharma and ICICI bank are largely unknown in the West.[19] These companies and thousands like them will be spending the next few decades transitioning from primarily domestic to primarily global enterprises. Yet India's future multinationals, in order to expand overseas, will need capital. Fortunately, India's well-developed capital markets will be there to provide the funds, and do so efficiently.

Capital in Search of Return

India's capital market system is another advantage in the race to go global. India has more listed firms than China, Russia and Brazil combined.[20] Many Indian firms have been listed for years, and India's overall capital markets are more mature than any major developing economy.

A long history of capital market activity is not sufficient to spur growth. A country's markets must also be efficient at allocating capital, in order for economic efficiency to be maximised. For this to happen, investors need to have access to reliable financial statements (produced by well-trained accountants); the government needs to report accurate macro-economic data; and a clear, stable regulatory framework must be in place at the national level.[21] India has all of these features; China does not.

India, of course, has its shortcomings in corporate governance. There are the well-publicised accounting scandals that the Security and Exchanges Board of India (SEBI) catches.[22] Then there are the frauds that go un-prosecuted or even un-detected. These are some typical frauds that Indian promoters of listed companies and their co-conspirators engage in: kickbacks from suppliers, payments to family-owned companies, 'pump-and-dump' stock manipulation[23] and various other forms of insider trading. These criminal actions are the dark side of India's success, well-known to those inside corporate India but invisible to many of those on the outside. They happen every day, and unwitting investors (both in India and overseas) are paying the price in the form of lower returns. The Indian economy also pays a price, as capital is siphoned off in ways that do not produce growth. All the while some crooked promoters line their pockets.

Corruption is especially endemic in industries where the Indian government has a regulatory role. The link between business and politics in India has recently been exposed by a scandal, which came to light in late 2010, over the government's 2008 allocation of licenses to telecom companies for the Second Generation (2G) wireless spectrum. As the Central Bureau of Investigation (CBI) continues to collect its evidence against an array of politicians, high-ranking civil servants, and business leaders, a picture is emerging of a spectrum allocation process by which the airwaves were for sale – not to the highest bidder – but at deep discounts to those companies in the favour of government officials granting the licenses. The 2G scandal is alarming in its scale and brazenness, but by no means unique. There is no doubt that Indian government officials are routinely bought and paid for by corporations wishing to profit from their favour, in transactions that enrich corrupt officials and corporate shareholders (both complicit promoters and unwitting shareholders) at the expense of the larger public.

While not minimising the extent or seriousness of corporate malfeasance by Indian listed companies, it could be worse. The United States has had more than its share of multi-billion dollar corporate scandals: fraud at Enron, fraud at WorldCom, and most recently reckless risk taking at financial institutions that led to a $700 billion bailout by the American taxpayer.

Within the global and historical context, India's capital markets function as well as many developed nation markets, and better than any major developing nation markets, save for China's. In 2010, Indian companies raised $8.3 billion in equity capital, a three percent share of the global total.[24] Though Chinese exchanges raised far more (over $70 billion in Shenzen and Shanghai together), India's total is just short of London's ($8.9 billion) and exceeds that of Australia ($7.9 billion), Korea ($7.8 billion) and Brazil ($6.4 billion).[25] India's capital market has proved adept at getting capital to the businesses that need it, even smaller ones. The average size of Indian IPOs in 2009-10 was $200 million.[26] For companies still too small to list on a public stock exchange, a vibrant Indian private equity market is there to fill the funding gap.

India's capital market system is not perfect; no nation's is. Yet India's markets are well-regulated, largely transparent and do the job well of providing liquidity to growing companies. The proof is in the returns. Apart from China's market, no stock market in the recent past has provided better returns with less volatility than India's.[27]

India's domestic consumption, fuelled by favourable demographics, will continue to provide a solid base of growth for Indian companies. For Indian firms to continue to offer top returns to investors, however, they will need to move beyond their home market, and take their businesses global. The biggest risk as they expand overseas is that they will be tempted to see growth by acquisition as a fast track to global success. While acquisitions are certainly a useful tool for accelerating international growth, for Indian companies today they hold more risks than rewards. How a given Indian company uses acquisitions to expand globally could well mean the difference between success and failure.

Buyer Beware

Indian companies have been on an overseas buying spree. It is not clear, however, whether a continuation of the recent pace of acquisitions is in the interest of India's companies, or in the interest of India's overall economy. Research in the United States has demonstrated that half of all mergers and acquisitions (M&A) fail to create any value for shareholders, and that many destroy value.[28] There is no reason to believe the success rate for Indian companies would be any better, particularly in overseas acquisitions where geographic distance and cultural differences make realisation of potential synergies all the more difficult. When those overseas acquisitions involve targets in low-growth (and high-cost) Western markets, the risk of failure becomes greater for Indian buyers.

Because India is in a demographic-economic sweet spot, as we saw in Chapter Four, its companies can afford to be patient and disciplined about overseas acquisitions. India is forecast to grow 7.5 percent in 2012, the Eurozone at 1.1 percent and the United States at 1.8 percent.[29] India's growth is already the envy of the West, and will be even more so if a five-to-six-percent growth gap between India and the United States/ Europe persists.

Today it no longer makes sense to speak of developed and developing economies. Instead, there are low growth and high growth economies. Low growth economies (the 'developed' world) are those where massive wealth has been created in the past, like the United States, Western Europe and Japan. Today their productivity levels are high, as are living standards, but further growth is increasingly difficult to wring out of a highly productive and expensive labour force, especially when populations are ageing.

High growth economies (the 'developing' world) lack the productivity of their richer neighbours, and this is the source of their advantage: They can create wealth more easily through rapid productivity gains. Today they are worse off than the low-growth economies, but the gap is closing fast, as they outgrow richer nations. Often productivity gains are enhanced by favourable demographics: a high birth rate, a youthful population spurring demand, or both.

India, as a high growth economy, must be wary about how it expands into low growth economies, lest it dampen its own growth prospects in the process. In order to avoid diluting their own growth, Indian companies must take a highly cautious approach to acquisitions abroad.

The good news is that the Indian promoter is a cautious creature by nature. He rarely rushes into decisions, particularly those, such as acquisitions, involving a large cash outlay or high degree of operational risk. Instead of pouncing on his prey immediately, he is likely to stalk it for months or years, waiting for the optimal time to strike.

For every overseas acquisition that Indian companies have made, they have examined dozens of others, many in great detail. Indian promoters show a healthy ability to walk away from deals when something is not to their liking, be it pricing, legal terms or even personal rapport with the target's management team.

While a certain caution towards acquisitions is certainly present in Indian companies, they lack a framework for evaluating when acquisitions do and do not make sense. Every target company offers unique risks and opportunities to a potential Indian buyer. There are no immutable rules Indian companies can apply to test the attractiveness of a potential acquisition, especially as prices can always vary. An acquisition target that might be unattractive at a given price could well make sense at a lower price.

Still, considering India's position in a changing global economy, it is possible to outline a broad framework that Indian corporations can use for approaching M&A. The framework must be long-term in its outlook, addressing the opportunities (and risks) for Indian companies over a period of decades rather than years. As such it must be based on a 'long-run' consideration of global economic trends, rather than a 'short-run' view of business opportunities.

Of course, compelling business opportunities (short- and long-term) must be present in any prospective acquisition. Buyers must evaluate these, and incorporate them into their valuation of the target. Before any target screening takes place, however, the buyer must have developed an overall acquisition strategy that can be applied to particular cases.

Ten Rules for Overseas Acquisitions

In the coming decades the race for growth, market share and profits will take place in the developing world. Indian companies, blessed with a large, fast-growing domestic market, have an enormous strategic advantage. The smart ones will cement that advantage through focused acquisitions at home and abroad; big deals get headlines, but smaller deals create value. The coming years will see fewer Indian companies doing deals to double their size overnight, and more doing deals to position themselves for long-term sustainable growth.

Below is a set of principles that Indian companies can use when developing an acquisition strategy. A strategy developed according to these guidelines can help Indian buyers focus their time and attention on deals that are most likely to succeed. The result will maximise potential return for the company's shareholders, while minimising overall execution risks.

1. **Smaller is Better:** Indian promoters occasionally declare their ability to acquire targets larger than their own companies, sometimes twice or more as large. The law of nature says that a small fish cannot swallow a big one. In acquisitions, it can happen successfully, but rarely. Big deals increase the risks of something going wrong in the integration of the two companies. Going out and buying a company twice one's own size is little different than travelling to Vegas and placing the company's share certificates on the roulette wheel. Far more prudent is to limit an acquisition target to twenty percent of the buyer's size in turnover. Such deals are large enough to have an impact on the acquirer, but small enough not to sink the ship if cost savings and/or sales growth do not materialise to the degree expected.

2. **Avoid Chasing Global Scale:** The temptation for Indian companies to take their businesses global at a single stroke can be great. A target with a leading position in a given sector in the United States or Europe

(or both), could instantly transform an Indian company into a global player. Buying such a company could also take the steam out of the Indian company's growth. It is dangerous to pursue global scale when half of the globe's economy (the United States, Europe and Japan) is well past its steep growth phase. Indian companies must pursue acquisitions based on unique capabilities of the target, not ill-defined notions of becoming a global player.

3. **Instead, Fill a Gap:** Indian acquirers should approach acquisitions with the objective of filling a clear gap in their product or technology profile. Though India has top-notch engineering talent, Indian companies are often far behind their American and European counterparts in product design and intellectual capital. This shortfall is equally present in consumer-facing and industrial businesses in India. Acquiring the technology for a new product, or technology that vastly improves · an existing product, can be highly attractive for an Indian company, especially when the target firm has good technology as well as low fixed costs. Europe in particular has a number of small, family-owned companies that have focused on developing great products for niche markets. In Germany alone, the so-called 'Mittelstand' (small-and medium-sized enterprises with fewer than 500 employees), accounts for approximately fifty-five percent of all employment.[30] A typical example is Micon GmbH, a maker of precision drilling tools with sixty employees based north of Hannover. Micron's products were instrumental in helping rescuers reach and free a group of Chilean miners trapped underground in 2010,[31] highlighting Germany's role as home to companies that, although small in size, are the best at what they have chosen to do. Acquiring such little leaders can be a growth accelerator for Indian companies, without the downside risk of a big deal.

4. **Look at Tomorrow's Markets, Not Yesterday's:** If an Indian company's motivation in making an acquisition is to boost top-line growth overseas, it should forget the United States, Europe and Japan. Those are yesterday's growth stories. Instead, it should look to the growth markets of tomorrow: China, Africa, Southeast Asia and

Latin America. A deal in Africa may not add as much immediately to an Indian acquirer's turnover as a larger acquisition in the United States, but the average African target will likely grow much faster. Today's China, with a preponderance of large state-run enterprises, offers relatively few acquisition opportunities in comparison to its size. This is bound to change: As India-China trade rises and the Chinese economy liberalises further, China should be at, or near the top, of the list for Indian acquirers.

5. **Don't Forget Growth at Home:** Indian companies intent on global expansion can often forget that they are sitting in the world's premier growth market. While acquiring new turnover overseas is important, acquisitions that add to the top line at home offer an added upside. Buying new products or new technologies from more mature overseas markets, and bringing them back to India, can allow acquirers to leapfrog the competition where it matters most, at home.

6. **Look for Intellectual Capital, Not Fixed Costs:** Much of what overseas acquisitions have to offer Indian companies is in technology, application engineering, brands, distribution channels, and customer relationships. They must beware of the fixed costs – plant, machinery, property and labour contracts – that often come along with the acquisition and can drag down future profitability. This is particularly true when doing deals in mature markets like the United States and Europe; their mix of high costs and low growth can be poison for Indian companies. In continental Europe especially, laws requiring severance to retrenched workers can make shutting plants and offices prohibitively expensive.

    The Tata Group's experience with recent big-ticket acquisitions highlights the risks of acquiring fixed costs in Europe, as well as the opportunities to be had when managing those risks. When Tata Motors acquired Jaguar-Land Rover (JLR) from Ford in 2008, in exchange for $2.3 billion, it was saddled with three plants in the United Kingdom with some 20,000 employees, just as worldwide vehicle demand began to fall off. Tata cut 3,000 jobs at JLR, which lost over $450 million in the first ten months of Tata's ownership.[32] Although Tata Motors has been able to turn JLR around in spectacular fashion – the subsidiary earned after tax profit of $1.7 billion in FY 2010/11[33] – the Tatas have not been so fortunate with their other big European acquisition. Tata Steel bought Anglo-Dutch steelmaker Corus for nearly $13 billion in 2007. While Corus was a respected steelmaker, it offered little unique technology. Demand for structural steel in the United Kingdom began falling soon after the acquisition, and still is only two-thirds of the levels in 2007. Tata Steel eliminated 1800 United Kingdom jobs in 2010,[34] and in May 2011 announced plans to shut two British plants, which would likely lead to the loss of a further 1500 jobs (eight percent of Tata Steel Europe's United Kingdom workforce).[35] Tata may yet turn Corus into the success that JLR is, but it will be a tough battle considering Corus's high European labour costs.

7. **Focus on Cost Savings, not Revenue Gains:** Acquisitions are a risky business, and plans that look good on paper can often be devilishly difficult to realise in practice. It is notoriously difficult to increase sales by cross-selling products of the acquired and the acquirer; cost savings offer a better immediate return. Every Indian company that buys overseas should be able to identify three immediate actions that it can take post-acquisition to improve the cost structure and efficiency of the acquired entity. Number one on any Indian company's list of cost synergies should be off-shoring of labour. Both in services (such as IT or BPO) and in manufacturing businesses, no Indian company should buy a business in Europe or the United States unless it can be certain of relocating at least some labour to lower cost locations. Second should be improving the target company's sourcing of low cost components from India (or elsewhere in Asia). Many European companies lowered costs in the past two decades by sourcing components from Eastern Europe, but few were able to master the complexity of sourcing effectively from Asia. Indian companies can improve the sourcing strategy of most European companies, especially those that have a turnover of $100m and below, which are typically less global in sourcing components than larger firms. Third should be the optimisation of R&D. Indian acquirers can adopt an onshore/ offshore model to R&D, whereby the R&D resources of the acquirer

and target are melded together in a single team that works around the clock. A sensible structure would have twenty percent of R&D headcount on shore with the target, to benefit from proximity to the customer. The remaining eighty percent of R&D headcount would be located in India, to leverage the lower cost of engineering and design talent. Such an approach lowers costs by greatly reducing the time-to-market for new products.

8. **Use acquisitions as a Source of Talent:** For Indian multinationals to become truly global they will need global workforces. Smart acquirers the world over see new talent as one of the benefits of doing deals; Indian companies must adopt the same approach. Just as selective acquisitions can be a fast-track to global revenues, they can also be a fast-track to building global management teams.

9. **Don't be Seduced by Brands:** Indian companies are often eager to acquire established Western brands, figuring those brands will help unlock global growth. Tata Motors took on $2 billion in debt to acquire JLR in 2008. Although Tata has been able to turn around JLR, the acquisition nearly crippled the company: By early 2009, Tata Motors' JLR-induced debt burden, combined with a worldwide recession, had erased sixty percent of the value of its shares.[36] While brands have value for Indian companies looking to go global, most would be better off investing in their own brands than paying a premium to acquire established global brands. The perception that Indian brands have less value than Western brands is short-sighted. The world is in the midst of a shift of economic activity from the United States and Europe to Asia. As Asian consumers take over from American consumers as the arbiters of taste, so will Asian brands take over as the embodiments of those tastes. Japan (Sony, Toyota) and Korea (LG, Samsung) created global brands, and India can too. But it will take time: Japanese cosmetics company Shiseido launched its first overseas brand forty years ago; today nearly sixty percent of its sales are still in the domestic market.[37] Building brands will also take money – money which must be directed single-mindedly towards marketing the Indian brand, instead of being spent on acquiring costly 'already global' brands.

10. **Broken, but Fixable:** The United States and Europe together account for half of the world's GDP, and no Indian company intent on becoming global can ignore these markets entirely. The best course for most Indian companies buying in the United States and Europe is to focus on distressed companies that can be bought for the net value of the assets on the books or less. Either because of mismanagement or because of increasing competition, such companies need fresh capital and a new business model. Ideally such companies will make good products underpinned by proprietary technologies, yet lack a globally competitive cost structure and access to growth markets. Indian buyers can offer these companies a new lease of life by revamping the cost structure and helping the company tap into India's growth. Attractive targets would include companies in sectors such as automotive, power equipment and industrial automation, whose steep growth phase is over at home, but is only just beginning in India. Companies that need an 'Indian solution' offer the best way for acquirers to minimise the substantial risks in buying overseas.

Big ticket M&A deals such as Tata-Corus, Tata-Jaguar/Land Rover and Hindalco-Novelis have broken all, or many, of the above rules. Time will tell whether the shareholders of these companies will benefit from the transactions; given the prices paid, in many cases it will be hard for the acquirers to squeeze out an attractive return on capital.

A disciplined overseas acquisitions strategy is essential for any Indian company intent on becoming a global enterprise. But acquisitions alone must be only part of the strategy. Far more important to the health and long-term competitiveness of Indian enterprises is organic, innovation-led growth at home. Acquisitions overseas are a supplement to, not a substitute for, a company's own growth. Indian companies who want to be global multinationals must first do the hard work of establishing themselves as dominant players in their chosen market segments in India. Only then can they selectively use acquisitions to build global strength. There are no shortcuts.

A 3x3 Strategy for Going Global

Godrej Consumer Products Limited (GCPL), the $2.6 billion[38] maker of personal and home care products, has a leading position in India in categories such as soaps, hair colour and household insecticides. But leadership at home in India was not enough for GCPL. Beginning in 2006, it embarked on a strategy to become a major global player in home and personal care. GCPL called it the 'global 3x3 strategy', developing a presence in three core categories (home care, personal wash and hair care) in three continents (Africa, Asia and Latin America). Over the course of the next five years the company has followed a disciplined strategy to reach its objective, acquiring businesses in South Africa, Nigeria, Indonesia and Argentina.[39] The result was the transformation of an Indian leader into a global leader, with exposure to the fastest growing regions of the world. Since 2006, GCPL has increased its revenues by more than a factor of three.[40] It accomplished this growth with patience and strategic focus. The company avoided large acquisitions, and (with the exception of a single acquisition in the United Kingdom) avoided developed markets as well. GCPL's strategy of pursuing inorganic growth through niche acquisitions in emerging markets represents the future of Indian mergers and acquisitions deal making.

Rupee Strategy Wanted

In 2010, the Indian Ministry of Finance announced a competition for a new symbol for the Rupee. According to Ministry of Finance Circular No 10/8/06-Cy.II,[41] the Dollar, Pound Sterling, Yen and Euro have an identification symbol, but not the Indian Rupee. The winning design was to be chosen by a jury of seven, comprising representatives of the Government of India, the Reserve Bank of India and 'art institutes of repute'. The winner was to receive 250,000 rupees, in exchange for surrendering the copyright for the winning design to the Indian government.

While the winning design (₹) is a perfectly fine sign for India's currency, symbols can only take India so far. Now the Indian government must devote its attention to developing a strategy for making the Rupee into a global currency.

China wants the Renminbi to be a global currency, and has a long-term strategy for making it one. Though China is the world's single largest holder of dollar reserves ($2.6 trillion in 2010), it has also criticised the dollar's domination of the international financial system.[42] China knows that it will be a long time before the Renminbi can rival the dollar as a global currency, so it favours expanding the use of the IMF's Special Drawing Rights (SDRs), whose value is derived from a fixed basket of currencies (United States Dollars, Japanese Yen, British Pounds and Euros).

In the meantime China is readying the Renminbi for the world, and readying the world for the Renminbi. The People's Bank of China (PBOC) is working hard to circumvent the dollar where possible in international trading. Since December 2008, the PBOC has announced currency swap arrangements with seven nations,[43] whereby importers can borrow Renminbi from those nations' central banks to pay Chinese suppliers.[44] In June 2009, China and Brazil agreed in principle to settle trades in their respective currencies, bypassing the dollar.[45] The move is all the more significant because China is now Brazil's largest trading partner.

The world's developing nations are accounting for a greater share of world trade, and trading more with each other. Brazil, Russia, India and China together now account for thirteen percent of world trade, and have produced half of the world's economic growth since 2007.[46] Trade among developing nations ('South-South trade') reached $2.8 trillion in 2008, having grown at an average annual rate of eighteen percent since 2000.[47] As South-South trade outpaces both 'North-South' trade and 'North-North' trade, it will become increasingly pointless to settle trades in dollars. More common, as China eclipses the United States as the world's largest economy, will be countries settling trades (whether they involve China or not) in Renminbi.

The Indian Rupee has as much claim to future global currency status as the Renminbi. What is missing in India is an activist government with the vision and confidence to promote the Rupee as one of the leading currencies in the world. As it is, the Indian government is more worried about maintaining a Rupee/dollar exchange rate that supports IT services earnings growth for the next two quarters than it is about devising a Rupee strategy that supports India's growth as a world power for the next two decades.

India needs to take a page from China's play book and think long term. India should announce a goal to make the Rupee, along with the Dollar and the Euro, one of the top three global currencies by 2025. The statement alone would be a show of self-confidence on India's part and generate far better national publicity than a new Rupee symbol. No nation will treat India as a future global economic power until it begins behaving like one.

400 Million Reasons

The world needs the Indian economy to reach its full economic potential. Gone are the days when the United States can be the engine that drives the global economy. Between 2000 and 2007, United States consumer spending accounted for over seventy-five percent of the nation's real GDP growth.[48] Given that the United States has, for the past two decades, itself accounted for a quarter of world GDP, the global economy was highly dependent on the American consumer for growth until 2007. This unhealthy state of affairs could not persist indefinitely, as the economic crisis that began the following year abruptly demonstrated. Today we are in the midst of a seismic shake-up in the global economy, as activity shifts from West to East (and North to South).

As we saw in Chapter One, this is not so much a new era but rather a return to the norm that pertained for much of the past two millennia. The past two centuries, where (relatively) small countries could control outsized portions of the global economy, were an anomaly. Now economic activity is again becoming aligned with population, just as it has been for most of organised human history.

This realignment will mean decades of faster growth in (former) developing countries like India, as their economies regain ground lost to the (former) developed countries. As this takes place, Indian companies will become much more important generators of wealth, not just at home, but abroad as well.

It is already happening. Indian companies invested $26.6 billion in the United States from 2004-09, creating over 56,000 jobs over the period.[49] The United States and other low-growth economies like Europe and Japan need Indian multinationals to continue to grow and claim their rightful place as corporate giants of the twenty-first century.

As much as the world economy needs India to continue to grow, there are even more pressing reasons for Indian companies to take their businesses global. Though India's economy has shown impressive growth rates in the past decade, there are still 400 million people in India (about one-third of the population) who live in grinding poverty, earning less than $1.25 a day.[50]

The Indian government, as noble as its intentions may be, can never adequately care for the nation's poor. The fate of India's poor lies in the hands of India's business community. Only the Indian private sector can generate the wealth that will be needed for widespread poverty reduction.

Fortunately, Indian business has already shown it can reduce poverty. The Sensex has risen twenty-fold since 1991. Over a similar period, India has been able to lift 100 million people out of poverty.[51] Or, put more correctly, Indian business lifted 100 million people out of poverty; as the Sensex went up, poverty rates went down. For growth to continue at a pace sufficient to reduce poverty yet further, Indian businesses must now expand globally, as American companies did last century.

These Indian multinationals can be, as their American counterparts have been, instruments of national power. They are emerging in an era when India is in a demographic-economic sweet spot. By combining the power of Indian multinationals with assertive government trade policies (including, where called for, protectionism), India can achieve the economic might needed to support its development as a global political power. Wealth will beget more power, which will beget yet more wealth. The United States has enjoyed this virtuous cycle, as the United Kingdom did before it. Now it is India's turn. This will be good news for all of India's citizens, rich and poor alike.

Indian industry, even with thousands of powerful multinationals, cannot single-handedly make India into a world power. As we will see in the next chapter, economic strength and geopolitical strength go hand-in-hand and are mutually reinforcing. India can only become wealthy if it is a global power, and vice versa. First India has some work to do; it must abandon its decades-old timidity in foreign affairs, invest in defence and, where necessary, shed blood to prevent emerging threats.

I have always been fond of the West African proverb: 'Speak softly and carry a big stick; you will go far.'

– Theodore Roosevelt, 26th president of
the United States (1901-09)

7

BIG STICK: FOREIGN POLICY FOR A SUPERPOWER

China Beach

Hambantota is a dusty hamlet on the southern coast of Sri Lanka. With traffic it is about a six hour drive from Colombo on the coastal road. During Sri Lanka's quarter century civil war it was one of the last towns on the coast firmly in government control; drive past Hambantota and south becomes east, what was then LTTE country. This is also the southern tip of South Asia; look south from the beach and there is nothing but water between you and Antarctica.

Hambantota is about 550 kilometres from Jaffna, the cultural and commercial centre of Tamil Sri Lanka on the northern tip of the island. Sri Lanka's President Mahinda Rajapakse was born in Hambantota District, making him literally just about as far removed from the island's Tamil heartland as physically possible.

The town is actually closer to the southern tip of India than it is to Jaffna. This is why the activities of Hambantota's newest and most unusual residents should be causing alarm in New Delhi. On the coast near Hambantota, hundreds of Chinese workmen have been working to build what is to be one of South Asia's most advanced and largest ports, with a co-located oil refinery. The Chinese have been sent there nominally by China Harbour Engineering Co Ltd, the company with the contract to build the port;[1] in reality they have been sent by their government. They are there to establish a Chinese beachhead less than 500 kilometres from Kanyakumari, the southern-most tip of India.

The official rationale of the project is Hambantota's proximity to the major shipping lanes that run just off the southern coast of the island. The idea is that crude oil on the way from the Middle East to Asia can be refined in Hambantota. Other goods can be transhipped in the port as well.

It all makes good sense. But the commercial reasons are only part of the story. The Hambantota port is also part of China's larger geopolitical strategy to encircle the only country that can threaten its complete dominance of Asia: India.

Rajapakse is all too glad to welcome the Chinese to his hometown. Thanks to poor roads, his home district has always been remote from Colombo, and remote from Colombo's links with the world. His ambition is to turn Hambantota into Sri Lanka's second largest city after Colombo, and the new port is a central part of the strategy. With the port, Hambantota and Southern Sri Lanka will be isolated no more: Like a restaurant just off the highway, much of the passing traffic will find the port too convenient to pass up.

Rajapakse is adept at playing regional powers off on one another for what he perceives to be Sri Lanka's benefit. He did this during the nation's civil war by procuring arms, in turn, from India, Pakistan and China, running up bills from one until, his credit exhausted, he turned to the next.

Now Rajapakse is parlaying Sri Lanka's location into investments from foreign powers who want a piece of the island to help fulfil their own geopolitical strategies. It is a dangerous game for Sri Lanka, one that could bring various types of foreign domination that are not in the island's interest.

The Chinese for their part insist that the port is no more than a business investment, designed to help Sri Lanka develop its infrastructure.[2] Pull out a map of the world to see the real story. The eighty kilometres of the Palk Strait that separate India and Sri Lanka practically disappear on a world map. From the air, the chain of small islands linking Rameshwaram and Mannar (so-called 'Adam's Bridge')[3] is clearly visible, a geological umbilical cord linking Lanka to Mother India. These are the stepping stones that literally once connected Sri Lanka to India: Geological studies and historical records indicate that the causeway may have been passable up until the fifteenth century.

Beijing is 5000 kilometres from Rameshwaram. By this measure, the eighty kilometres of the Palk Strait separating India and Sri Lanka are a rounding error. With a presence in Sri Lanka, the Chinese have made it over ninety-eight percent of the way to India. They are no doubt delighted to have a foothold on what is virtually part of the Indian subcontinent.

It is not hard to imagine Chinese naval vessels one day securing basing rights in the newly constructed port. From there, Red Army troops can easily move up the coast of Sri Lanka to Mannar, which is but a hop, skip and a jump to the Indian mainland.

United States General Douglas MacArthur (1880-1964) called Taiwan an 'unsinkable aircraft carrier' off the coast of China.[4] By that analogy Sri Lanka is an unsinkable aircraft carrier off the coast of India, and the Chinese are about to come aboard.

Indian security analysts and retired Indian officials have expressed concern over China's encroachment into their backyard.[5] India's policy makers, however, have not taken any action to counter China's moves. It is as if India's leadership does not view China's Sri Lanka foothold as a direct threat to India's security.

Taiwan is one hundred miles off the coast of China. Would the Chinese allow India to build a port in Taiwan? China will not even countenance the notion that Taiwan is a separate country, much less allow a potential Asian rival to establish a beachhead there.

More to the point, would the idea ever even occur to India that it should have a foothold somewhere near China?

Experts believe that by 2020 the United States may no longer be able to defeat China in a war over Taiwan; China's air power will have become too great.[6] If the United States – with the world's largest military and bases in Japan and throughout the Pacific – cannot defeat China in a battle over Taiwan, India on its current defence spending trajectory has no hope of defeating China in a battle over Sri Lanka.

Contrast India's indifference to Sri Lanka with America's policy towards islands in its own backyard. During the First World War, the United States purchased Denmark's Caribbean territories Saint Croix, Saint John and Saint Thomas (now collectively the United States Virgin Islands) for the sum of $25 million.[7] It was an offer Denmark could not refuse; not because the price was attractive, but because Denmark must have known that the only alternative to a sale would have been seizure by the United States. With the United States readying to enter the war, it was not about to take a chance that Denmark's islands would fall into German hands.

The United States even cares more about security in the Indian Ocean, half-a-world away from Washington, than India does. The United States and the United Kingdom jointly operate a military base on Diego Garcia, home to scores of American naval vessels and long-range bomber aircraft. According to Naval Support Facility Diego Garcia's official Mission and Vision statement, it supports 'US and Allied forces forward deployed to the Indian Ocean and Arabian Gulf'.[8] In other words, Diego Garcia helps America show its muscle in, among other places, Iraq and Afghanistan.

For centuries Diego Garcia was home to former slaves, originally brought there by the French to farm coconut plantations. In 1971, the United Kingdom forcibly depopulated the island, removing its inhabitants, so that it and the United States could do as they please, free of the prying eyes of the natives. This is how great powers behave when their interests are even remotely threatened; India should take note.

Powerful nations have geopolitical strategies to protect their national interests and, where needed, expand their influence. India, by contrast, does not even have a geopolitical strategy. It has at best a regional strategy. That strategy – which could be summarised as 'keep Pakistan and China at bay' – is geared towards maintaining India's tiny sphere of influence, not expanding it.

India needs a geopolitical strategy, and it needs one fast.

A Finland of the South

Hambantota is not the only instance of India's foreign policy leadership being asleep at the wheel. China is also building ports in Bangladesh, Myanmar and Pakistan in what American military observers have called a 'string of pearls' strategy.[9]

If India is not careful, it could find itself choked by China's string of pearls. China's strategy will give it multiple access points to threaten the Indian mainland within a one hour missile flight.

Great powers have traditionally sought to establish a security perimeter well beyond their own territorial borders, as an extra protection against foreign incursions. As a young nation, the United States declared in 1823 that it would not tolerate any further European territorial expansion in the Western Hemisphere.[10] A century later (before, during and after the Second World War), the United States staked claims in the Pacific to limit Japan's territorial ambitions; in addition to the State of Hawaii today the United States has territories far and wide across the Pacific.

Cuba and American Power

The United States has its own Sri Lanka. For more than a century it has wrestled with the question of how to manage the potential strategic risk from Cuba, 150 kilometres off Florida's Key West.

The United States fought a war in 1898 to expel the Spanish from Cuba. The United States won, and after the war, acquired a perpetual lease to its base on the island at Guantanamo Bay. The purpose of Guantanamo is clearly spelled out in the 1903 agreement between United States and Cuba granting the lease: To enable the United States to maintain the independence of Cuba.[11]

For the United States 'independence' for Cuba meant freedom from European influence, not freedom from American influence. By the 1950s Cuba was full of American hotels and casinos, a playground for East Coast Americans. With Fidel Castro's revolution in 1958-59, the island became a thorn in the United States' side. Since then American policy has focused on ensuring that the island does not become a threat to American national security. During the 1962 Cuban Missile Crisis, John F. Kennedy was willing to go to the brink of war, maybe even nuclear war, to force the Russians to withdraw missiles from Cuba. For Kennedy, his cold war rival having a military strike capability so close to America's shores was an unacceptable situation.

Over the past fifty years American policy towards Cuba has included a failed invasion, active support for dissidents and – since 1961 – a trade embargo. Whatever the success of America's Cuba policy, no one can accuse any administration of allowing the island to compromise American national security. The United States has a radio program – Radio Marti – whose sole purpose it is to send pro-American and anti-Cuba propaganda to the Cuban people. Radio Marti and its sister television broadcaster TV Marti are funded with an annual budget of $30 million from the United States government.[12]

The fall of the Soviet Union deprived Cuba of financial support from its long-time patron, and Cuba's economic model has been slowly crumbling over the past two decades. Fidel Castro has handed power over to his younger brother and largely disappeared from public life. The United States is hoping that democracy will soon return to Cuba, and with it a more friendly government free of influence from other powers (except its northern neighbour, of course).

The United Kingdom has always regarded occupation of the low country ports of Holland or Belgium by another major power as a direct act of aggression. That is about as clear a warning as one country can send to another.

More recently, in August 2008, Russia fought a war with Georgia to send clear messages to North Atlantic Treaty Organisation (NATO) and the West: that Georgia lies within Russia's sphere of influence, and that Russia will never allow Georgia to join NATO. Nor should current NATO members, after serious reflection, want Georgia to join the alliance, for it would be bound by Article V of the NATO Charter to defend Georgia in case of attack.[13] The war of August 2008 proved that NATO is not willing to go to war with Russia over a country of five million people, located three thousand kilometres from Brussels.

It is puzzling that India's policy makers have ignored all these examples in developing their own regional strategy. India's acquiescence in China's South Asian land grab flies in the face of common sense as well as historical precedent. No self-respecting global power can allow an island a fraction of its size and lying kilometres off its shores to exercise a fully independent foreign policy, much less cavort with a rival power.

Sri Lanka, for its part, may feel that it is in its own interest to play India, China and potentially other powers against each other, to maximise its regional standing and leverage. This is a dangerous game. Sri Lanka's situation is fundamentally different from that of Nepal or Burma, which are sandwiched between India and China, and must pay heed to both. If India becomes a major power, there is only one situation of equilibrium for Sri Lanka – as a client state of its neighbour.

Any substantial influence or presence of a power other than India in Sri Lanka is certain to be a de-stabilising influence on both Sri Lanka and India. Sri Lanka must realise what Finland realised when it entered into a Friendship, Cooperation, and Mutual Assistance Treaty with the Soviet Union after the Second World War: When a major power is at your doorstep, it is better to accommodate it and retain a degree of independence than to risk losing independence altogether. Finland's actions set the example of 'Finlandisation' and brought the nation four decades of security throughout the Cold War.

India must now concentrate on the Finlandisation of Sri Lanka. The sooner this happens, the greater the chances for a long term stable balance of power between India and China.

In the short term this will mean preventing any further non-Indian involvement in Sri Lanka's affairs. India must use all available tools of coercion to demonstrate to Sri Lanka that its future lies in close ties with India and India alone. India's greatest tool is its commercial weight, both in channelling direct investment to the island and in serving as a market for its goods and services.

The Free Trade Agreement (FTA) India and Sri Lanka signed in 1998[14] and their follow-up Comprehensive Economic Partnership Agreement (negotiated but not yet signed) have established a framework for increased trade. The FTA has worked: Trade has grown nearly tenfold in the years since the agreement.[15] But this is just a start. India still only has a thirteen percent share of Sri Lanka's overall trade, behind the European Union [EU] (twenty-two percent).[16] Given the proximity and size of the Indian economy, India ought to be Sri Lanka's largest trading partner.

Currently the United States is Sri Lanka's largest export market, driven primarily by apparel exports. This trade, a legacy of the United States import quota system for apparel, has declined by ten percent since the expiration of quotas in 2004.[17] It is likely to decline further as it becomes increasingly difficult for Sri Lankan manufacturers to compete against lower labour costs in both India and China.

Furthermore, smart Sri Lankan companies are realising that consumer markets in India are a great export opportunity. MAS Holdings, one of Sri Lanka's largest companies, has built a $700 million business largely by exporting lingerie to brands in the United States. Now MAS is directing more of its energy and investment to developing its own brand of lingerie marketed in India and manufactured in Sri Lanka.

The United States-Canada trade relationship demonstrates the potential for cross-border trade between two mature neighbouring economies. In 2010, the United States consumed three-quarters of Canada's exports, making it by far Canada's largest market.[18] Canada, though only about one tenth the size of the American economy, is also the United States' largest export market, consuming one-fifth of exports in 2010.[19]

Sri Lanka is fortunate to be located next to what will be the world's third largest economy by 2030.[20] The Chinese can build a port in Sri Lanka, but they can never bring the everyday trade opportunities to Sri Lankan businesses that India can. India can further strengthen its trade links with the island by building a bridge across the Palk Strait. The engineering of such a bridge is entirely feasible; all that is missing is the political will and strategic vision in both nations to make it happen.

Even without an international bridge, it is possible within two decades for India to consume three-quarters of Sri Lanka's exports. Along the way the Indian Rupee and the Sri Lankan Rupee, inevitably, will begin to be linked, with further implications for Sri Lanka's monetary and fiscal policies.

As this economic integration between the two nations proceeds, the Indian government must pursue a parallel strategic integration. India will have to persuade Sri Lanka that the two nations have common security interests. It will be no easy task, considering the depth of suspicion many Sri Lankans still hold about their larger neighbour. But a close economic and strategic alliance with India is Sri Lanka's fastest route to prosperity and security. The alternative – to keep India at arm's length while courting the Chinese and others – will isolate Sri Lanka from the economic benefits that only India can bring it.

Sri Lanka has no external enemies; all its past wounds are self-inflicted. India is a close friend, but it needs to become more than that. As a true multi-ethnic, multi-religious society with a rapidly growing economy, India is just the kind of brother Sri Lanka needs.

For India, bringing Sri Lanka firmly into its sphere of influence will require changing not only its policy towards that nation, but building a new capability to neutralise emerging strategic threats, and do so aggressively. In the short term this reform is needed to prevent further strategic mis-steps in its neighbourhood like the Hambantota port; in the longer term it will be necessary if India is to fulfill its promise as a superpower.

Blind Faith

India's policy towards its island neighbour is part of a broader foreign policy passivity that has characterised most of its history since Independence. The problem has been both a lack of institutional capability and a mis-adventure with the NAM.

India's foreign policy apparatus is understaffed and underfunded.[21] New Zealand and Singapore have more diplomats in the field than India.[22] India's overseas embassies and missions operate on a budget of $300 million, entirely insufficient for a nation of 1.2 billion people.[23] Even India's corps of talented diplomats cannot perform the miracle of conducting superpower diplomacy on a developing country budget and a

Former Indian prime minister, Rajiv Gandhi, being garlanded by a supporter at an election campaign in Morena, Central India on 15 May 1991. Six days later Rajiv Gandhi was assassinated at a similar event in South India by a suicide bomber who approached him with a garland. (AP Photo)

The scene in Sriperumbudur, South India, moments before Rajiv Gandhi's assassination. The suicide bomber Dhanu, centre, stands waiting to approach Rajiv Gandhi, with garland at the ready; under her clothes was an explosive belt. India's Central Bureau of Investigation recovered this image from the assassination squad's official photographer, who was himself killed in the blast while attempting to capture it on film. (AP Photo)

Indian prime minister, P. V. Narasimha Rao, meets with United States president, Bill Clinton at the White House on 19 May 1994. Rao had taken office one month after Rajiv Gandhi's assassination, to lead a nation in mourning and an economy in crisis. Rao responded by mortgaging yet more gold to pay India's bills, and by giving his finance minister, Manmohan Singh, political cover to implement economic reforms that laid a foundation for two decades of growth. One and a half years after this photo was taken Rao aborted a planned nuclear test, after the United States ambassador to India confronted Rao's principal secretary with satellite photographs showing unusual activity at India's desert test site. (AP Photo/Doug Mills)

Having been caught preparing a nuclear test once by the United States (in December 1995), India was more circumspect when it was again ready to test two and a half years later. The 11 May 1998 tests led to widespread international condemnation of India. This photo, released by the Indian government, shows Shakti 1, one of four nuclear test sites in India's Thar desert, on the day of the tests. (AP Photo)

United States Deputy Secretary of State Strobe Talbott, left, and Indian Foreign Minister Jaswant Singh address the media in New Delhi on 30 January 1999. The Talbott-Singh dialogue on Indo-American relations was critical to repairing the rupture in bilateral relations caused by India's nuclear tests. (AP Photo/Ajit Kumar)

Indian Army troops fire artillery rounds on 30 May 1999 during the Kargil conflict with Pakistan. India and Pakistan went to the brink of nuclear war after Pakistani troops invaded the town of Kargil in Jammu and Kashmir in May 1999. The United States, through personal diplomacy by President Bill Clinton, managed to convince Pakistan to withdraw its troops – an outcome that pleased India and further strengthened the Indo-American relationship. (AP Photo/Aijaz Rahi)

Indian commandos take their positions as they work to repel an attack by Pakistan-based terrorist groups on the Parliament house in New Delhi on 13 December 2001. The attack, coming only three months after the attacks of 9/11 in the United States, helped unite India and the United States in shared opposition to terrorism. Nonetheless, India has since continued to be frustrated by the United States' limited action against Pakistan-based terrorists. (AP Photo/Manish Swarup)

United States President George W. Bush and India's Prime Minister Manmohan Singh on 18 July 2005 at the White House. That day Bush and Singh announced in a joint statement the framework for an agreement to cooperate on civil nuclear technology. The Indo-US nuclear agreement, finalised in 2008, capped a remarkable decade-long transformation in the bilateral relationship after India's 1998 nuclear test. White House photo by Eric Draper

Infosys employees on the sprawling company campus in Bengaluru. India's outsourcing industry, in spite of its strong record in job creation and in generating export earnings, is holding India back from reaching its true economic potential. Until India can focus its tremendous software and engineering talent on creating its own innovative technology products, it will continue to be caught in the trap of providing low-margin, outsourced services to Western clients. (AP Photo/Gautam Singh, File)

Students attend classes at a cram school in Kota, on 5 August 2010. Cram schools offer extra tuition, for a fee, to students who are preparing to sit for ultra-competitive entrance examinations to the IITs and other elite Indian universities. India's acute shortage of tertiary education institutes – less than five hundred universities for a nation of 1.2 billion people – is holding back the country's economic development. (AP Photo/Saurabh Das)

The partial wreckage of an Indian Air Force MiG-21 jet dangles from the ceiling of a house after the jet crashed in Jalandhar, Punjab, on 3 May 2002. The crash killed at least seven people and injured twenty. India's accident-prone fleet of Russian-made MiGs is an emblem of the sad state of India's military hardware. (AP Photo/Devinder Luthera)

While India's armed forces suffer with antiquated and low quality equipment, China has methodically been building a world class navy. China's first aircraft carrier Varyag returns to port after its maiden voyage, in Dalian in northeast China's Liaoning province on 14 August 2011. (Photo By Liu Debin/Color China Photo/ AP Images)

RUSSIA

KAZAKHSTAN
MONGOLIA
JAPAN

UZBEKISTAN
Xinjiang
TURKMENISTAN
KYRGYZSTAN
TAJIKISTAN
Beijing
N. KOREA
S. KOREA
Pacific

AFGHANISTAN
C H I N A
East China Sea
Ocean

PAKISTAN
Tibet

BHUTAN
NEPAL
BANGLADESH
TAIWAN

INDIA
MYANMAR
LAOS
South China Sea
PHILIPPINES

THAILAND
CAMBODIA
VIETNAM

MALAYSIA
SINGAPORE

Indian
I N D O N E S I A

Ocean
AUSTRALIA

Approximate zone of Chinese influence   Countries that will resist Chinese influence

Thanks to increasing economic and military power, China is rapidly expanding its sphere of influence in Asia. Only India and Japan could possibly resist an expansionist China. With Japan economically weakened and rapidly ageing, India alone stands between China and complete domination of the Asian continent. That is why an India that becomes a global power is China's worst nightmare. Reprinted by permission of Foreign Affairs, May-June 2010. Copyright 2010 by the Council on Foreign Relations, Inc.
Note: This map does not depict precise political borders.

Chinese workers boring a hole during the construction of a harbour in Hambantota, on the southern coast of Sri Lanka, on 30 January 2008. The harbour, one of several China is building in countries in India's neighborhood, represents a potential Chinese foothold a mere 500 kilometres from the southern coast of India. (AP Photo/Gemunu Amarasinghe)

A 16 April 1994 United States NASA photograph of the south coast of India (top) and the north coast of Sri Lanka (bottom), separated by the Palk Strait. In the middle right portion of the image a chain of islands (so-called 'Adam's Bridge') practically connects the two countries. This virtual link underscores how serious the threat to India is from China's incursion into Sri Lanka, which is just a hop, skip and a jump from the Indian mainland. Image Science and Analysis Laboratory, NASA-Johnson Space Center. "The Gateway to Astronaut Photography of Earth." http://eol.jsc.nasa.gov.Image STS059-229-25.

United States President Barack Obama and Indian Prime Minister Manmohan Singh walk towards the East Room of the White House on 24 November 2009, during Singh's state visit. The Obama-Singh era began with high expectations for a continuation of the rapid development of the Indo-American relationship that had taken place under President George W. Bush. But most observers, Indian and American alike, have been disappointed by the progress in bilateral relations during the first three years of Obama's term. (White House Photo by Chuck Kennedy)

Singh repaid the hospitality by welcoming Obama to India one year later. Obama speaks to the Indian Parliament at the Parliament House in New Delhi on 8 November 2010. In his speech, he offered a vague assurance of American support for India's bid for a permanent seat on the UNSC. Indians were thrilled with Obama's gesture. But real power will come to India only when it has sufficient economic and military might to inspire respect among its friends and fear among its enemies. For the United States, an India that becomes both its closest ally and a true global power would be a dream come true. (White House Photo by Pete Souza)

skeleton staff. India needs to double its Foreign Service staff as soon as feasible, and chart a course for building a foreign policy establishment on a par with China by 2020.

Compounding the staffing and budget shortfall is a lack of foreign policy resources outside government. The United States benefits from a network of think tanks, universities and consulting firms whose staff spend their time reflecting, writing and speaking on foreign policy issues. These researchers cover practically every conceivable foreign policy topic. One recent publication of a leading American think tank, the Council on Foreign Relations, included research on topics ranging from German economic policy to American drone strikes in Pakistan to South African land reform.[24]

Many of these foreign policy experts are former administration officials whose political party is currently out of power. As a group they constitute a kind of 'shadow' state department that provides the public with an opposing view on many of the administration's policies. They also incubate and develop ideas that the more bureaucratic government organisations are not yet able, or ready, to consider. Even the consulting and lobbying firms pushing the interests of American companies, foreign companies and foreign governments fulfill a valuable function of American democracy by bringing views of additional parties into the legislative and policy-making process.

This ecosystem is almost entirely lacking in India. The few think tanks and universities working on foreign policy make a valuable contribution, but far short of what is required to ensure a full public debate on the pressing international issues facing the country. The Indian government should recognise the role these organisations fill and create an environment where they can grow in number and thrive. As in the United States, the main funding for such organisations will have to come from political parties and the private sector (individuals as well as corporations and foundations).

India's ill-conceived identification with NAM has also stunted its growth as a global power. It is still paying the price today for its NAM mindset, and its refusal to quit the organisation even now is a display of self-defeating stubbornness.

There is a certain absurdity to countries aligning themselves in an organisation of non-aligned countries. Still, for many small former colonies NAM did have a degree of logic when it was established in 1961. Take an African nation such as Ghana, which declared independence from the United Kingdom in 1957, and was a founding member of NAM. For Ghana of the early 1960s, with a population less than seven million and a GDP per capita of $180,[25] the post-colonial world might have looked like a scary place. After the initial rush of freedom wore off, Ghana could have rightly concluded that being independent carried substantial risks as well as rewards. The world's weak nations, especially those of sub-Saharan Africa, needed a means for pooling their power. For this purpose 'Non-alignment' with the existing blocs was a reasonable pretence; one could hardly have expected NAM to bill itself as a weak nation movement.

India's mistake was thinking that it had any place in such an organisation. The NAM's membership criteria[26] refer repeatedly to prospective members keeping their distance from 'great powers' and their conflicts. While India was not a great power then, it need not have declared that fact so clearly by helping to conceive NAM and then being one of its leading voices. Joining NAM was itself an admission of impotence, one a nation of nearly 500 million people should never have taken.[27] The world took India at its word that it was a weak nation, and India has had to fight that perception ever since.

If India had truly wanted to be non-aligned it would have joined no international organisations. Switzerland is an example of a truly independent country; it did not even join the United Nations until 2002.

The ultimate irony was that India, in spite of its NAM affiliation, did align itself during the Cold War with what turned out to be the losing side. Nehru's Cold War tryst with the Soviet Union left India with the worst of both worlds: official alignment with self-declared powerless countries, and unofficial alignment with a soon-to-be former great power.

India's NAM mindset was strengthened by Nehru's holding the post of minister of external affairs for his nearly seventeen-year tenure as prime minister. During that time there was no one to challenge his views on foreign policy in general and the NAM orthodoxy in particular. By the time Nehru died in 1964, NAM was fully entrenched in India's post-independence world view.

Even today India continues to defend NAM. Before departing for the 2009 NAM Summit in Egypt, Manmohan Singh said that NAM 'has been the bedrock of India's foreign policy since [Nehru] and remains an article of faith for us'.[28] India would do well to question this article of faith if it wishes to realise its ambitions to become a world power.

Even if there was justification for India participating in NAM decades ago, any rationale has long since disappeared. China participates in NAM only as an observer state.[29] If China does not consider NAM worthy of its full time and attention, then India should not either.

Remaining in NAM today is also out of step with the commitment Nehru made at independence for India to serve 'the larger cause of humanity'. The future that beckoned to India in August 1947 surely was not one, over sixty years later, summiting in Sharm El Sheikh with the likes of pariah states Cuba, North Korea and Venezuela. NAM's only European member, Belarus, is a puppet state of Russia ruled by an oppressive dictator, hardly the company India should be proud of keeping.

Blind Hope

If membership in NAM is an article of faith for India, then a permanent seat in the UNSC is an article of hope. For many years Indian prime ministers have been beating the drum for reform of the UNSC system. In the words of Manmohan Singh, the UNSC must 'reflect the realities of contemporary age rather than being embedded in [an] era which is dead and gone'.[30]

India has long been pressing the United States to support its bid for a permanent UNSC seat. It got what it wanted during President Barack Obama's November 2010 visit to India. In a speech to Parliament, Obama declared, 'In the years ahead, I look forward to a reformed United Nations Security Council that includes India as a permanent member'.[31]

Yet Obama's vision for a 'reformed' UNSC falls far short of a commitment to support India's case. Even if the United States were to press India's case with the other permanent UNSC members – China, the United Kingdom, Russia and France – India is unlikely to get the seat it covets.

The permanent members made immense sacrifices to fashion the peace that has largely reigned since 1945. In the First and Second World Wars – arguably a single conflict with a pause of two decades[32] – the permanent members lost a total of 25 million people.[33] France alone lost 1.4 million in the First World War and Russia 20 million in the Second World War. They have earned the right to wield power for as long as the UN is a relevant world body.

India, which itself contributed 37,000 lives to the allied war efforts, can appreciate the level of sacrifice the permanent members have made. Although India did not win the power of a UNSC seat in return for its sacrifices, it has benefitted from the UN system in another way: More than six decades of global stability have allowed it to grow and prosper into an emerging world power.

India and others (notably Germany, Japan and Brazil) who want to expand the UNSC's permanent membership argue that the composition of the USNC is outdated. They are correct: The world has changed a lot since the end of the Second World War. New powers like India and Brazil are on the rise. Russia, France and the United Kingdom are in their twilight years as major powers.

Pleading for admission to a select club does not work; one has to earn an invitation. An invitation to the UNSC club is unlikely for India, or for any other aspirant. It is the height of naiveté for India and others to believe that the permanent members would in any way dilute their power by admitting a new member. Admitting one new member also raises the question of fairness to other nations. If India, why not Brazil? Brazil (population nearly 200 million), like India, is an emerging power. Furthermore, South America currently has no permanent representation on the UNSC. If Brazil, why not South Africa? Should Africa be alone among continents with no permanent representation on the Security Council? And so on.

Precisely because the world has changed, India should forget the UNSC Seat. It is a needless distraction from the real work facing India: preparing itself for the conflicts of the twenty-first century that will decide tomorrow's great powers.

The world today is free of large scale international conflicts. To be sure, Afghanistan has been in the midst of a protracted civil war for a decade, and civil strife began toppling dictators throughout the Middle East in early 2011. Fortunately these episodes are localised and have not sparked large regional wars. The threat from terrorism, meanwhile, is serious (especially with the possible use by terrorists of nuclear, chemical or biological weapons) and widespread, but unlikely to ignite a global conflict. Compared to the first half of the twentieth century, the world today is enjoying relative peace and stability.

Peace, however, can slip away suddenly, as it did in Europe in 1914; four years later the First World War had killed 37.5 million people. One century later India must use today's precious years of peace to prepare for the conflicts that tomorrow could well bring. India must be willing to shed its blood to win these future wars. Then, when the conflict is over, India cannot and will not be denied a seat at the great power table.

Joining the Asian Arms Race

India has a lot of work to do to prepare for a large scale conflict. Its advantage is that it has an outstanding military tradition with highly dedicated and professional soldiers, sailors and airmen. The disadvantage: India lacks the equipment and technology to do justice to its troops.

India's fleet of MIG fighters dates from the 1960s. Maintenance problems are common, and over forty percent of the aircraft procured by India since 1963 have been destroyed in accidents.[34] For the period from 1971 to 2004, the Indian Air Force (IAF) suffered an average rate of 1.09 accidents per 10,000 hours of flying, equating to the loss of twenty-three aircrafts and death of ten to fourteen pilots every year.[35]

India's development of a credible nuclear attack capability has been a great leap forward in its defence posture. However, nuclear arms are no substitute for conventional arms for a nation that has global power ambitions. The investment of time, money and attention that India has made in its nuclear capability has come at the cost of developing non-nuclear arms. Today India has a nuke-heavy posture with a large but ill-equipped conventional force.

To right the conventional-nuclear balance, India must increase its defence spending dramatically. India's defence spending amounted to $41 billion in 2010, placing it ninth in the world (right behind Germany and just ahead of Italy).[36] As a percentage of GDP, India's expenditure (2.7 percent) puts it behind Russia (4.0 percent) and Saudi Arabia (10.4 percent).[37]

China has the right approach. It started to increase its defence spending dramatically in the 1980s. Between 2001 and 2010, China's spending grew by 189 percent, versus 54 percent for India.[38] In 2010, China spent $119 billion on defence, or 2.1 percent of its GDP.[39] With this money China is building armed forces that will make it both a major land and sea power. It already has an army of 1.6 million, the world's largest.[40] Experts predict that by 2025, China's submarine force could be larger than the United States Navy's.[41]

China's aggressive military build-up supplements its natural geographical advantages. Its southern border is close enough to the Indian Ocean to reach it by road and through energy pipelines.[42] Its enormous interior shares borders with mostly weak states (Mongolia, Kazakhstan, Kyrgyzstan) and sparsely populated Russian Eurasia.[43] With little prospect of challenge from most of its neighbours, China does not have to concentrate its forces along its land borders to repel potential invasions;[44] it can even entertain the prospect of territorial gains there if it wishes. The lack of military distractions means China can afford to devote its defence spending to naval power, the ideal mode of military strength for a country with a coastline stretching 14,500 kilometres from its border with South Korea to its border with Vietnam.

The giant of the region is enhancing its natural advantages with massive defence spending, and so an Asian arms race has begun. Right now it is a one nation race, with China halfway down the track; India has not even left the starting block.

India must urgently create the kind of military its soldiers, airmen and sailors deserve: one that will both project its power and protect its people. A research report indicates India is to spend $200 billion on defence equipment between now and 2022.[45] However, most of this spending is to replace outdated equipment, to compensate for a lack of suitable acquisitions over the past twenty years. Replacing ageing equipment is not sufficient;

India also needs to expand and accelerate all manner of acquisitions if it is to close the arms gap with China.

Even if China only maintains its average defence spending growth rate from the past decade, it will reach $225 billion in spending by 2020 and $425 billion by 2030. Closing the arms gap with China by 2030 will require India's spending at least $380 billion over the next two decades on defence, or $320 for every Indian alive today.

Even this level of spending might not enable India to catch up with China; China could well accelerate its own military expenditures even as India does. But, spent efficiently, an extra $380 billion can bring India into a credible second place in Asia.

Of course India has other pressing development priorities that it must address, notably in infrastructure and education, and government funds are finite. It must balance its security needs with the imperative of lifting 400 million people out of poverty. There will be difficult choices to make. But it would be short sighted for India to continue to under-fund its military forces. Widespread economic prosperity cannot exist without national security. More to the point, security threats (whether foreign or domestic) can destroy economic growth and job creation. India and Indians cannot achieve financial security without achieving military security.

Wanted: Military-Industrial Complex

Beyond providing the umbrella security for growth, Indian defence can and must itself become a job-creation engine, as it has been in the United States for the past sixty years. United States President Dwight Eisenhower, on leaving office in 1961, warned of the growth of what he called the 'military-industrial complex' and its potential for 'unwarranted influence' on government policy. Eisenhower noted that prior to the Second World War the United States had not had a defence industry, relying instead on the makers of ploughshares to, 'with time and as required, make swords as well'.[46] After the war the United States had reached the point where instant defence readiness was a necessity, which in turn required a permanent defence industry.

India too has reached the point where it needs a defence industry that is capable of supplying the 2.6 million soldiers, sailors and airmen of India with world-class equipment. While heeding Eisenhower's warning about the potential influence of a sector whose livelihood depends on defence spending, India should move forward to create its own military-industrial complex.

India has to do no less than create an entire new industry that will propel further employment. The experience of the United States since the end of the Second World War indicates that defence will create jobs, breed new technologies with cross over applications for other industries and, most importantly, help keep the peace.

The United States defence sector employs 1.1 million people, accounting for one in ten American manufacturing jobs.[47] American defence companies generated $6.8 billion in export sales in 2009.[48] With its combination of technology, size and export muscle, the defence industry is critical to the health of the overall American economy.

India's defence sector is minuscule in comparison. It consists of mainly nine state-owned enterprises,[49] which together control eighty-five percent of the $5.3 billion domestic defence industry. The Indian government opened up the defence sector to privately-held Indian companies in 2001, and there are now six major private defence contractors and hundreds of smaller firms.[50] The private firms, however, face bureaucratic procedures to participate in procurement tenders, and sometimes are not allowed to bid at all.[51] India's total defence exports, from private and public entities combined, currently amount to $22 million,[52] and are low-tech in nature.

If India's defence industry were to reach a level of national importance equivalent to America's, large enough to account for one in ten Indian manufacturing jobs, it could mean direct employment for 2.5 million Indians.[53] These would be good manufacturing, engineering and support jobs that would create the growth and additional indirect employment needed to lift millions of Indians out of poverty.

Increased defence spending must not come at the expense of investments in infrastructure and direct aid to India's poor, both of which are critical to India's future growth and social harmony. But if India is going to direct funds to any industry, it should direct them to defence. India currently spends over $32 billion directly subsidising a range of industries, including farming, food, and fuel.[54] Some of these may be worthy causes. But none of them can claim to offer the overall national security benefits that a government-sponsored defence industry will.

India is ideally positioned to be a major global defence player. It has the engineering capabilities and a major steel-making industry. As defence technology fuses more with IT, India's experience in coding software and designing chips will give it an edge on rivals. If Indians can work in Bengaluru designing chips for American and European clients, they can also design the chips and systems that will control a new generation of precision guided missiles, made in India with Indian technology.

Combining its engineering and IT talent with robust government defence spending will allow India to develop unique technologies that it can sell selectively to other nations. These defence sales can not only become a major export industry, but also become a tool of Indian power and influence globally. Deciding what nations can and cannot have access to defence technology is a major instrument of American foreign policy, and it can be for India as well.

Buy American

Building stronger defence ties with the United States (and its allies) is the only way for India to create the defence industry it needs over the next decade.

For its part the United States recognises India's growing military capabilities, and wants to encourage their further development. The United States Defence Department's Quadrennial Defence Review (QDR) stated that 'India's military capabilities are rapidly improving through increased defence acquisitions and they now include long-range maritime surveillance, maritime interdiction and patrolling, air interdiction and strategic airlift'.[55]

The United States wants to help develop India's capabilities – and enrich American defence firms – by selling India the equipment it needs to become a major military power. So far the Indian government has been highly receptive. In June 2011, the Indian cabinet approved the purchase of C-17 military transport aircraft from United States based Boeing; the contract is for ten aircraft worth $4.1 billion, with an option for India to buy six more.[56] This follows India's 2009 order of Boeing reconnaissance aircraft for $2.1 billion, and its 2008 order of $1 billion worth of transport aircraft from United States based Lockheed Martin Corporation.[57] Although the American government was 'deeply disappointed' that no American firms made the April 2011 shortlist of India's biggest procurement contract in history (an $11 billion contract for 126 new fighter aircraft),[58] it can be consoled that American arms sales to India are gaining rapid speed.

It is a promising start, but there is still a long way to go. Even with these announced purchases, India is only spending a fraction of what it needs annually to start credibly to close the China gap.

The principle behind India's forthcoming investments must be to bring the world's best technology and equipment to the country. The ideal model will be for Indian companies to tie up with American and allied defence companies in Joint Ventures (JVs). Mahindra and Mahindra has a 75/25 JV with BAE Systems (BAE is nominally based in the United Kingdom but sixty percent of its $6.9 billion in turnover comes from the United States.)[59] In February 2010, the partners agreed to invest $21.25 million into the JV to tap the growing market for defence equipment in India.[60] Such integration allows world class technology to come to India while supporting the domestic Indian defence sector to improve its capabilities and create jobs in India. In a recent example of such technology transfer, BAE is supplying the technology for production of bullet-proof vests to an Indian company, for manufacture in India.[61]

Indian policy requires that any defence contract worth more than $65 million carries so-called 'offset' business of at least thirty percent.[62] Offsets require a foreign company supplying defence equipment to India to buy a certain amount of goods from the buyer's home country, to offset part of the funds outflow. While offsets can take many forms (including the counter-purchase of goods having nothing to do with defence), there is one type of offset – the co-production agreement – that would be of particular value to India. India should focus on co-production offsets to accelerate the development of its own defence technology base, and thereby enhance its long-term national security.

Here's how it can work. India, for example, places an order for $1 billion worth of transport aircraft from an American defence company. In the contract the Indians require the American supplier, when constructing the planes, to source at least $300 million in components (thirty percent of the total contract value) for the planes from Indian suppliers. These components would be produced in India, by Indian companies, with American technology. That technology could either be licensed to the Indian company, or managed by an Indo-American joint venture entity. Everyone wins: The American company gets the order and most of the manufacturing work; India creates jobs manufacturing some components, and vital technology along the way.

To be a global power India cannot simply buy American equipment and learn how to operate and maintain it. India has to have a role in the entire production process, so that it can master the technology behind the equipment. Once the American technology is infused in India's defence companies, they can build on this knowledge to create entirely new technology platforms as well as innovations on existing American platforms. This technology transfer is the key to India developing indigenous defence technology, and offsets can speed up the process dramatically. Then India can become a seller, not a buyer, of advanced defence equipment.

As Chapter Eight will demonstrate, the Indo-American relationship has the potential to be as close in the twenty-first century as the Anglo-American relationship was in the twentieth century. A strong India supported by American defence technology will be a critical element in this future alliance.

Toy Boats

In 1897, an ambitious American in his late thirties was intent on securing a particular position in the administration of newly elected United States President William McKinley. The young man marshalled the help of a dozen influential Americans in his quest: congressmen, cabinet secretaries, major party donors and even their wives. For months they besieged the president-elect and his key advisors with entreaties on behalf of the aspirant.[63]

He got the job he wanted. In April 1897, Teddy Roosevelt became secretary of the navy, a job that became a springboard for him to positions of even greater power. By 1901, he became McKinley's vice president, and later that year Roosevelt ascended to the presidency himself upon McKinley's assassination.

The strategy worked so well that fifteen years later his distant cousin, Franklin Delano Roosevelt, decided to emulate it: secretary of the navy from 1913 to 1920, president by 1932.

These leaders of a young United States understood the importance of the navy in building a nation as well as in building a career. When he was president, Teddy Roosevelt sent sixteen American battleships on a worldwide tour. When the 'Great White Fleet' returned from the fourteen-month, 69,000-kilometre voyage in February 1909, the press called it 'the most impressive pageant... that ever made the American breast swell with pride in his country and his flag'.[64] The United States had arrived as a world power. It was less than forty-five years after the end of the American Civil War.

Yet sixty-plus years after Independence, India's navy is suffering from years of under investment. India's navy is the fourth largest in the world – in manpower terms. That highlights precisely what is wrong with India's military investment – strong on people, weak on equipment and technology. People are not expensive in India, with a navy captain making a monthly salary of around $420,[65] a fraction of what his American counterpart makes. It has been all too tempting for India to increase its navy staff to create an illusion of power on the cheap.

When measuring naval power, the number of sailors is not decisive; gross tonnage of vessels is. In terms of tonnage, India is eighth in the world. Even Germany, whose coastline is only one third the length of India's, ranks ahead of it in naval tonnage.

A century ago, the United States was a rising power just like India. Yet it made sure that it was climbing the ranks of world tonnage. It was a wise investment from a country that, like India today, was battling grinding poverty, inadequate infrastructure and uneven access to education. In spite of all these competing needs for government spending, the United States made sure to prioritise its navy. In 1916, the United States Congress, viewing from afar the naval battles of a World War America was soon to join, authorised one of the greatest naval build-ups in the history of mankind: fifty destroyers to be built over a three year period.[66]

Navies win wars – it has been that way since Admiral Nelson and shows no signs of changing as long as two-thirds of the earth is covered by water. India must not forget that. Bangladesh certainly will not. It owes its existence as a nation in no small part to the Indian Navy's blockade of Karachi in 1971.

India's Kind of War

While India is building its nuclear and conventional military capability, it should also devote resources to mastering the twenty-first century's emerging global battlefront: cyberwar. Countries will of course continue to fight battles on the land and sea and in the air. Today, however, soldiers, sailors and airmen are being joined by a new comrade: the IT genius tapping at a keyboard. This soldier will use technology as a weapon to attack other nations' computer and defence systems. He can hack into enemy databases to download battle plans, drop virus 'bombs' into enemy email applications, or shut down enemy command and control systems. In the future one IT engineer with a computer and an internet connection will be able do more damage than an entire infantry battalion.

Cyberwar is already with us. Georgia accused Russia of hijacking Georgian government websites during their 2008 war.[67] In 2010, an unknown attacker unleashed a virus on the industrial control system in Iran's nuclear facility, in an attempt to slow progress on the country's nuclear programme.

Cyberwar is India's kind of war. It has a base of 2.2 million IT sector employees[68] who collectively know more about computer systems than any group of men and women on the planet. They have built, debugged and quality tested almost every conceivable type of IT network. They are fiercely patriotic, and can be India's secret weapon in the twenty-first century.

First India will need to mobilise them. The United States, United Kingdom and Russia have all set up initiatives to use technology as an offensive weapon and to defend against technology attacks by enemies.[69] China boasts of being able to win 'informationised (sic) wars by the mid-twenty-first century'.[70] To do so it has allocated a $55 million annual budget to computer attacks, and has a force of 10,000 cyber soldiers who learn in Chinese military schools how to write viruses that disable enemy systems and steal confidential information.[71]

India, meanwhile, is falling just as far behind China in cyberwarfare as in conventional warfare. The Indian Army insists it is aware of the threat from cyberwarfare, and has established a Computer Emergency Response Team (CERT) to respond to enemy cyber-attacks.[72] Defensive actions, however, will not suffice; India needs to develop an offensive cyber capability, lest it be spending all its time and resources fighting off attacks. Despite having the best potential 'IT army' in the world, India is letting this potential strategic advantage go unutilised.

The best way to mobilise India's IT talent to make the nation into a cyberwar superpower will be to appoint one of the nation's top technology executives to lead the initiative. Indian prime minister Manmohan Singh put ex-Infosys CEO Nandan Nilekani in charge of implementing a national Unique Identification (UID) card system in 2009. Singh should appoint an IT leader of equal status to develop and implement a cyberwar strategy.

The United States was caught by surprise when Japan attacked Pearl Harbor in December 1941; it then commenced the greatest military production programme yet known to mankind. In January 1942, United States President Franklin Roosevelt announced army production targets for the next two years: 185,000 airplanes and 120,000 tanks.[73] It was possible only because the United States had the largest industrial base on earth, some of which had been underutilised during the Great Depression of the 1930s; the military commandeered every spare bit of that industrial capacity.

Today India has the greatest IT production base on earth. The Indian government must not wait until its Pearl Harbor to mobilise this force. Today India must develop a plan to deploy its private sector IT strength in support of national security. The Indian government should develop the plan in consultation with and full support of the IT services industry, so that Bengaluru is equally committed to defending the homeland as it is to winning that next big outsourcing contract. Together the public and private sectors can create an IT army ready to be activated virtually overnight in case of need.

If India is to become a superpower it must do so in both conventional weapons and cyberwarfare. India has fallen behind the rest of the world in the former, and must now work hard to catch up. The battlefield of cyberwar, however, is only just beginning to take shape, and India's talent base gives it a natural edge over rivals. India can partly compensate for its conventional arms disadvantage by becoming the world's undisputed cyberwar superpower.

Pax Indica

Beyond all the other benefits such as job creation, export growth and innovation, the most important consequence of a strong India will be enhanced security for the Indian people and the region as a whole: a *pax Indica*.

Though arms races have a bad reputation, the history of America's defence build-up since the Second World War has been overwhelmingly positive. 520,000 Americans died in wars in the first half of the twentieth century, 95,000 in the second half.[74] While the Cold War arms race with Russia was a period of tension in both nations, with sometimes a real threat of nuclear war, in retrospect it was largely a period of peace.

Moreover, the United States owes much of its defence and space technology to the impetus provided by the Cold War.[75] It was competition on earth with Russia that propelled American astronauts to the moon. Today, having outspent and out-innovated the Soviet Union during the Cold War, the United States is reaping continued benefits from its investments. In military technology, the United States now has such a dominant advantage that it will take any would-be rival decades to catch up. Even China admits that it is twenty years behind the United States in defence equipment, weapons and systems.[76]

Defence technology innovations have also allowed the United States to fight wars with less loss of life than otherwise would be required. Over the course of seven years in Iraq and ten in Afghanistan, the United States has sustained just over 6,000 deaths. This compares to 58,000 during nine years in Vietnam.[77]

Investments in defence have kept generations of Americans secure. Thanks to the dominant technological advantage the United States has achieved, its defence sector will continue to keep Americans secure for many years to come. A twenty-first century rivalry with China can be for India what the Cold War was for America: a motivation to develop a superior base of technology in defence and aerospace that will keep the peace. Indians should demand no less of their government, for themselves and future generations.

Locking up the Resources

A strong defence alone cannot keep India and its people secure. India will have to supplement its aggressive military policy with an equally aggressive policy to lock up the natural resources needed to fire the factories that will, in turn, build its naval vessels, tanks and fighter jets.

India has seventeen percent of the world's population living on two percent of its landmass. By 2030, India will be the world's most populous nation, with 1.5 billion people crammed into a nation less than one-third the size of the United States.[78] Managing the disparity between a growing population and finite resources is a critical challenge for India in this century. If India is to achieve a level of global power commensurate with its population, it will have to find a way to overcome its space and resource constraints.

Throughout history great powers or would-be great powers, faced with limitations of space and resources, have sought various ways to overcome them. The dawn of sea exploration allowed small European states to exercise power and influence disproportionate to their size by colonising far-flung peoples. More recently Germany started two wars in the twentieth century in part to find more *Lebensraum* (living space).

During its own rapid growth phase the United States moved continuously westwards, muscling out indigenous peoples and colonial powers to reach the Pacific Ocean. Having fought a Civil War to preserve the Union in the 1860s, by the turn of the century the United States had expanded to forty-five states, bringing under its control many of the vast states that now make up the American West.

The relentless march westwards was in part fuelled by America's industrial expansion in the East. The United States was fortunate to have the coal, oil and labour to enable the expansion of its industrial production in the late 1800s. As a result, it was able to enter the twentieth century poised for great power status.

Where the United States has lacked resources, it has, throughout its history, unapologetically filled in the gaps by forays overseas. These have included political deals for oil supplies (pre-revolution Iran, Saudi Arabia today), private sector deals for metals (aluminium in South America), and outright purchases of large territories from foreign powers in need of cash (the 1803 Louisiana Purchase from France, and the 1867 purchase of Alaska from Russia).

The result: America has become the world's dominant power, with a growing population, dynamic economy and access to seemingly limitless natural resources at home and abroad, all framed within a stable and scalable political system.

India has all these advantages except for the natural resources. If India is to achieve the global power its population warrants, it will have to address its resources shortfall. Without resources to fuel its continued growth India risks becoming a large, but largely irrelevant, player on the global stage.

China is faced with a similar predicament. The difference is that China is doing something about its resources shortfall, while India is not. China has a clear strategy for locking up resources to fuel its growth: Strike political deals with resource-rich (but otherwise under-developed) countries in Africa and South America to ensure a steady flow of natural resources to Chinese factories. To win those deals, China offers a combination of development aid, political support and attractive, long-term purchase agreements.

China Development Bank (CDB), for example, has pioneered the use of energy-backed loans (EBLs) to procure the resources the nation needs to grow. China's EBLs are structured for the long term (as much as twenty years) and for big impact (sizes up to $20 billion), which gives CDB a unique offering for nations looking for cash today in exchange for resources tomorrow.[79]

South America has responded to China's overtures with enthusiasm. The two struck a simple bargain: China gets access to the region's natural resources (copper, iron ore, zinc, soy and oil), while South America gets cash for development. In recent years China has signed deals worth $100 billion with South American nations:[80] $32 billion in loans to Venezuela, to be paid back in oil shipments over a decade; a $2 billion joint venture in copper with Chile; $1.4 billion in irrigation infrastructure for Argentina, in exchange for twenty-year rights to grow corn, wheat and other crops for export to China; the list goes on.[81] The long-term nature of these contracts has proven valuable to China; when copper prices doubled after its deal with Chile, China was able to secure the mineral at well below market prices thanks to a fifteen-year, partially fixed price contract.[82]

China is not afraid to flex its new-found trade muscles in South America when its interests there are threatened. In 2010, Argentina announced duties on Chinese shoes to protect local producers. China's response? An immediate halt to its $1.5 billion annual soy purchases from Argentina.[83] China began buying the soy again after six months, only after the two nations agreed on a $12 billion project for China to work on in rail projects in Argentina.[84]

Unlike America, which has often used foreign policy to spread democracy with the zeal of a missionary, China does not seek to export its values abroad; its foreign policy is simply about securing the resources to support a continued rise in living standards for one-fifth of humanity.[85] Chinese priorities are illustrated by its commercial and political relationship with Sudan. The Sudanese government has come under widespread international criticism for documented human rights abuses in the Darfur region; but not from the Chinese, for whom Sudan was the sixth largest supplier of oil in 2010.[86]

China's global resources strategy is working. China now accounts for one quarter of all global metal consumption, up from ten percent in the late 1990s.[87] In 2009, it also consumed about half of the world's production of coal, zinc and aluminium.[88]

India must take a similar aggressive approach to sourcing the resources it needs. With South America dominated by America and now China, Africa is the key battleground. Fortunately, Africa has much of what India needs: oil (Nigeria, Angola, and others); gold and diamonds (South Africa); coal (Mozambique); and uranium (Malawi and Niger).[89] Unfortunately, in Africa, India is again playing catch up with China.

China has deluged the continent with investments and with people. There already may be as many as one million Chinese immigrants living in

Africa.[90] They are running businesses, making investments and constructing infrastructure funded by Chinese government loans and grants.

China's investments in Africa dwarf India's. During 2009 and 2010, both nations made six financing and investment deals above $5 million in Africa. India's totalled $230 million, and were exclusively loans (one of which was concessionary). China's deals included concessionary loans, one grant and Foreign Direct Investments (FDI). Their total value? Over $5 billion.

India's leadership sees the problem and is working hard to catch up with China in Africa. At the May 2011 Afro-Indian summit in Addis Ababa, Indian Prime Minister Manmohan Singh pledged $5 billion in soft loans to Africa and $1 billion in other aid.[91] This is the kind of quantum leap in engagement that India needs to close the Africa gap with China. Now India has to convert this financial commitment to commercial deals in Africa, especially in resource rich countries.

India cannot match China's state-run enterprises dollar-for-dollar in spending. Apart from a handful of state-owned companies like Indian Oil Corporation (IOC) and Oil and National Gas Corporation (ONGC), India does not have the potential to direct the power of the state to gain a foothold in Africa. To penetrate Africa and catch up to the Chinese there, India will have to unleash its greatest weapon: private sector entrepreneurs.

India should consider giving its private sector companies specific incentives to invest in Africa. These could include duty-free import of natural resources back into India or tax breaks for investments overseas into certain mineral-rich areas. The Indian government can and should provide overall political cover for these investments, but the driving force must come from the private sector. India's private companies can develop the valuable promoter-level connections on both sides of the Arabian Sea that can propel the Afro-Indian commercial relationship forward.

One bright spot in India's race for resources is its potential for access to nuclear fuel from the nuclear suppliers group. India will need 1300 Gigawatts of power by 2050, and nuclear power can satisfy around a quarter of this demand.[92] But nuclear power cannot compensate for shortfalls in basic resources such as coal, copper, and iron ore that are the building blocks of any industrial base. India will have to get these from other nations, and get them before China does.

The Indian Experiment

If India aspires to truly be a global power in the twenty-first century, a globally aggressive natural resource policy is essential. Only with the resources to fuel continued economic growth can India finance the defence investments necessary for a true 'big stick' foreign policy. Only with a 'big stick' foreign policy can India truly enjoy the security necessary to pull 400 million people out of poverty.

If a 'big stick' seems out of character with India's tradition of non-violence, it is worth remembering that India – as a pluralistic democracy in the developing world – sets an important example for other nations. Can a democratic political system like India's create the same wealth in the next two decades that China's centrally-planned system has created in the past two decades? The outcome of what might be called 'the Indian experiment' will tell.

India must not allow that experiment to fail. It must secure a future of prosperity and security for its people, even if it has to strong-arm neighbouring countries like Sri Lanka and the resource-rich countries of Africa along the way. If India prospers it will set an example to countless other nations and peoples who dream of living in democratic freedom under the rule of law and a capitalist system. India has an obligation to be strong, not just for its 1.2 billion citizens, but for those the world over who will look to it as an example in the twenty-first century, just as they look to the United States as an example today.

To protect and project their shared values, India and the United States must do more to be strong as individual powers. They must develop an alliance that will be to the twenty-first century what the Anglo-American alliance was to the twentieth century: a guarantor of freedom and, if needed, saviour of the world.

PART THREE

The United States and India:
An Alliance for the Twenty-First Century

Beware, I say; time may be short. Do not let us take the course of allowing events to drift along until it is too late. If there is to be a fraternal association of the kind I have described, with all the extra strength and security which both our countries can derive from it, let us make sure that that great fact is known to the world, and that it plays its part in steadying and stabilizing the foundations of peace. There is the path of wisdom. Prevention is better than cure.

– Winston Churchill, *The Sinews of Peace*, Westminster College, Fulton, Missouri, 5 March 1946

8

A NEW SPECIAL RELATIONSHIP

From Cold Shower to Warm Embrace

The decade between 1998 and 2008 saw a transformation in Indo-American ties. India's 1998 nuclear test had been a cold shower for America. The outrage that the test provoked was only partly due to American concerns about non-proliferation. An equal cause was the perception that India had challenged the post-Cold War international order that the United States had constructed.

Many Americans at that time, especially American government officials, believed that the United States was the sole superpower, and would be for some time. Europe was at peace, apart from some trouble in the Balkans. Russia was weak, and the EU and NATO were expanding at will eastwards to absorb former Soviet states. China was a rising power, but any prospect of Chinese dominance seemed to be distant, thanks to America's own economic strength at the time. Islamic terrorism seemed to be no more than a fly that had to be swatted away occasionally. There were small threats out there – Saddam Hussein's Iraq, a recalcitrant North Korea – but nothing that would challenge America's primacy.

Along came India to upset Washington's dreams of a *pax Americana*. At the time of the test, it looked like a reckless act in an otherwise orderly world. Yet, as we saw in Chapter Three, the shock of the cold shower gradually wore off, and the United States came to accept a nuclear India (and later a nuclear Pakistan).

The first two years of the twenty-first century saw a change in the worldview of many Americans. After 9/11, the latent threats of five years before (Saddam Hussein and Islamic terrorism) had developed into real ones, certainly in the eyes of many in the administration of President George W. Bush and many Americans as well. By 2002, America's own economy was in a deep recession; suddenly China's dominance did not seem that far off.

India, ever wary of both Pakistan and China, saw dangers on the horizon at the close of the twentieth century that the United States did not see, or could not see, until the opening of the twenty-first. It is now clear that India's nuclear test was not only prudent for India, but a boon to the United States as well. The test marked the emergence of a new partner for America, one that the United States must embrace as its primary ally of the twenty-first century.

America's New Britain

The Anglo-American 'special relationship' was the dominant alliance of the twentieth century for both nations. Together, the United States and United Kingdom liberated Europe, kept it free and made it whole. Along the way the citizens of both nations enjoyed decades of security and prosperity. It will be remembered as one of history's great alliances.

As effective as the relationship with the United Kingdom was for the twentieth century, it is insufficient to meet the security challenges that the United States is likely to face in the remainder of the twenty-first century. The United States must develop a new special relationship with a superpower of tomorrow that shares its values and security concerns. India must become America's new Britain.

Three strategic realities argue for the United States putting India on the fast-track to a special relationship.

First, the United Kingdom is not the global power it was fifty years ago, let alone in its age of Empire. In the coming century the United Kingdom will be ill-suited to enhance American security: It is too small, suffers daunting economic challenges and is located in the wrong part of the world. The era when a small nation like the United Kingdom can exercise power out of proportion to its size is ending. The world is in the midst of a historical realignment of power, back to what it was before the Industrial Revolution. As we saw in Chapter One, throughout most of human history, economic activity has been concentrated in countries with the largest populations. The Industrial Revolution, in retrospect, was a distortion of this historical norm – a distortion that allowed small countries to accumulate great wealth, underpinned by technological advantages. This technology-driven wealth translated into great commercial and military power. A small island off the coast of Europe was the primary beneficiary of this distortion; the United Kingdom will also be the main loser as the distortion disappears.

While the United Kingdom will be a close American ally for the foreseeable future, the partnership will increasingly become little more than symbolic as the gulf between American and British strength continues to widen. The United Kingdom's decline leaves a void that the United States must fill.

The second strategic reality that compels the United States to develop a closer alliance with India is a shift in the global centre of gravity – economically and militarily – from the transatlantic region to Asia.

The odds of a major war in Europe this century are low. One cannot say the same for Asia.

The Second World War was started by countries with rapidly growing populations looking for room to expand. Germany had only a relatively small stretch of coastline on the North Sea, and by land it was hemmed in by France to the West and Poland to the East. Japan, for its part, felt its chain of islands in the northern Pacific insufficient to meet the demands of its growing population. The territorial ambitions of these two nations plunged the world into a conflict that claimed sixty million lives.

Today Japan and Germany are wealthy and peaceful, with greying populations; the rebellious teens have become docile seniors.

Now the world faces a new generation of nations that, like Germany and Japan a century ago, are capable of precipitating wars through aggressive territorial expansion or through domestic instability. Iran is the Germany of today: a distinct ethno-linguistic group (the Persians) surrounded by other medium-sized states and no local superpower to fear. With a fast growing population, ambitions of greater power, and a religious fervour comparable to Germany's Nazi cult, the parallels are unsettling.

Saudi Arabia, though on the surface a stable state, is a cultural powder keg. A few thousand princes, who with their families make up a tiny portion of the overall population, control a sizeable share of national oil revenues and national wealth. The United States largely ignores the situation because the Saudi royal family is a strong ally. Yet revolutions can topple friendly dictators overnight, as the United States learned from the Shah's Iran in 1979 and Hosni Mubarak's Egypt in 2011. Saudi Arabia could well be a contemporary version of pre-revolutionary Iran; simply substitute 'House of Saud' for 'Peacock Throne'.

A democratic Iraq is unlikely to start conflicts itself, but might be weak enough to be prey for an aggressive Iran. Afghanistan and Pakistan bring their own form of instability to the picture. Together these five states – from Saudi Arabia in the West to Pakistan in the East – make up the most dangerous zone in the world. Add oil and communal tensions to the mix and the prospect of a major conflict erupting in the area is substantial.

Further afield, the frightening insanity of North Korea – a nation with little to lose by going to war – and the increasing militarism of China solidify Asia's status as the world's next potential source for large scale conflict. In this neighbourhood, the United States needs an ally it can rely on tomorrow as much it relies on the United Kingdom today. It needs India.

The third reason India should become America's primary global ally is that India is uniquely capable of taking over this role from the United Kingdom. It shares American security concerns in Afghanistan and Pakistan, and has a strategic location near the most dangerous countries in the world. It has a thriving economy and technological base that – given sufficient investment – can fuel enough military might to compensate for the United Kingdom's decline. Finally, India possesses the same core values that underpinned the Anglo-American relationship: democracy, human rights, the rule of law and the free market.

As the United States and the United Kingdom came together to save Europe, so the United States and India may have to come together to save Asia.

The Intel Club

The Anglo-American relationship, formed quickly and out of necessity in the crucible of the Second World War, has strengthened further in the years since. Now the two nations' military, diplomatic and intelligence structures are so well-coordinated that cooperation on matters large and small is the default mode.

It will take years, decades perhaps, for the United States and India to elevate their relationship to this level. It is in the strategic interests of both India and the United States to begin the process now. They must not wait for a Third World War.

In addition to closer military ties, a critical component of Indo-American cooperation in the twenty-first century must be intelligence sharing.

There are only four countries that the United States shares intelligence with completely – the United Kingdom, Canada, Australia and New Zealand. It is the world's most exclusive club, one where the members don't have any secrets from each other.[1] The members share an alliance so strong that they cooperate on the state's most intimate activity: spy craft. For decades they have worked together in secret to protect themselves and each other, fighting the small battles and making the large sacrifices that the general public will never learn of.

The club should make way for a new member: India. It qualifies to join on all counts, sharing values, strategic interests, and strong democratic institutions with the current members. It is no accident that the nations who fully share intelligence also have a common British heritage. These values guide their collective security interests, as well as how their spies work on a daily basis to safeguard these interests.

While the current members cover much of the world, there is a gap of 14,000 kilometres between Australia and the United Kingdom. In this gap falls West Asia, precisely where trouble is most likely to originate in the twenty-first century. The United States and its closest allies need a nation capable of being the club's member-on-the-scene in Asia. India is the logical candidate for the job.

India is already taking an active role in intelligence matters in Afghanistan, and is also putting its money to work in a multi-billion dollar aid program.[2] India's involvement in Afghanistan clearly unnerves Pakistan. A Pakistani intelligence official interviewed in the American press wondered aloud what role an Indian consulate in Afghanistan serves, if there is no Indian population there.[3] Whatever objections Pakistan may voice, India must keep a firm foothold in Afghanistan and the region, led by both intelligence gathering and targeted international development assistance.

Joining the club would dramatically enhance India's national security. While access to new intelligence would be one benefit for India, of equal value would be the opportunity to improve its intelligence gathering capabilities. To work efficiently with its new intelligence partners, India would need to increase funding and staffing for intelligence activities. India's Research & Analysis Wing (R&AW) was estimated in 2000 to have a budget of around $150 million, with a strength of eight to ten thousand agents.[4] Even assuming a doubling of budget and agents in the past decade, R&AW is still too small to serve the foreign intelligence needs of a nation of 1.2 billion with ambitions of global power.

China's Ministry of State Security, which covers both domestic and foreign intelligence matters, is estimated to have staff in excess of 30,000.[5] The budget of the Ministry is, of course, secret; but China does disclose its total spending on non-military security (including intelligence, police, armed civil militia, courts and jails). Chinese non-military security spending will reach $95 billion in 2011, an increase of nearly fourteen percent from 2010.[6] There is no way to know exactly how much of this spending is on foreign intelligence, in order to compare Chinese spending with R&AW's budget. If, however, only one percent of China's non-military spending is on foreign intelligence, it is still several times greater than R&AW's likely current budget.

Neither India nor China comes anywhere close to the United States in intelligence spending. The American intelligence budget for 2010 was $53.1 billion (including the CIA and fifteen other federal intelligence agencies, but excluding intelligence programmes run by the military).[7] While India cannot possibly match American levels of spending, it should work to close the intelligence funding gap with China.

An increased investment in intelligence would be well worthwhile for India. In the near term, new agents and the information they gather would help India defend itself against terrorist attacks from neighbours. In the long term, better intelligence gathering would help establish India as the dominant power in South Asia, capable of resisting China's influence on the all-important secret battlefields of espionage. Never again should India be surprised by the actions of a potential adversary (as when China attacked it in 1962). More importantly, an India with strong intelligence capabilities can prevent such surprises from happening in the first place.

Admission to the intelligence club will come at a price for India. In return for membership, the United States and its allies will require the full and irrevocable pledge of the Indian government to protect the club members' shared values and security interests. India's agents will have to put their lives at risk alongside American, British, Canadian and Australian agents. Beyond covert action, India's new allies will require an overt and public commitment to a common foreign policy framework.

This is not a club that can abide part-time or temporary members. Once joining, non-alignment for India will be finished, and there will be no going back. Nor could India any longer cultivate relationships with regimes such as Iran, whatever the perceived Indian interests.

Learning from 26/11

In March 2011, David Coleman Headley, an American citizen partly of Pakistani descent, pleaded guilty in a Chicago court to helping the Pakistan-based terrorist group the Lashkar-e-Tayyeba (LeT) plan 26/11, and also to helping plan a foiled terror attack in Denmark. The case is an emblem of the shortcomings of pre- and post-26/11 Indo-American intelligence sharing as well as an emblem of the potential benefits of bringing India fully into the Unites States-led intelligence sharing network.

Headley was born in 1960 in the United States to a Pakistani father and American mother.[8] During much of his life he bounced back and forth between Pakistan and the United States. He was arrested twice by the United States on drug charges (in 1988 and 1997), and became an informant for the United States Drug Enforcement Agency (DEA) in exchange for lighter sentences.[9] The DEA sent him to Pakistan on multiple occasions to gather intelligence.[10] He remained a DEA informant until at least 2003, by which time he had already begun preparing for his new career – terrorism – by receiving training in explosives and small arms at Pakistan-based camps.[11]

Until 2006, Headley was known by his given name Daood Sayed Gilani; he adopted the European-American sounding name to facilitate travel to India. It worked: Over the next two years, he made five trips, undetected, to scout locations for the 26/11 attacks.

Headley's role in 26/11 did not come to light until he was arrested in October 2009, on his way to Pakistan with surveillance videos that had been taken in connection with the planned attack in Demark. The history of official United States involvement with Headley demonstrates multiple missed opportunities to uncover his links to Pakistani based terrorism and warn the Indian government about him. One month after 9/11, an ex-girlfriend of Headley's reported him as a suspected terrorist sympathiser.[12] The Federal Bureau of Investigation (FBI) questioned Headley, but he was able to convince them that his visits to known radical mosques in Pakistan were in connection with his work for the DEA.[13] The information went unshared with India.

In 2005, his American wife reported his reported his ties with LeT to American authorities, and in 2007, his Moroccan wife (he was married to three women at the same time) informed the United States Embassy in Islamabad of her suspicions that he was planning an attack. The United States again shared neither tip with India.

In 2010, India's Union Home Secretary G.K. Pillai publicly expressed his 'disappointment' in the United States' failure to share intelligence about Headley prior to his arrest a year after 26/11.[14] Disappointment is no doubt a diplomatic nicety for the anger that Pillai and his fellow government ministers felt.

Also in 2010, in part due to Indian dissatisfaction with American handling of the Headley case, the United States Director of National Intelligence led an official inquiry into how American law enforcement and intelligence agencies missed Headley as a threat to India. In a statement to the *New York Times* in connection with an article on the inquiry, an unnamed 'senior United States official' said that 'had the United States government sufficiently established [Headley] was engaged in plotting a terrorist attack in India, the information would have most assuredly been transferred promptly to the Indian government'.[15]

The official's excuse – we could not tell India that Headley was a threat because we did not know ourselves – misses the point of intelligence sharing. A piece of information that the United States dismisses as unreliable or insignificant may well be reliable or significant to India, when viewed through a different cultural lens and in a different national security context. As far as the Indian officials who approved Headley's Indian visas knew, he was just a typical United States citizen travelling on business. They had no idea of his Pakistani ancestry, nor his name change, nor the tips of his ex-girlfriend and wives. Had the United States shared any of these facts with Indian intelligence officials, they would have seen through Headley's rouse in a second. Had broad intelligence sharing between the United States and India been in place when Headley was scouting Mumbai targets for LeT, 26/11 would never have never taken place.

Your Terrorists are Our Terrorists

It is not too late to prevent the next 26/11. To do so, both the United States and India have to adopt a new motto in intelligence gathering: 'Your Terrorists are Our Terrorists'.

It is already the motto of the Anglo-American intelligence cooperation. It was, after all, the United Kingdom that fingered Headley as a terrorist. Headley had moved freely between the United States, Pakistan and India for years, first training as a terrorist and later helping plan 26/11. American officials only became aware of what Headley was doing after the British authorities informed their American counterparts of Headley's August 2009 meeting with al Qaeda operatives in the United Kingdom.[16] It was just the kind of routine intelligence sharing that Indian and American intelligence need to adopt to avoid future attacks on both nations.

The killing of Osama bin Laden in a Pakistani garrison town, Abbottabad, in May 2011 could further hasten the process by which the United States adopts India's terrorist enemies as its own. Both 26/11 and the bin Laden killing proved what the Indian government has been saying for years: that Pakistan is a sanctuary for terrorists who threaten both India and the United States. After 26/11 the United States came to see that sharing intelligence on Pakistani-based terrorism can save lives. With the killing of bin Laden, number one on the United States' Terrorist Most Wanted List, the American intelligence and military can now focus on eliminating people like Ilyas Kashmiri (the senior al Qaeda leader reportedly killed in an American missile strike in June 2011), who are threats to both the United States and India.

The next step in the evolution of joint Indo-American counter-terrorism will be for the United States to eliminate terrorists who threaten India, even if they pose no direct or immediate threat to the United States. Then cross-border terrorists based in Pakistan will have acquired a new enemy – one with advanced intelligence collection capabilities, and the military reach to use that intelligence to kill terrorists with the push of a button. Such a development would be a great step forward for Indo-American relations, and for India's overall national security.

The United States and India increased bilateral intelligence sharing substantially after 26/11. They signed a bilateral agreement on counter-terrorism cooperation in July 2010,[17] which Home Secretary Pillai credits with making Indo-American intelligence sharing 'far more broad-based'.[18] Still, the current arrangement falls far short of full sharing. Instead of letting India have access to select pieces of information, the United States should – as it does with the United Kingdom – commit to a full exchange of information. As the Headley case demonstrated, the only way to ensure crucial information does not go unused is to share it all.

The benefits to India to full information sharing with the United States would be enormous. India's current ability to collect intelligence within Pakistan is limited, to say the least. Indian access to the United States' information on the activities and movements of Pakistan-based terrorists who plan cross-border attacks would instantly improve India's terrorist interdiction capabilities.

Indo-American intelligence sharing would, at least for the next few years, be largely one way: The United States has much more to share with India than vice-versa. For the sharing to make sense for both nations, India would have to commit to vastly increasing its intelligence gathering capabilities in its own neighbourhood. India's intelligence operatives can operate effectively nearly anywhere there is a substantial Indian diaspora; in places like the Gulf nations and Africa, Indian human intelligence capabilities could be a valuable complement to existing American activities.

If the United States opens its intelligence databases to India, however, it must do so with an important condition: India must commit not to use intelligence for any purpose other than self-defence. Pre-emptive attacks on terrorists in Pakistan by India would be fair game, but attacks to destabilise Pakistan would not.

Though Pakistan is a source of terrorism that threatens both India and the United States, there is a scenario worse than the status quo: the disintegration of the Pakistani state. The United States and India must, as they target their common terrorist enemies in Pakistan one by one, take great care to keep the architecture of a functioning government in place in Pakistan. It is a careful balance that the United States and India must strike together; if they push Pakistan into anarchy, all three nations lose.

Desi Yankees

Rapidly improving nation-to-nation ties constitute only one element of the emerging Indo-American alliance. Equally powerful and long-lasting are the people-to-people ties the United States and India share.

The community of Indian Americans[19] will be the cornerstone of Indo-American relations in the twenty-first century. Their wealth, their growing political influence and their interest in both nations will ensure that Indo-American relations continue to strengthen.

The potential influence of the Indian-American community in United States' foreign policy is a thousand times greater than it is today. Indian Americans have all the ingredients of a powerful group, and they have tapped just a fraction of it. When they are activated – either by choice or by compulsion of events – they will help turn India into America's most important and strongest bilateral relationship.

The population of Indian Americans is growing at an annual rate above ten percent, and far faster than the overall United States population.[20] From just a sliver of the overall American population fifty years ago, Indian Americans now are 2.8 million strong,[21] nearly one percent of the national population counted in the 2010 census. Between 2000 and 2010, the Indian American population grew by sixty-nine percent.[22]

A steady stream of new immigrants from India is adding to the numbers. India was the third largest source of immigrants to the United States in 2010, and accounts for over half of the H-1B and L (intra-company transfer) visas issued.

Indian Americans are not only growing in number, they are wealthy. Their household income is nearly twice that of the average American household.[23] They achieved this wealth, as a group and as individuals, through a combination of hard work and education. Two-thirds of Indian Americans have bachelor degrees (or higher) and forty percent hold a Master's, a PhD or other advanced degrees.[24]

Many first generation Indian Americans had their degrees already when they landed in America. Others came with little formal education, but with an entrepreneurial spirit that allowed them to build wealth and give their children the educations they lacked. Frequently it took the less educated Indian Americans only a generation to catch up with the better educated peers, as their children also became doctors, lawyers and engineers. No matter where Indian American families start – whether run-down government clinics of Tamil Nadu, or the dusty villages of Gujarat – it often does not take long for them to reach the wealthiest levels of the world's largest economy.

Just as the population of Indian Americans is growing and becoming more highly skilled, it is also becoming more Americanised. The first wave of Indian immigrants to the United States began arriving in the 1960s and 1970s; their children are now coming into positions of professional responsibility. Second generation Indian Americans are leading conventional middle class American lives. Some are choosing high-income professions like their parents. Yes, they are becoming doctors and engineers, but they are also entering professions their parents did not: law, investment banking, management consulting, and venture capital/private equity.

Others are departing even farther from their parents' career paths and choosing public service by going into politics, federal government service or working at non-profits. The parents came to the United States for a better life and got it. Now the children, having grown up with material wealth, are often more interested in improving society than they are in making money. With this second generation, Indians have truly arrived in upper middle class America, where people listen to National Public Radio, read the *New Yorker* and are captivated by the ideals of public service. The freedom *not* to pursue money is a great benefit of American prosperity, one the first generation did not have.

The Indian American community's wealth-minded and service-minded wings together have the potential to impact materially the course of American government policy towards India. They need only to pool their money and influence into an organised effort to pursue that most American of political activities: lobbying the federal government.

The Lobbyists

In a June 2011 speech to African leaders, United States Secretary of State Hillary Clinton initiated a 'very frank conversation about corruption' and promised to elevate 'corruption as a major focus of our diplomatic efforts'. She proceeded to describe a new American law that requires resource companies that raise capital in the United States to document the royalties they pay foreign governments, to 'ensure that Africa's natural wealth benefits the people of Africa rather than corrupt officials'.[25]

United States policy makers should not forget that there still are plenty of corrupt officials at home. In 2005, a United States Congressman was caught by the FBI with $90,000 in cash in his freezer; he is now serving a thirteen-year prison sentence for bribery, racketeering and money laundering.[26] In 2006, a corruption investigation connected to government lobbyist Jack Abramoff led to the convictions of a Congressman, two White House officials and several former Congressional aides.[27] Corruption has also reached higher levels of government: In 1973, United States Vice President Spiro Agnew resigned, rather than face charges of having accepted bribes throughout his political career, including $17,500 handed to him in envelopes while he was vice president.[28]

Yet in a certain sense the United States has moved beyond corruption of the developing world variety. The United States has institutionalised corruption and given it a name: political contributions. In places like India politicians get a paper bag full of cash; in the United States they get a check contributing to their next campaign.

As long as there is political power and money, there will be people who seek to trade one for the other. The best a society can hope for is that these transactions do not happen in secret, but are subject to full legal and public scrutiny. The United States regulates the exchange of money for political power. Both those who make contributions (wealthy citizens, corporations and their lobbyists) and those who receive them (holders of political office, or those who aspire to be) are legally required to disclose what they give/receive and to/from whom. So when a politician casts a vote or advocates a certain policy, the public can check if the politician has received money from a person or group with an interest in that vote or policy.

The result of the United States' regulated political contribution system is that money can be a big influence on policy, including foreign policy. The Indian American community, if it wishes, can have an enormous impact on the course of American policy towards India. It has all the makings of a powerful advocacy group – wealth, an increasing civic awareness, and an affection for both the United States and India.

In the past few years, the 'India lobby' in Washington has come out of nowhere to be a significant force in American foreign policy. Several organisations – foremost among them, the US India Political Action Committee (USINPAC) – already operate as registered lobbyists, dedicated to India matters. Long-time Washington lobbying firms have also begun to see big business potential in representing India interests to the American government, and have created new India practices. In the negotiations on the Indo-American nuclear deal, the Indian government hired Washington lobbying firm Barbour, Griffith & Rogers to help win support of the deal, signing an initial contract worth $700,000. India grasped the workings of the American political system quickly; Barbour, Griffith & Rogers point person on the India account: former United States Ambassador to India Robert Blackwill.[29]

Even small countries, with focused lobbying efforts, can change American policy. Little Armenia (population 3 million) has used its population of Armenian Americans (1.2 million Americans are of Armenian descent)[30] to great effect. The Armenian Americans have been persistently lobbying the American government to declare the massacre of Armenians by the Ottoman Turks during the First World War a genocide. It is working. In 2008, then presidential candidate Barack Obama promised, if elected, to use the term 'genocide' in describing the massacre.[31] Then, in 2010 a Congressional committee passed a resolution calling the massacre a genocide, prompting Turkey to recall its ambassador from Washington in protest. (Turkey sent the ambassador back after the resolution did not make it to the floor of the House of Representatives.)[32] The Armenians have achieved all this despite Turkey being a key NATO ally and, as a secular Muslim nation, a key positive example in American hopes for de-radicalisation of the Muslim world.

The key to the Armenians' success? Money. The Armenian Assembly of America, an umbrella lobbying group, boasts 10,000 members and an annual budget of over $3.5 million – enough to keep four influential Washington lobbying firms on the payroll, and enough to keep Armenia on the agenda of the United States Congress.[33] On a per capita basis the Armenian Americans have far outspent other immigrant groups.

If Armenian Americans can be so effective, imagine the impact Indian Americans can have on American foreign policy. Their coming of age as an interest group coincides with the strengthening of the Indo-American relationship. The India lobby – with money and motivation – can further accelerate the development of bilateral ties.

Big Business

Apart from Indian Americans, there is a yet bigger force lobbying for stronger Indo-American ties: the American business community. As Indo-American trade and investment grows, American companies will only intensify further their efforts to bring the two countries closer together.

United States-India trade stood at $49 billion in 2010, having grown by over $20 billion since 2005. Recent trade is heavily weighted in India's favour, with the United States running a persistently high trade deficit with India (reaching $10 billion in 2010).[34]

In spite of the large trade gap, the American business community sees big money in the Indian market. It is no longer merely a place to go for an American corporation to outsource services or to source cheap goods; it is a place to drive revenue growth.

Early American corporate entrants to the Indian market have seen the revenue. Ford sold more than 50,000 India-produced vehicles in the first five months of 2011, up by more than seventy percent from the same period in 2010.[35] Pepsi is now the fourth largest consumer products company in India, having entered the country in 1989.[36] General Electric earns $3 billion in revenue in India, and is aiming for $6 billion by 2015.[37] American companies have tasted Indian success and they want more.

To make sure India stays open to American business, and indeed becomes more open, American companies are making sure official Washington knows how important the Indian market is to their financial results.

The US-India Business Council (USIBC) is a Washington-headquartered advocacy organisation dedicated to lobbying the American and Indian government on commercial matters. It describes itself as a 'business advocacy organization...whose aim is to deepen two-way trade and strengthen commercial ties [between the United States and India]'.[38] The USIBC has over 150 members, including many of the largest American corporations, who pay up to $20,000 a year in membership fees.

The sale of defence equipment is an area where American companies see particular potential in India. As we saw in Chapter Seven, India needs to invest heavily in defence to modernise its equipment and close the growing arms gap with China. Even at current forecast levels of defence expenditure, India is at least a $120 billion market for weapons and weapon systems over the next five years.[39] If India further accelerates its military spending, as it should, this number could increase substantially.

India is already the world's ninth largest defence market;[40] India's planned level of expenditure would instantly catapult the country into one of the top markets for American defence exports. Exports, however, are a tricky endeavour for American defence companies. Even when there is a willing customer, sometimes the American defence industry must walk away from a potential sale. American law requires government approval for export of sensitive equipment or technology, and the interpretation of 'sensitive' is often broad. Washington's political and strategic considerations come first, and business comes second.

The American government will bar sales to countries that pose even a remote threat to American interests, or that Washington has determined to have violated human rights. The State Department lists twenty-five countries where arms sales are either fully or partially embargoed. The list includes traditional enemies (Cuba, North Korea and Iran), strategic threats (China) as well as human rights abusers (Sudan, Burma and Belarus).[41]

If the United States catches a person or company violating export control laws, it will prosecute the case vigorously. In 2010, the Department of Homeland Security, through its Project Shield America, arrested 247 individuals for unlawful export of sensitive technology, and obtained convictions in half those cases.[42]

Other countries may meet Washington's standards for defence exports, but may be difficult for American suppliers to penetrate. Some countries are historically or culturally closer to other main defence suppliers like Russia or the Europeans, making it difficult for American firms to win business. Other countries may be unwilling or unable to pay the premium prices that American firms expect for their products and technologies.

So when American defence executives see a nation that is politically close to the United States, that wants to buy American equipment, and that has no human rights problems, they become excited. Even more so when that nation is the world's second most populous, with an economy growing at nearly ten percent annually, and with an urgent need to modernise ageing military hardware. For the executives of the American defence industry, India is a once-in-a-career business opportunity. They intend to grab it.

As described in Chapter Seven, there have already been some early successes, with recent major Indian aircraft purchases from Boeing and Lockheed Martin Corporation. Further accelerating American defence sales to India will require intensive, and expensive, lobbying by American defence suppliers. They will have to conduct this offensive on multiple fronts simultaneously: asking the American government (the State, Commerce and Defence Departments) to push the sales with their Indian counterparts; convincing the Indian government and armed forces to favour American equipment; and helping to steer both nations towards a closer overall bilateral relationship. The American defence industry is doing all of this and more. In the process it is becoming the most powerful non-governmental actor in Indo-American ties.

American big business – propelled by the defence industry – and the Indian American community – bolstered by its wealth – together are putting the Indo-American relationship into overdrive.

Preserving a Common Heritage

The list of promising factors in the Indo-American relationship is long: common security interests, enhanced intelligence sharing, an influential Indian American population and thousands of American corporations eager to expand in India. As we will see in the next chapter, none of these elements is nearly as important as the common heritage that both nations share as offshoots of the British Empire. This heritage has bred the common values that underpin the Anglo-American relationship, and will underpin the future Indo-American relationship as well.

The emerging Indo-American alliance is not simply a matter of promoting mutual interests; the alliance is critical to the endurance of the values that both India and the United States have inherited from Britain. The twenty-first century is certain to see renewed attempts by some nations to practice tyranny at home and spread it abroad; to rule by force instead of by the will of the people; to favour certain ethnic or religious groups instead of promoting equality; to use the power of the government to control the economy instead of unleashing the power of human ingenuity to drive economic activity. The danger of such regimes is present everywhere, and particularly in Asia, where one half of humanity is competing for ever scarcer resources.

When tyranny strikes – and it is a question of when, not if – it will take an India at full strength, with the United States by its side, to preserve freedom and restore the peace, for Asia and for the world.

War is an ugly thing, but not the ugliest of things: the decayed and degraded state of moral and patriotic feeling which thinks nothing worth a war, is worse....As long as justice and injustice have not terminated their ever-renewing fight for ascendancy in the affairs of mankind, human beings must be willing, when need is, to do battle for the one against the other.

– John Stuart Mill, 'The Contest in America' (1862)

9

HEIRS TO THE CROWN

Decline and Fall

In 408, the Hun leader Alaric I was amassed with his armies outside Rome. A two-year siege of the city began. The Roman Senate tried to buy him off with titles and territories, to no avail. In 410, Alaric's army breached the gates of the city, and Rome fell to a foreign army for the first time in 800 years.

Though Rome was sacked, the Roman Empire lived on. 'Rome' had become more than a city in what is now Central Italy. It was a way of life of one-fifth of the world's people,[1] stretching from Britain in the West to Asia Minor in the East.

Rome's emperors had taken precautions to protect that way of life. In 330, Emperor Constantine chose a city on the edge of Europe (now

Istanbul) as a capital of the Eastern Roman Empire. Through Byzantium, Rome lasted for over a thousand years more, until it finally fell to the Ottoman Turks in 1453.

It is all too easy to look at the broad sweep of history and forget that long-term trends, such as the millennium-long decline of the Roman Empire, would have looked different to those living at the time. Humans may fail to see what epochs they may be living through or over-emphasise the impact of individual events (e.g., the sacking of Rome). One advantage of studying history is that we might, having studied the past, look at the present beyond the restricted frame of our own lifespans and glimpse of the long view that future historians will place us in.

In the last century, we witnessed the disintegration of history's second greatest empire after Rome: the British Empire. In the space of twenty years, the United Kingdom went from being the seat of an empire ruling about a fifth of the world's population[2] to being merely an island in the North Atlantic, with a few overseas territories and dominions. With the independence of India alone, the British Empire lost three quarters of its population.[3]

The contemporary view is that the United Kingdom is in the midst of a steep, and unstoppable, decline in wealth and power. Some commentators have suggested that former United Kingdom Prime Minister Tony Blair allied his nation so closely with the United States (especially as the two nations went to war in Iraq and Afghanistan) to bask in America's power[4] and thereby preserve a modicum of global influence for the United Kingdom.[5] The United Kingdom's current economic strains (a budget deficit over ten percent of GDP, a debt burden over sixty percent of GDP, and eight percent unemployment) only encourage those who believe in the demise of what was, a century ago, one of history's greatest empires.

One could look at these events and pronounce the end of the British Empire. It certainly does not have the direct power it had a century ago. Future historians, however, may well assert that the United Kingdom did not perish with the loss of its colonies, just as the Roman Empire did not perish with the fall of its capital. Britain's values and influence could live on for another thousand years, guarded and nurtured by its former colonies, the United States and India.

The British (Values) Empire

The British Empire could be ruthless in its application of power. It exploited its colonies' resources. It put down rebellions with excessive force, often with little regard for civilian casualties. The United States fought a bloody war for independence from Britain, and in India, millions suffered and died during Partition as the colonial system fell apart. The British Empire was far from a benign ruler.

This record of abuse and violence stands in contrast to the noble values that Britain displayed to the world and bequeathed to its former colonies: democracy, the rule of law, respect for human rights and a free market system. Britain was not the first government to adopt these features, and it fell short of the ideal on all of them at one time or another. Yet, compared to contemporary nations, and especially to contemporary empires, Britain upheld its core values better than any other. Better than the empires of Europe – Spain, Portugal, Holland and Belgium. Certainly better than the empires of Asia – the Ottomans and the Japanese.

The story of man's improved system of government over the past millennium has largely been the story of Britain and its offshoots. If cruelty crept into British rule, it did so because of the shortcomings of human nature, not any inherent shortcomings in Britain's system of government. Run as it was by men, Britain did the best it could with the leadership it had. As time went on, it bettered its record.

The result of this constant striving has been that Britain's two most consequential offshoots – the United States and India – have adopted, and improved on, many of its values. When the United Kingdom, the United States and India are counted together, one fifth of humanity is part of a New British Empire – one of British values.

For much of the twentieth century, the United States was the main exemplar of these values. It displayed a regular and orderly change of governments, elected by the people. Its economy grew to become the world's largest. It showed tolerance for people of many ethnicities and religious beliefs. Where parts of the government stumbled in protecting equality and human rights, other parts intervened: Lincoln freed the slaves, women got the vote, and racial discrimination was outlawed.

The United States also became the main global guarantor of the values it shares with Britain, helping to free Europe from tyranny (twice) and stamp out oppression in Asia and the Americas. Though the United States does not always live up to its own ideals, its belief in freedom for all mankind never falters.

As we saw in Chapter Eight, today the United States finds itself in a world much changed from the one it knew during the last century. The centre of global economic activity is shifting from Europe and America to Asia. Power will shift as well.

In this new global structure the United States will no longer be the sole standard-bearer for British values. It will be joined by a new partner: India.

The First Half Century

The first fifty years of Independence were difficult for India. Armed conflicts with Pakistan and China, as well as secessionist movements in various corners of the nation, threatened India's security and territorial integrity. Occasional communal violence interrupted India's otherwise peaceful diversity. Apart from the members of the Nehru-Gandhi family, India was unable to find stable political leadership; and even that family was sometimes prone to misrule.

Independent India's economy did not grow fast enough in its first half century to achieve widespread poverty reduction. In a world split between capitalism and communism, India understandably refused to place all its chits with either side. The result was a middling performance. Though India did not get the benefits of full capitalism, it did not bear the costs of full communism either. In the end, however, the first half century was far from wasted: India developed a strong and diverse industrial base. After the economic reforms of 1991, this industrial base would serve as a runway for India's future growth.

Independent India can be excused for getting off to a slow start: moving to self-government after centuries of colonial rule is no simple task, especially for the world's second most populous nation. It is to India's lasting credit that it was able to reform its economy so quickly, with so little disruption to society. Indians can be proud that, whatever the setbacks of the first fifty years, India survived with its democracy intact; and that by 1991, it had put itself in a position to thrive.

Island of Calm

India's achievement as a pluralistic, free-market democracy is all the more impressive for the neighbourhood it lives in. Tranquil India is surrounded by a sea of chaos.

Sri Lanka is the counter-example to India's democratic pluralism. Having become independent around the same time as India, Sri Lanka successively squandered its advantages over its larger neighbour. With no external enemies, it went to war with itself. As a result, despite opening its economy in 1979 (a full twelve years before India), it has lagged India in growth for all but a handful of years in the last two decades.

Notwithstanding the annihilation of the LTTE in 2009, Sri Lanka remains a deeply fractured society, with no hope for ethnic harmony on the horizon. Its constitution, once as strong as India's, has become a vehicle for the tyranny of the majority. An amendment to the constitution further strengthening the Executive Presidency, passed by Parliament in 2010, could well stamp out the dying embers of democracy on the island. In the absence of a government representative of all peoples, the nation is at risk of slipping back into armed conflict again. Meanwhile, as we saw in Chapter Seven, Sri Lanka is opening its arms to China, in a serious strategic threat to India.

Nepal is a Himalayan version of Sri Lanka, beset by internal conflict and scarcely able to govern itself. For India, the only advantage is that, whatever Nepal's future troubles may be, they are unlikely to spread southward. Furthermore, Nepal, wedged as it is between China and India, acts as a useful buffer between the two strategic rivals.

Bangladesh, four decades after independence, is still struggling to overcome the neglect that it suffered at the hands of (West) Pakistan. Its people drew the short straw in South Asia, crowded into a river delta with few natural resources and prone to natural disasters. This weak state, like Sri Lanka, is easy prey for Chinese influence.

Pakistan – where to start? The very premise of its existence – a nation for Muslims – has been proven to be flawed. Since independence, it has devolved into a military dictatorship overlaid on a feudal society, where the military sees hostility against India as key to its power. Faced with this national intransigence, India can only subdue Pakistan by building overwhelming military and economic strength through a closer relationship with the United States.

As the United States and India develop a special relationship for the twenty-first century, they both must take care not to leave Pakistan behind. An isolated Pakistan would only fall further under the sway of Islamic extremism or China (or both). To avoid this fate, the United States must strike a delicate balance between supporting Pakistan with enough funding and military support to ensure some degree of cooperation on counter-terrorism and cohesion of the state, but not so much that Pakistan is emboldened to threaten India. India, for its part, must continue to engage Pakistan in talks to promote better cross-border relations. Whatever challenges Pakistan's behaviour presents to the United States and India – and there will doubtless be many in the years to come – each country must remember that even a deeply flawed Pakistan is preferable to a second Afghanistan. The closer the United States and India stay to Pakistan, the better their prospects for leading Pakistan towards stability and prosperity.

China is India's inevitable strategic rival. China's demographic advantage is waning, and thanks to its ill-conceived one-child policy, India will outgrow China decades sooner than it otherwise would have. This gives China a window of opportunity of twenty to thirty years to build an unassailable economic, military and technological advantage over India. It is already well on its way: The Chinese economy outperforms India's; China's military expenditures are three times India's;[6] and China is out-innovating India through superior universities and scientific research. Meanwhile, China is extending its influence into India's backyard, exploiting weak states such as Pakistan, Bangladesh, Myanmar and Sri Lanka. India is the only thing standing between China and domination of the Asian continent, including South Asia.[7]

This is a dangerous neighbourhood, a mixture of weakness in some states and bellicose ill-will towards India in others. In the middle of it all is the relative calm of India itself. Whatever the problems inside India – poverty, corruption, communal violence, Naxalite uprisings – they are insignificant compared to what is happening just outside its borders.

India's relative social tranquillity is worth protecting. Thus far, India has been able to keep its enemies and potential enemies at bay by fighting border skirmishes and building a credible nuclear deterrent. It has not yet faced threats to its very existence. One day it might. To prevent this day from coming, and be ready in case it does, India must start behaving like the world power it so desperately wants to be.

Global powers earn their status by building military power and projecting it far and wide. India will not become a superpower overnight. In the meantime, it needs to align itself as closely as possible with the United States, the only global power that shares its core values. This alliance will give India the time it needs to develop the military strength to defend against a threat to its very existence.

Secure the Perimeter

China is not content to limit its influence within its national borders; it knows that to have a secure nation, it needs to project its power well beyond. India needs to do the same, or else fall victim itself to Chinese power.

As it builds its military strength, India must also establish a secure perimeter around the country, well beyond the current borders. As we saw in Chapter Seven, as a first step India should use its considerable economic weight to bring Sri Lanka firmly and irrevocably into its strategic orbit.

The same is true for Bangladesh. India already practically surrounds Bangladesh in a geographic vice grip. Still, Bangladesh, because of its access to the Bay of Bengal, holds vulnerabilities for India. India cannot tolerate any further Chinese incursion into Bangladesh, where the Chinese are already expanding the Chittagong port and now plan to construct a deep sea harbour further down the coast with a road linking it (through Burma) to China.[8] India should treat the Bay of Bengal as its own waters: Permitting the Chinese Navy to dock in a Bangladeshi port is little different than letting it sail up the Ganges.

Bangladeshis fear undue influence from India, and India must dispel this notion. India's current aid to Bangladesh is insufficient (notwithstanding a \$1 billion line of credit announced in 2010).[9] As India grows richer, it should share the wealth with its poorer neighbour through targeted development aid and preferential trade agreements. Bangladesh will have no choice but to welcome India's embrace, and will itself grow richer and more stable in the process. A closer relationship with Bangladesh will help India counter the growing trend of its neighbour breeding anti-Indian terrorist cadres.

India must also redouble its aid efforts in Afghanistan. India has pumped \$1.5 billion into Afghanistan in recent years, and Prime Minister Manmohan Singh pledged another \$500 million in development aid during his May 2011 visit to Kabul.[10] This is an investment in India's long term security, and money well spent. If India can help Afghanistan to become a functioning state, Pakistan will have that much greater a chance at stability. In the meantime a strong Indian presence in Afghanistan can act as the second part a pincer movement on the Pakistani state.

Further afield, India's navy must develop a true regional presence. This will require forward naval bases from the horn of Africa to the straits of Malacca. Fortunately, a power friendly to India already has such bases: the United States. Joint Indo-American naval exercises already take place regularly, most recently in April 2011 off the Japanese coast (with the Japanese navy also participating).[11] India and the United States should now begin to negotiate an agreement for the United States to allow the Indian Navy to have blanket basing rights within a defined perimeter of Indian territory. A logical starting place would be for the United States and United Kingdom to bring India in as a joint partner at their naval base at Diego Garcia. From there India could broaden its presence to American bases in Bahrain and Singapore.

The goal for both nations should be for the American and Indian navies to cooperate as closely in the Indian Ocean and Bay of Bengal as the American and British navies have done in the Northern Atlantic. Common bases will increase exponentially the opportunities for joint training with India and for the transfer of military technology to India. Such intensive naval cooperation will have the added benefit of speeding

India's development as a naval power, one that can act as America's eyes and ears in a region far from Washington.

Becoming a Winner (Again)

For the lifespan of anyone alive today, and indeed for the past two centuries, India has had an image of a poor nation, barely able to see to its own people's most basic needs. Empirical evidence supported this image.

Today India is in urgent need of a new narrative, developed by Indians and unencumbered by holdover biases from the old, Western-dominated narrative.

The core of this new narrative: that India is returning to its former economic glory at the same time as the West's run of economic good fortune is coming to an end.

As we saw in Chapter One, for most of human history, wealth has been concentrated in countries with large populations, and economic growth has been driven largely by population increases combined with urbanisation. Then came the Industrial Revolution, which made it possible to generate substantial wealth through productivity gains alone, without large population increases. Small states, like those in Europe, could control amounts of wealth far out of proportion to their size. Such states could continue to maintain (or even increase) their wealth if their populations were static or growing only slowly.

Now, however, the benefits of the Industrial Revolution – previously enjoyed almost exclusively by Western Europe and its offshoots – are open to all takers. Capital and production will flow to where the demand is. The West's head start has vanished, and the world will return to the norm that has prevailed for most of the past two thousand years, where wealth and power are concentrated in the hands of more populous nations.

The twenty-first century will produce a new field of 'winners' in the global economy: large states with young and expanding populations. India will be foremost among them. China by virtue of its size alone will be a big winner as well, even though its population growth has slowed to 0.5 percent.[12] Other winners will be Nigeria (population 155 million, growing at 2.3 percent), Brazil (population 194 million, growing at 0.9 percent) and Indonesia (population 230 million, growing at 1.1 percent).[13]

The last few centuries have been tough for India. Becoming a winner (again) offers it the opportunity to write a new narrative for its own history. Perhaps the colonial era and first half century of Independence will come to be considered India's 'dark ages'. Perhaps the nation is on the verge of its own Renaissance, where India's own historical achievements in science, culture and government will be rediscovered and newly appreciated.

Perhaps a resurgent, confident and strong India will join together with another great power, which also sprung from the British Empire, to protect their shared values and, one day, save the world.

Heirs to the Crown

India and the United States have much in common: democracy, diversity and a free market system. These traits are underpinned by a common heritage as part of the British Values Empire.

If the nineteenth century belonged to Europe, and the twentieth to America, then the twenty-first will belong to Asia. As the centre of global economic activity shifts from the transatlantic region to Asia, the centre of military power will follow, as will the prospect for large scale armed conflict. The Anglo-American alliance saved Europe after two world wars. Asia needs a similar alliance for the twenty-first century. Only the United States and India can provide it, as the true heirs to the British Empire. In the past the sun never set on the British Empire; in the future it will never set on the Indo-American alliance.

The second half of the twentieth century was far more peaceful than the first half, when tens of millions died in two world wars. If human history is any guide, the twenty-first century may well see a return to bloody large scale conflicts as nation states continue to battle for limited resources. Small local conflicts are happening all the time; the risk is that one of these will spark a regional conflict, which will in turn draw in major powers.

If World War III happens, there is only one outcome that will preserve freedom and democracy: an Indo-American victory. America, hobbled by debt and an ageing population, may not be able to win on its own; it needs India's help. The United States has shown that it is ready to fight. Now it is time for India to join the United States as a nation courageous enough to fight for a free world, and strong enough to win.

Non-violence and Power

India's shaking off the bonds of colonial rule without violence was one of the great achievements of the twentieth century. For as long as mankind is on this earth, India's independence struggle will serve as an example to oppressed people who wish to be free.

Gandhian principles of non-violence have been a part of India's national identity, political philosophy and security policy ever since. Non-violence has gained India the respect of all people and nations that value freedom. India's ability to maintain a stable pluralistic democracy, as states around it have slipped into chaos or oppression, has gained it further respect.

Respect of those nations that value freedom, however, is not enough for India. It must have the respect of every nation on earth, including those bent on oppression and territorial expansion. Such nations do not respect India for its moral standing; they respect only military power, and the willingness to use it. Such nations show respect only when it is born of fear. It is time for India to become a nation that commands both respect and fear.

Non-violence is a suitable philosophy for a people struggling for independence, but not for a nation that has won it. A nation has responsibilities. It must protect the freedom of its people from threats to them and their way of life. As a nation that will soon be the most populous on earth, India has a proportionally great responsibility to protect freedom. This responsibility calls for strength first, and adherence to non-violence principles second.

India must not abandon its commitment to non-violence, which has given the nation moral authority in the eyes of the world. Rather India must combine moral authority with raw power. Moral authority alone, without power and the willingness to use it, will not keep enemies at bay; power alone without moral authority is hollow. Moral authority and power together will enhance each other and India's standing in the world.

The 1998 nuclear test was a down payment on India's future as a global power. True to its tradition of non-violence, nuclear India declared a no-first-strike policy three months after its test. In the words of then Prime Minister Atal Bihari Vajpayee, 'These tests were not intended for offence, but for self-defence...we will not be the first to use nuclear weapons'.[14] It was an example of combining moral authority and power, and the perfect model for the balance that India needs to strike in its next half century.

The Future Beckons

India has entered the twenty-first century in a demographic-economic sweet spot that will give its economic growth continued momentum. This momentum will not be sufficient to vault India into a position of global economic, much less political, leadership. To fully capitalise on its demographic advantage, India will have to leave the world of outsourcing behind and build its own intellectual property. India has too long used its talent to innovate for others. Now it is time for Indian firms to deploy this talent to build the sustainable, proprietary advantages in technology that will create tomorrow's great global companies. The resulting profit margins will fund further R&D, in a virtuous cycle of innovation.

India's multinationals will play a critical role in making it an economic power. Indian firms have strong advantages in the quality of their management teams, as well as the strong base of demand at home. They have the potential, unlike China's firms, of becoming as globally powerful as American multinationals. But there are no shortcuts to going global. To achieve lasting global strength, Indian firms will have to use acquisitions highly selectively. Indian firms' scarce capital is better spent investing in their own intellectual property and brands than in buying companies overseas.

Even if India embraces innovation and develops global companies, its future as a superpower is not assured. Economic power alone is not enough; India has to develop a muscular foreign policy to defend and multiply its growing wealth.

For decades, India's political leadership has been neglecting emerging security threats. In the meantime, China has established itself as the premier power in Asia, buoyed by a massive military build-up, an aggressive hunt for resources overseas, and the establishment of footholds in strategic locations. If India continues to let China extend its reach unchallenged, the Sino-Indian power gap will soon become unbridgeable. India can still avoid falling under China's thumb, but only with immediate and aggressive action to accelerate its own military build-up, secure its own supply of resources, and expel China from India's rightful sphere of influence. There is not a moment to lose.

India's Choice

The history of mankind has been a history of conflict. The twenty-first century will be no different: There will be nations that attempt to gain power by invading, annexing or dominating other nations. These nations will govern through tyranny at home, and will be bent on extending this tyranny abroad.

The Indian way of life is based on diversity, tolerance and consent of the governed. Tyranny anywhere is a threat to this way of life.

When tyranny threatened the world in the twentieth century, the United States and the United Kingdom fought against it. Indian soldiers fought alongside them, even when the threat was half a world away. In this century, an independent India will have to make its own choice whether to fight tyranny, wherever it is, or to look the other way.

When the history of this century is written, it can be the triumph of freedom, liberal values, pluralism and democracy; or it can be the return of the tyrants. The United States will fight for freedom again, but by itself it cannot be certain of prevailing. It needs India to join the fight, and join it with a raw power enhanced by moral authority.

It is India's choice to make. The world is waiting.

Epilogue

TWO PROFESSORS AND
A COWBOY

When Barack Obama took office in January 2009, the future looked bright for Indo-American relations. The two countries had just completed a tremendous period of rapprochement, beginning with Bill Clinton's March 2000 visit to India and culminating in the Indo-American civil nuclear agreement of October 2008.

There was every indication that bilateral relations would continue to strengthen rapidly, with Barack Obama replacing George W. Bush. After all, Manmohan Singh and Bush had been, for all their success, an unlikely pair: the soft-spoken Punjabi economics professor and the brash Texas cowboy.

Obama, by contrast, had much more in common with Singh. Though born twenty-nine years apart and a world away from each other, the two leaders had strikingly similar, and equally compelling, personal histories. Born to modest means, they were both raised in part by grandparents and learned the value of an education. They both grew up to attend elite institutions, and later became university teachers before entering government. In addition, America's first non-white president and India's first non-Hindu prime minister both, in early 2009, commanded the respect (even if not the political support) of majorities of their nations' citizens.

So it was tempting to wonder, as Obama began his presidency: 'If the cowboy and the professor could produce the nuclear deal, what even greater things can the two professors achieve?'

The early signs were indeed positive. The two leaders gushed heartfelt praise for each other in public. (Singh on Obama: a 'ray of hope'; Obama on Singh: a 'wonderful man'.) Together they showed an easy rapport that eluded Bush and Singh. (Try as he might, Singh had never been able to seem completely at ease standing next to Bush, especially when Bush's arm was draped casually around his shoulder). Reciprocal visits (Singh to the United States in November 2009, and Obama to India in November 2010) brought the leaders even closer together and served as successive announcements to the world of the importance of the bilateral relationship. Indians and Americans alike were expecting their leaders to deliver a far deeper and more consequential relationship.

Indians' expectations were heightened further by Obama's statement, in a speech before Parliament during his November 2010 visit to India, that he '[looks] forward' to India being on the UN Security Council as a permanent member.[1] Parsing Obama's language, he made no commitment whatsoever to India of American support for a permanent UNSC seat; that did not stop Indians from being overjoyed with Obama's gesture.

Yet in 2011, three years after Obama's election, the relationship has not progressed to the extent that many in India and in the United States had hoped. The economic situation at home is foremost on most Americans' minds, with low GDP growth, high unemployment and a growing national debt burden. The attention of America's foreign policy establishment remains focused on matters other than India (the Middle East uprisings, the sovereign debt crisis in Europe, the trade imbalance with China, and international terrorism, to name a few).

India, meanwhile, has failed to live up to a key American demand connected with the 2008 Indo-American nuclear deal: that India enact legislation protecting nuclear equipment makers from liability in case of a nuclear accident. Without such legislation, American nuclear equipment suppliers like GE will be reluctant to risk supplying India's $150 billion nuclear energy market. Washington also wants India to open up sectors such as retail, financial services and insurance more fully to foreign participation.[2]

With the recent slow-down in the Indo-American relationship all too apparent, many Indians are coming to believe their long-held suspicion that bilateral relations are better off when a Republican is in the White House than when a Democrat is.

The truth is that the strength of Indo-American relationship depends not on which party is the White House, but instead on the quality of leadership in both Washington and Delhi. The professors have been in charge, and it shows. The first three years of the Obama-Singh era have resembled a long-term academic seminar on the growing strength of the Indo-American relationship. To be fair, the two professors-in-chief have team-taught this seminar with insight and eloquence, saying all the right things about shared values and a common future.

Somewhere along the way, however, the world stopped listening. For all the words that Singh and Obama put forth about each other and the bilateral relationship, it turns out that they were missing one important thing: action. It turns out the Indo-American relationship could have used a little less professor and a little more cowboy.

Mutual affection among political leaders can only take the Indo-American relationship so far. The strength of a bilateral relationship is measured not in kind words, but in firm deeds: the earnings of commercial deals signed; the technologies transferred; the intelligence shared; the joint military exercises conducted; the terrorists captured or killed; and – most of all – the sacrifices of blood made together for a common cause. It is by these standards that the United States' relationships with its key allies (foremost among them the United Kingdom and Australia) have been proven, time and time again. The same standards will determine whether the Indo-American relationship remains one of kind words and good intentions, or whether it becomes both nations' primary alliance of the twenty-first century. For the sake of Indians and Americans alike, it must become the latter.

★

John Quincy Adams said of the young United States in 1824, on the forty-eighth anniversary of the Declaration of Independence: 'She goes not abroad, in search of monsters to destroy...she is the champion and vindicator only of her own.'[3] Much has changed since then; from the time of its entry into the Second World War, the United States has been in a continuous search for monsters abroad. Furthermore, the United States' pre-occupation with its enemies has crowded out much other strategic thinking on foreign policy.

The pattern has repeated itself several times: The United States defines an enemy, then devotes all its attention and resources to achieving total victory. First the enemies were the aggressors of the Second World War: Nazi Germany and Imperial Japan. Then the enemy was communism, over which the United States waged two wars (in Korea and Vietnam) and the Cold War. Since 9/11, the enemy has been international terrorism. All of these total wars have left little room to develop a long-term strategy for alliances that can position the United States for greater wealth, power and influence in the twenty-first century.

Although it would hardly seem possible, India has done even less long-term strategic thinking than the United States. India's obsession with Pakistan has exceeded even the United States' obsession with its successive enemies. As a result, the Indian government has, with the exception of the development of its nuclear programme, shown little ability to think beyond the short-term and beyond its next-door neighbour. Meanwhile China, in a matter of three decades, has transformed itself from a backwards agrarian society to a budding economic and military superpower.

At its current slow pace of development, the Indo-American relationship could well look much the same in 2020 as it does today: many warm words, but little in the way of joint action. That would be a tragedy for the people of both nations, because the world could well look very different – and much more dangerous – in 2020 than it does today.

Now is the time for the United States and India to look ahead in this century, and envisage the worst case scenarios that can arise: an aggressively expansionist China; nuclear arsenals in Iran and North Korea; revolution in Saudi Arabia, driving oil to $200 a barrel; rising commodity prices causing persistent worldwide inflation; a steep drop in global trade, fuelled by a long-term recession, increased protectionism and an outbreak of currency wars. None of these worst case scenarios can be ruled out, and it is possible, if not probable, that several of them could occur simultaneously well before 2020.

Even the possibility of such developments should frighten Singh, Obama and their senior officials enough to ensure India and the United States come together now, before the world falls apart. The two nations must take out insurance on all of the above threats by putting in place the architecture of an alliance that will maximise both nations' wealth and power tomorrow, regardless of what misfortunes befall the world. The United States' strengths today (technology, raw military power, innovation and economic might) and India's strengths today (brainpower, size, labour cost advantages, a youthful population, and massive economic growth potential) are a potent combination. No conceivable alliance of nations, and certainly no single nation, can be as resistant to the dangers of the twenty-first century as India and the United States will be standing together.

Getting India and the United States to a twenty-first century special relationship will require intensive and sustained leadership from both the prime minister and the president. During the decade after the Indian nuclear test the two nations were on an accelerated journey towards closer relations. The pace of this journey has slowed in the past three years, but fortunately the relationship has not stalled completely. The Indo-American strategic dialogue, begun in 2002, has continued to gain momentum since, including during the Obama Administration. In 2009, Secretary of State Hillary Clinton and Minister of External Affairs S.M. Krishna re-focused the strategic dialogue around five key pillars[4] covering all the critical issues in the bilateral relationship. The dialogue can be the ideal forum for the Indo-American alliance, provided both nations are committed to making giant leaps forward, not just small steps.

Speed is the need of the hour. As Churchill said of the Anglo-American relationship after the Second World War, 'Do not let us take the course of allowing events to drift along until it is too late'. The Indo-American relationship under Singh and Obama has been drifting. Happily it is not yet too late, but there is no time to spare. There have been enough words. Now is the time for deeds.

It should therefore be a leading objective of the American and Indian governments that their fraternal association be fully in place by 2020. That is the best way for the people of both nations to prevail in mankind's brutal – and, alas, never-ending – struggle for freedom.

ENDNOTES

Chapter 1

1. 'Number of poor in India has gone up: World Bank', Indo-Asian News Service, 26 August 2008. http://ibnlive.in.com/news/number-of-poor-in-india-has-gone-up-world-bank/72227-3.html.
'Report of the Expert Group to Review the Methodology for Estimation of Poverty', Government of India Planning Commission, November, 2009. http://planningcommission.nic.in/reports/genrep/rep_pov.pdf
2. World Development Indicators 2011, World Bank. 2009 figures are in current United States dollars.
3. World Development Indicators 2011
4. 'India's Rising Growth Potential', Goldman Sachs, January 2007.
5. Standard Chartered Bank forecasts India's growth to accelerate over the coming decade, and for India to become the third largest economy in the world by 2020. See 'India and the Super Cycle', Standard Chartered Bank Research 2011.
6. American GDP per capita in United States dollars in 2009 was thirty-eight times India's ($46,000 vs. $1,200). Adjusting for purchasing power, India's per capita income rises to $3280, one-fourteenth the level of United States income. See World Development Indicators 2011.
7. John F. Richards, *The New Cambridge History of India* I.5 'The Mughal Empire', Cambridge University Press, 2002.
8. Angus Maddison, *The World Economy: Historical Statistics*, OECD 2002, tables 8a and 8b.
9. The population of England in 1600 was around four million while the best estimate of the Indian population in 1600 is 100 million. See Ifran Habib,

The Cambridge Economic History of India, Volume 1, Cambridge, 1982. Extract retrieved at http://histories.cambridge.org/extract?id=chol9780521226929_CHOL9780521226929A010

10. James Talboys Wheller and Michael Macmillan, *European Travelers in India*, Susil Gupta (India) Ltd, 1956, p. 77.

11. Wheller and Michael Macmillan, 77.

12. Wheller and Michael Macmillan, 113.

13. Vipul Singh, Jasmine Dhillon, and Gita Shanmugavel, *Longman 7 History & Civics for IC*, Chapter 11: 'Creation of an Empire: Akbar (1556-1605)', p. 69. Dorling Kindersley (India) Pvt. Ltd., 2010.

14. Sohaib Arshad, 'The Visionary King', *The Friday Times*, 15-21 January 2011. http://www.thefridaytimes.com/14012011/page16.shtml

15. N.R. Farooqi, 'Six Ottoman Documents on Mughal-Ottoman Relations during the Reign of Akbar', *Journal of Islamic Studies* 7:1,1996, pp. 32-48.

16. Includes 123 parishes of London. See Stephen Inwood, *A History of London*, Macmillan, 1998, p. 158.

17. 'City Development Plan AGRA', AGRA Nagar Nigam, Urban Development Department, Government of Uttar Pradesh. http://jnnurm.nic.in/nurmudweb/toolkit/AgraCdp/Cdp_Agra.pdf

18. Inwood, 157.

19. Inwood, 166-7.

20. Inwood, 167.

21. Inwood, 159.

22. Inwood, 177.

23. Inwood, 161.

24. Inwood, 163.

25. Amartya Sen, *The Argumentative Indian*, Penguin, 2005, pp. 18-19.

26. Sen, 76.

27. Antonia Fraser, *Faith and Treason: The story of the Gunpowder Plot*, Anchor 1997, p. 223.

28. Wheeler, J.T., *The History of India from the Earliest Ages* Volume IV Part 1: Mussulman Rule, Elibron Classics, Trübner and Co. London, 2005, p. 137.

29. Maddison, *The World Economy: Historical Statistics*, 242.

30. Maddison, *The World Economy: Historical Statistics*, 242.

31. Maddison, *The World Economy: Historical Statistics*, 242.

32. India throughout history has meant different things and had different geographic boundaries. For the purposes of this work, any references to India's economy in history assume that the present day geographic boundaries of India also

applied then. Therefore any changes in national income have not been affected by increases or decreases in India's territory over time.

33. Maddison, *The World Economy: Historical Statistics*, table 8b.
34. The following analysis of James Mill's attitude towards India is based on Sen, 147-149. Quotations from Mill's work are also taken from Sen.
35. Sen, 79-80

Chapter 2

1. Angus Maddison, *The World Economy: A Millennial Perspective*, OECD 2001, Table B-18.
2. Maddison, *The World Economy: A Millennial Perspective*, Table B-18.
3. *The Hindu*, January 1, 1991. As it happens, the Rajiv Gandhi-led Congress did withdraw its support for Shekhar's government, in the wake of a scandal in which Congress accused Shekhar's government of spying on Gandhi. Shekhar resigned on 6 March 1991, prompting fresh elections.
4. *The Hindu*, 1 January 1991.
5. *The Hindu*, 2 May 1991.
6. World Development Indicators 2011
7. World Development Indicators 2011
8. Unless otherwise noted, data on the causes of India's 1991 financial crisis are taken from: Valerie Cerra and Sweta Chaman Saxena, 'What Caused the 1991 Currency Crisis in India?' IMF Staff Papers, Vol. 49, No. 3, 2002. http://www.imf.org/External/Pubs/FT/staffp/2002/03/pdf/cerra.pdf
9. Two years later, in December 1992, the Babri Mosque was destroyed by a Hindu mob, following a BJP political rally. The destruction sparked communal riots across India that killed an estimated 2000 people.
10. The following descriptions of the planning and execution of Rajiv Gandhi's assassination is based primarily on Rajeev Sharma, *Beyond the Tigers: Tracking Rajiv Gandhi's Assassination*, Daya, 1998.
11. Arunabha Ghosh, 'Pathways Through Financial Crisis: India', *Global Governance* 12 (2006), p. 418.
12. Ghosh, 418.
13. Ghosh, 418.
14. 'Standard And Poor's Ups India's Credit Rating To Investment Grade', *Agence France Press*, 31 January 2007.
15. Ghosh, note 17.
16. Ghosh, 418.

17. Yashwant Sinha, *Confessions of a Swadeshi Reformer: My Years as Finance Minister*, Penguin Viking, 2007, p. 19.
18. Sinha, 19.
19. Ashok V. Desai, *My Economic Affair*, Wiley Eastern Limited 1993, p. 107.
20. 'Sri Lanka: The Untold Story Rajiv Gandhi's Assassination', Ministry of Defence of Sri Lanka. http://www.defence.lk/new.asp?fname=20060521_02
21. Sharma, 56.
22. Sharma, 67-8.
23. Sinha, 20-21.
24. Sharma, 16-17.
25. Sharma, 17.
26. Sharma, 16-17.
27. Sri Lanka: The Untold Story Rajiv Gandhi's Assassination.
28. Sinha, 22-23.
29. For the account of the negotiations on the gold with the Bank of England and subsequent transaction, see Sinha, vi-viii, and 22-24.
30. The *New York Times* reported that the 200 tonnes of gold was sold for $11.7 million a tonne, or $234 million in total. See '20 Tons of Gold Sold by India', *New York Times*, 7 June 1991.
31. The *New York Times* reported that the gold was sent on 24 May (not 21 May), 'on SwissAir flights apparently to Zurich'. See '20 Tons of Gold Sold by India'.
32. Sinha, vi-viii, and 23.
33. Statement of the minister of finance Manmohan Singh before Parliament, 22 November 1991. http://parliamentofindia.nic.in/ls/lsdeb/ls10/ses2/13221191.htm
34. Ghosh, 419.
35. Ghosh, 419.
36. Statement of the Minister of Finance Manmohan Singh before Parliament, 22 November 1991.
37. 'Nalini's plea against denial of release adjourned', *Times of India*, 16 April 2010. http://articles.timesofindia.indiatimes.com/2010-04-16/chennai/28115802_1_premature-release-prison-advisory-board-nalini
38. Vaijanthi Prakash, 'Rajiv murder case is not closed', *Sunday Times* (Sri Lanka), 16 May 1999. http://sundaytimes.lk/990516/specrpt.html
39. See T.S. Subramanian, 'Unraveling the plot', *Frontline*, 7-20 February 1998. http://www.hindu.com/fline/fl1503/15030170.htm
   See also Bhavna Vij and Swati Chaturvedi, 'Legal luminaries divided on death verdict in Rajiv assassination case', *Indian Express*, 30 January 1998. http://www.expressindia.com/ie/daily/19980130/03050184.html

40. Prakash, 'Rajiv murder case is not closed'.
41. T.S. Subramanian, 'The Final Verdict', *Frontline*, 23 October-5 November 1999. http://www.hindu.com/fline/fl1622/16221320.htm
42. 'Prabhakaran's Extradition: India awaiting Lanka's response', *Press Trust of India*, 21 February 2002. http://www.expressindia.com/news/fullstory. php?newsid=7684
43. 'Let's forget Rajiv; we need your help: Balasingham begs India . . . ,' Ministry of Defence of Sri Lanka. http://www.defence.lk/new.asp?fname=20060628_04
44. Statement of the Minister of Finance Manmohan Singh before Parliament, 22 November 1991.
45. 1991-92 budget speech of Minister of Finance Manmohan Singh, 24 July 1991. http://indiabudget.nic.in/bspeech/bs199192.pdf
46. Singh, 1991-92 budget speech.
47. Singh, 1991-92 budget speech.
48. 'Statement on Industrial Policy', Government of India, Ministry of Industry, 24 July 1991. http://siadipp.nic.in/publicat/nip0791.htm
49. 1991 Statement on Industrial Policy
50. 1991 Statement on Industrial Policy
51. 'Shri P.V. Narasimha Rao – A Profile', Office of the Prime Minister of India. http://pmindia.nic.in/pm_rao.htm
52. Interview with Manmohan Singh, *PBS*, 6 February 2001. http://www.pbs.org/ wgbh/commandingheights/shared/minitextlo/int_manmohansingh.html
53. PBS Interview with Manmohan Singh.
54. Vijay Joshi and I.M.D. Little, *India's Economic Reforms 1991-2001*, Oxford 1996, pp. 12, 14.
55. World Development Indicators 2011.
56. Singh, 1991-92 budget speech.
57. World Bank, 'World Development Indicators 2011'.
58. Although the LTTE's assassination of Rajiv Gandhi successfully kept India out of the Sri Lankan ethnic conflict, it also undermined the support the LTTE still enjoyed in Tamil Nadu. The killing of Rajiv Gandhi on Indian soil made it politically difficult for mainstream Tamil Nadu politicians to support openly the LTTE. The loss of financial and political support in Tamil Nadu in turn hurt the LTTE, and was an important factor in its ultimate international isolation.
59. Francis Wade, 'China port plan threatens India face-off', *Democratic Voice of Burma*, 2 June 2011. http://www.dvb.no/news/china-port-plan-threatens-india-face-off/15946

Chapter 3

1. The solution to the queue problem took place shortly before the author's arrival in Chennai. The visa officers cleared the queue simply by abandoning the policy that restricted the number of daily applicants, and opening the doors to any applicant who presented himself before a certain hour in the morning. The Consulate staff had to work hard for several days to serve the backlog of applicants in the queue – and those who showed up disbelieving the new policy would last – but it was worth it. After a short period, the ability to apply for a visa the United States Consulate was no longer a scarce resource: The queue disappeared and the confidence of South India in American efficiency returned.

2. The United States did not in 1998, and does not today, operate a formal Embassy in Cuba. Instead there was and is a United States Interests Section that operates under the legal protection of the Swiss government. However, the Interests Section looks and acts like an embassy in many ways, and is also staffed with Foreign Service officers.

3. Talbott, 2-3.

4. Talbott, 53.

5. 'Scientists not excited by lifting of sanctions', *Times of India*, 24 September 24 2001. http://articles.timesofindia.indiatimes.com/2001-09-24/india/27247829_1_ sanctions-indian-scientists-agrani

6. Talbott, 52.

7. Perkovich, 407.

8. Perkovich, 360.

9. The BJP had come to power for a period spanning less than a month after the eleventh general elections in 1996. Vajpayee, however, was unable to hold his coalition together, and the passage of a no-confidence motion in the Lok Sabha led to his resignation, fresh elections and a new government led by the Janata Dal.

10. Talbott, 74.

11. Talbott, 246 note 1.

12. Talbott, 91.

13. 'Trade in Goods with India', United States Census Bureau. http://www.census. gov/foreign-trade/balance/c5330.html#1998

14. K. Alan Kronstadt, 'India-U.S. Relations', *Congressional Research Service*, 23 February 2005. http://fpc.state.gov/documents/organization/42978.pdf

15. Talbott, 165.

16. Talbott, 169.

17. T.V. Parasuram, 'Vajpayee meets families of Indian 9/11 victims', *Indian Express*, 12 September 2002. http://www.expressindia.com/news/fullstory. php?newsid=14638

18. Two years later, Frank Roque was convicted of the murder of Balbir Singh Sodhi, and is currently serving a life sentence.

19. 'Press Release on the death of Mr. Balbir Singh in Mesa, Arizona', Embassy of India, Washington, D.C., 17 September 2001. http://www.indianembassy. org/prdetail1209/-press-release-on-the-death-of-mr.-balbir-singh-in-mesa%2C-arizona

20. 'Embassy Press Release on terrorist attacks in New York and Washington, DC', Embassy of India, Washington, D.C., 13 September 2001. http://www. indianembassy.org/prdetail1212/embassy-press-release-on-terrorist-attacks-in-new-york-and-washington%2C-dc

21. 'India condemns terrorist attack on J&K state assembly' Embassy of India, Washington, D.C., 1 October 2001. http://www.indianembassy.org/prdetail1204/-india-condemns-terrorist-attack-on-jandk-state-assembly

22. Though Blackwill undoubtedly transformed Indo-American relations, his management style also generated complaints and criticism within the State Department. The State Department's Inspector General blamed him, in two separate reports, for lack of civility towards subordinates and low morale at United States Embassy New Delhi. He left his post in India after two years. Later, while serving on the National Security Council at the White House, Blackwill was accused of physically hurting a State Department employee. See Glenn Kessler and Al Kamen, 'Ex-Adviser Reportedly Hurt Embassy Aide', *Washington Post*, 12 November 2004. http://www.washingtonpost.com/wp-dyn/ articles/A43756-2004Nov11.html

23. Steve Coll, 'The Stand-Off', *The New Yorker*, 13 February 2006. http://www. newyorker.com/archive/2006/02/13/060213fa_fact_coll?printable=true

24. Coll, 'The Stand-Off'.

25. Ibid.

26. 'More groups join US terror blacklist', *BBC News*, 21 December 2001.

27. Coll, 'The Stand-Off'.

28. Ibid.

29. Ibid.

30. Ibid.

31. 'Historical Changes of the Target Federal Funds and Discount Rates', Federal Reserve Bank of New York. http://www.newyorkfed.org/markets/statistics/ dlyrates/fedrate.html

32. 'United States National Index Q4 2010', Case-Schiller Home Price Index, Standard and Poor's. http://www.standardandpoors.com/indices/sp-case-shiller-home-price-indices/en/eu/?indexId=SPUSA-CASHPIDFF–P-US—

33. Alan Greenspan and James Kennedy, 'Sources and Uses of Equity Extracted from Homes', *Federal Reserve Board Finance and Economics Discussion Series*, 2007-20, Table 2. http://www.federalreserve.gov/pubs/feds/2007/200720/200720pap. pdf

34. 'Personal Saving Rate', U.S. Department of Commerce: Bureau of Economic Analysis. Compiled by the Federal Reserve Bank of St. Louis. http://research. stlouisfed.org/fred2/data/PSAVERT.txt

35. For American war dead in Iraq and Afghanistan see 'Faces of the Fallen', *Washington Post*. http://projects.washingtonpost.com/fallen/.
    For American spending on the wars in Iraq and Afghanistan see Amy Belasco, 'The Cost of Iraq, Afghanistan, and Other Global War on Terror Operations Since 9/11', *Congressional Research Service*, 29 March 2011.

36. For debt figures see 'Table A: Gross External Debt Position: December 31, 2010', United States Department of the Treasury. http://www.treasury.gov/ resource-center/data-chart-center/tic/Documents/debtad10.html.
    For GDP figures see 'National Economic Accounts', United States Department of Commerce, Bureau of Economic Analysis. http://www.bea.gov/national/ index.htm#gdp

37. An index of thirty leading United States stocks.

38. Daniel Markey, 'Terrorism and Indo-Pakistani Escalation', Contingency Planning Memorandum No. 6, *Council on Foreign Relations*, January 2010.

39. Markey, 'Terrorism and Indo-Pakistani Escalation'.

40. On 28 May 1998 Pakistan tested five nuclear devices in response to India's tests two weeks earlier. The then prime minister of Pakistan, Nawaz Sharif declared that Pakistan's tests were made inevitable by the tests performed by India. See '1998: World fury at Pakistan's nuclear tests', *On this Day*, May 28, *BBC*. http:// news.bbc.co.uk/onthisday/hi/dates/stories/may/28/newsid_2495000/2495045. stm

41. Peter Popham, '"The world's most dangerous place" is already at war', *The Independent*, 18 March 2000.

42. World Development Indicators 2011

43. Sridhar Krishnaswami, 'Of planes and plans', *Frontline*, 12-25 March 2005. http://www.hindu.com/fline/fl2208/stories/20050422002601000.htm

44. Ellen Dengel-Janic, 'South Asia', in Lars Eckstein (ed.), *English Literature across the globe: A companion*, W. Fink UTB, Germany, p. 135.

45. Minhaz Merchant, 'Dialogue is the key', *The Times of India*, 24 March 2011. http://articles.timesofindia.indiatimes.com/2011-03-24/edit-page/29181385_1_india-and-pakistan-india-s-gdp-composite-dialogue

46. Aysegul Aydin, 'The deterrent effects of economic integration', Journal of Peace Research, September 2010, vol. 47 no. 5, pp. 523-533. Abstract retrieved at http://jpr.sagepub.com/content/47/5/523.abstract?rss=1

47. 'Top Trading Partners – Total Trade, Exports, Imports', United States Census Bureau. http://www.census.gov/foreign-trade/statistics/highlights/top/top1012yr.html

48. For GDP figures see World Development Indicators 2011

49. For bilateral trade figures see United Nations Conference on Trade and Development (UNCTAD) Statistics. Calculated using estimates of bilateral trade available at UNCTAD statistics. http://www.unctad.org/Templates/Page.asp?intItemID=1584&lang=1

   For GDP figures see World Development Indicators 2011

50. 'Remarks by President Obama and Prime Minister Singh of India during Arrival Ceremony', The White House, 24 November 2009. http://www.whitehouse.gov/the-press-office/remarks-president-obama-and-prime-minister-singh-india-during-arrival-ceremony

51. 'The Treaty on the Non-proliferation of Nuclear Weapons', United Nations 2005 Review Conference of the Parties to the Treaty, May 2-27, 2005. http://www.un.org/en/conf/npt/2005/npttreaty.html

52. 'NPT discriminatory: PM', *The Hindu*, 27 January 2000. http://www.hinduonnet.com/thehindu/2000/01/27/stories/02270009.htm

53. Jaswant Singh, 'Against Nuclear Apartheid', *Foreign Affairs*, September/October 1998.

54. James Lamont, 'Indian PM attacks nuclear treaty', *Financial Times*, 29 September 2009.

55. David P. Fidler and Sumit Ganguly, 'India Wants to Join the Non-Proliferation Treaty as a Weapon State', *Yale Global Online*, 27 January 2010. http://yaleglobal.yale.edu/content/india-wants-join-non-proliferation-treaty

Chapter 4

1. World Development Indicators 2011. Figures in current USD.

2. India GDP per capita: $87. Egypt GDP per capita: $152. Figures available for Indonesia beginning 1967, when it had a GDP per capita of $55. World Development Indicators 2011. Figures in current USD.

3. 'The Non-Aligned Movement: Description and History', The Non-Aligned Movement (NAM). http://www.nam.gov.za/background/history.htm

4. Barack Obama, 'Remarks by the President to the Joint Session of the Indian Parliament in New Delhi, India', The White House, 8 November 2010. http://www.whitehouse.gov/the-press-office/2010/11/08/remarks-president-joint-session-indian-parliament-new-delhi-india

5. 'Remarks on India and The United States: A Vision for the 21st Century', Hillary Clinton, Chennai, India, July 20, 2011. http://www.state.gov/secretary/rm/2011/07/168840.htm

6. See Arvind Panagariya, 'India's Trade Reform: Progress, Impact and Future Strategy', 24 March 2004. http://www.columbia.edu/~ap2231/Policy%20Papers/IPF_India.pdf

7. World Development Indicators 2011.

8. Ibid.

9. Growth in Manufacturing Value Added in Constant year 2000 United States dollars. World Development Indicators 2011.

10. Ibid.

11. EUR 34.8 billion, converted to USD at a 2010 average exchange rate of 1.33 USD/EUR. See 'India-EU Bilateral Trade and Trade with the World', Directorate General for Trade of the European Commission, 17 March 2011. http://trade.ec.europa.eu/doclib/docs/2006/september/tradoc_113390.pdf

12. 'Trade in Goods with India', United States Census Bureau. http://www.census.gov/foreign-trade/balance/c5330.html#2009

13. World Federation of Exchanges. http://www.world-exchanges.org/statistics/annual/2010/equity-markets

14. T.E. Narasimhan, 'SMEs listed on BSE see 11% fall in five years', *Business Standard*, 5 January 2010. http://www.business-standard.com/india/news/smes-listedbse-see-11-fall-in-five-years/381626/

15. World Federation of Exchanges.

16. Michael Lind, 'Free Trade Fallacy', *Prospect*, New America Foundation, 1 January 2003 http://web.archive.org/web/20060110011059/www.newamerica.net/templets/Documents/print.cfm?pg=article&DocID=1080&Prt=Yes

17. 'Bangladesh: Trade Policy and Integration', World Bank. http://web.worldbank.org/WBSITE/EXTERNAL/COUNTRIES/SOUTHASIAEXT/EXTSARREGTOPINTECOTRA/0, contentMDK:20592516~menuPK:579454~pagePK:34004173~piPK:34003707~theSitePK:579448,00.html

18. 'India's average trade tariff rates high: CPI', *Business Standard*, 17 May 2004.

http://www.business-standard.com/india/news/indias-average-trade-tariff-rates-high-cpi/151018/

19. For Sri Lanka's assessment of non-tariff barriers in India see 'Our exports face non-tariff barriers in India, says Lankan Minister', *Business Line*, 30 September 2004. http://www.thehindubusinessline.in/2004/09/30/stories/2004093002990600.htm

20. 'The Himalayas of Hiring', *The Economist*, 7 August 2010.

21. Ibid.

22. Lind, 'Free Trade Fallacy'.

23. Ha-Joon Chang, *Kicking away the ladder: development strategy in historical perspective*, Anthem Press, 2003, p. 4.

24. The Doha Round refers to the free trade negotiations launched by the World Trade Organization in Doha, Qatar in November 2001. As of December 2011, the negotiations had stalled after five ministerial meetings (2003, 2004, 2005, 2006, and 2008) failed to produce an agreement. See http://www.wto.org/english/tratop_e/dda_e/dda_e.htm

25. List quoted in Chang, *Kicking away the ladder*, 4.

26. Chang, *Kicking away the ladder*, 3-4. See also Ha-Joon Chang, 'Economic History of the developed world: Lessons from Africa'. Lecture delivered in the eminent speakers program of the African Development Bank, 26 February 2009. http://www.econ.cam.ac.uk/faculty/chang/pubs/ChangAfDBlecturetext.pdf

27. Quoted in Lind, 'Free Trade Fallacy'.

28. Chang, *Kicking away the ladder*, 5.

29. Bruce Bartlett, 'The Truth about Trade in History', Cato Institute, 1 July 1998. http://www.cato.org/pub_display.php?pub_id=10983

30. Tariff Download Facility, World Trade Organization. http://tariffdata.wto.org/Default.aspx?culture=en-US

31. Lydia Polgreen, 'New Arrivals Strain India's Cities to Breaking Point', *New York Times*, 30 November 2010.

32. Richard Dobbs and Shirish Sankh, 'Comparing urbanization in China and India', *McKinsey Quarterly*, July 2010

33. Dobbs and Sankh, 'Comparing urbanization in China and India'.

34. World Development Indicators 2011

35. Ibid.

36. Ibid.

37. Ibid.

38. Ibid.

39. Ibid.

40. Campbell J. Gibson and Emily Lennon, 'Historical Census Statistics on the Foreign-born Population of the United States: 1850-1990', Population Division U.S. Bureau of the Census, Washington, D.C., February 1999. http://www.census.gov/population/www/documentation/twps0029/twps0029.html

41. World Development Indicators 2011

42. Ibid.

43. Arun Kumar, 'US pushing India for faster economic reforms', *Indo-Asian News Service*, 25 June 2011. http://news.in.msn.com/international/article.aspx?cp-documentid=5234455

44. 'China Overtakes Japan as World's Second-Biggest Economy', *Bloomberg*, 16 August 2010. http://www.bloomberg.com/news/2010-08-16/china-economy-passes-japan-s-in-second-quarter-capping-three-decade-rise.html

45. 'Trade in Goods with India', United States Census Bureau. http://www.census.gov/foreign-trade/balance/c5330.html

46. World Development Indicators 2011

47. Ibid.

48. 'The Child in Time', *The Economist*, 21 August 2010.

49. Dobbs and Sankh, 'Comparing urbanization in China and India'.

50. Anand Dibyesh, 'Anxious Sexualities: Masculinity, Nationalism and Violence', *The British Journal of Politics and International Relations* 9(2), 2007, pp. 257-269.

51. Jim Yardley, 'India Tries Using Cash Bonuses to Slow Birthrates', *New York Times*, 22 August 2010.

52. World Development Indicators 2011

53. Ibid.

54. Ibid.

55. Yılmaz Akyüz, 'Export dependence and future of growth in China and East Asia', South Bulletin 48, South Centre, June 30, 2010. http://www.southcentre.org/index.php?catid=144%3Asouth-bulletin-individual-articles&id=1339%3Asb48&lang=en&option=com_content&view=article

Chapter 5

1. Friedrich List, *The National System of Political Economy*, 1841. Translated by Sampson S. Lloyd, 1885.

2. List, *The National System of Political Economy*.

3. 'Noble or Savage?' *The Economist*, 19 December 2007. http://www.economist.com/node/10278703

4. 'Our History', University of Bologna. http://www.eng.unibo.it/PortaleEn/University/Our+History/default.htm

5. Outsourcing in this work is defined as IT services and Business Process Outsourcing (BPO)

6. 'Indian companies tighten grip on outsourcing: Nasscom', *Times of India*, 3 February 2011.

7. 'Industry Trends', NASSCOM. http://www.nasscom.in/Nasscom/templates/NormalPage.aspx?id=56966

8. 'Perspective 2020: Transform Business, Transform India', NASSCOM.

9. Robert J. Trent and Llewellyn Roberts, *Managing Global Supply and Risk: Best Practices, Concepts and Strategies*, J. Ross Publishing, 2010, p. 101.

10. Kalpana Pathak, 'Engineering graduates could become more "unemployable",' *Business Standard*, 7 July 2011. http://www.business-standard.com/india/news/engineering-graduates-could-become-more-%5Cunemployable%5C/396771/

11. 'Industry Trends', NASSCOM.

12. Pathak, 'Engineering graduates could become more "unemployable"'.

13. Penny Macrae, 'Nasscom forecasts sharp export rise', *AFP* 4 February 2010. http://www.livemint.com/2010/02/04184758/Nasscom-forecasts-sharp-export.html

14. 'Nasscom to sell outsourcing in US', *The Times of India*, 6 July 2010. http://articles.timesofindia.indiatimes.com/2010-07-06/outsourcing/28273839_1_service-industries-csi-som-mittal

15. 'The lowdown on teardowns', *The Economist*, 23 January 2010

16. Arik Hesseldahl, 'Deconstructing Apple's Tiny iPod Shuffle', *Bloomberg Businessweek*, 13 April 2009.

17. Market capitalisation $330 billion as of July 2011. For second quarter 2011 results see http://www.apple.com/pr/library/2011/04/20Apple-Reports-Second-Quarter-Results.html

18. David Barboza, 'Supply Chain for iPhone Highlights Costs in China', *New York Times*, 5 July 2010.

19. 'The Product Engineering Difference at Infosys', Infosys White Paper, July 2007. http://www.infosys.com/engineering-services/product-engineering/white-papers/pages/index.aspx

20. Infosys Financials, Operating Metrics. http://www.infosys.com/investors/financials/Pages/operating-metrics.aspx#Revenuesegmentation

21. Michael Bloch, Dejan Boskovic, and Allen Weinberg, 'How Innovators are changing IT offshoring', *McKinsey Quarterly*, 2010, Issue 1, pp. 21-23.

22. Vishwanath Kulkarni and Shamik Paul, 'IT firms spend more on R&D to offer new services', *Business Line*, July 19, 2009. http://www.thehindubusinessline. com/2009/07/20/stories/2009072050390200.htm

23. Kulkarni and Paul, 'IT firms spend more on R&D to offer new services'. INR 267 crore converted at INR 45 per USD.

24. World Development Indicators 2011. Calculated using constant 2000 United States dollars.

25. Ibid.

26. 'U.S. Companies Lead in R&D Spending', *Kiplinger News*, 27 May 2010.

27. 'From the Ashes', *Newsweek*, 23 and 30 August 2010.

28. Kirtika Suneja, 'Infosys expects increase in patent filings', *Business Standard*, 24 February 2010. http://www.business-standard.com/india/news/infosys-expects-increase-in-patent-filings/386673/

29. Teresita C. Schaffer, *Reinventing Partnership: India and the United States in the 21ˢᵗ Century*, Center for Strategic and International Studies, Washington, D.C., 2009, p. 25.

30. Bloch, Boskovic, and Weinberg 'How Innovators are changing IT offshoring'.

31. 'Xerox Launches Innovation Hub in India', Xerox Corporation Press Release, 17 March 2010. http://news.xerox.com/pr/xerox/PRN-xerox-launches-India-innovation-hub-155321.aspx

32. Pradeep Kanta Ray and Sangeeta Ray, 'Resource-Constrained Innovation for Emerging Economies: The Case of the Indian Telecommunications Industry', *IEEE Transactions on Engineering Management*, February 2010, Vol. 57 Issue 1, pp. 144-156.

33. Heather Timmons, 'Nestlé Plans Research Center to Focus on Indian Foods', 22 September 2010. http://www.nytimes.com/2010/09/23/business/global/23nestle. html

34. 'The End of 'I' in Business', *CNBC Business*, May 2010.

35. Maddison, *The World Economy: A Millennial Perspective*, 59-63.

36. Maddison, *The World Economy: A Millennial Perspective*, 57.

37. Maddison, *The World Economy: A Millennial Perspective*, 63.

38. Ibid.

39. '2011 Silicon Valley Index: Public Finance Crisis Undermining Economic Recovery', Silicon Valley Community Foundations, 14 February 2011. http://www.siliconvalleycf.org/news-resources/press-releases/11/pr-2-14-11.html

40. Richard C. Levin, 'Top of the Class: The Rise of Asia's Universities', *Foreign Affairs*, May/June 2010.

41. Levin, 'Top of the Class'.

42. World Development Indicators 2011.
43. Levin, 'Top of the Class'.
44. Ibid.
45. Ibid.
46. Ibid.
47. Ibid.
48. World Development Indicators 2011.
49. Levin, 'Top of the Class'.
50. 'Foreign Education Bill finally gets Cabinet nod', *Business Standard*, 16 March 2010. http://www.business-standard.com/india/storypage.php?autono=388740
51. For the number of seats allotted for the IITs for 2011, see 'Joint Entrance Exam 2011: A Guide to Candidates', Indian Institutes of Technology, Table 1. http://www.jee.iitb.ac.in/cb2011.pdf
52. Levin, 'Top of the Class'.
53. National Center for Education Statistics, Digest of Education Statistics 2010.
54. '1,000 new universities for India?' *The Telegraph*, 10 May 2010.
55. Robert M. Berdahl, 'The Privatization of Public Universities', Speech at Erfurt University, Erfurt Germany, 23 May 2000. http://cio.chance.berkeley.edu/chancellor/sp/privatization.htm
56. '24% hike in allocation for education', *Times of India*, 28 February 2011.
57. Levin, 'Top of the Class'.
58. Ibid.
59. Ibid.
60. 'Science funding: Budget 2011-12', Indian Academy of Sciences. http://www.ias.ac.in/currsci/10apr2011/964.pdf
61. Levin, 'Top of the Class'.
62. Ibid.
63. 'Big Shift in Bric's scientific landscape', *Financial Times*, 26 January 2010.
64. 'Another Way China May Beat the U.S.', *Time*, 11 April 2011.
65. 'Big Shift in Bric's scientific landscape', *Financial Times*, 26 January 2010.
66. Ibid.
67. QS Quacquarelli Symonds 2011 Asian University Rankings. http://www.topuniversities.com/university-rankings/asian-university-rankings/2011
68. Levin, 'Top of the Class'.
69. Ibid.
70. 'Will they still come?' *The Economist*, 7 August 2010.
71. Ibid.
72. Ibid.

Chapter 6

1. David Cameron, 'A stronger, wider, deeper relationship', *The Hindu*, 27 July 2010. http://www.thehindu.com/opinion/lead/article537003.ece?homepage=true

2. Manjeet Kripalani, 'India: The GE and McKinsey Club', *Business Week India*, 23 February 2006.

3. 'CIA chief promises spies "new cover" for secret ops', *Washington Post*, 26 April 2010. http://blog.washingtonpost.com/spy-talk/2010/04/cia_chief_promises_spies_new_a.html

4. CNN Money Global 500. http://money.cnn.com/magazines/fortune/global500/2010/

5. CNN Money Global 500: India. http://money.cnn.com/magazines/fortune/global500/2010/countries/India.html

6. 'A world of uncertainties', *Spectator Business*, June-August 2010.

7. 'Big U.S. Firms Shift Hiring Abroad', *Wall Street Journal*, 19 April 2011.

8. '3M Operating Earnings Rise; Overseas Sales Strong', *Reuters*, 29 January 2008. http://www.cnbc.com/id/22877113/3M_Operating_Earnings_Rise_Overseas_Sales_Strong

9. Daniel Gross, 'Death On Our Shores', *Newsweek*, 19 June 2010.

10. Gross, 'Death On Our Shores'.

11. GE Factsheet, http://www.ge.com/company/factsheets/corporate.html

12. 'Big U.S. Firms Shift Hiring Abroad'.

13. Joe Leahy, 'Up in the heir', *Financial Times*, 6 September 2010.

14. Speech by United Kingdom Prime Minister David Cameron in Bangalore, India, 28 July 2010. http://www.number10.gov.uk/news/speeches-and-transcripts/2010/07/pms-speech-in-india-53949

15. 'Growth and competitiveness in the United States: The role of its multinational companies', *McKinsey Global Institute*, June 2010

16. 'Growth and competitiveness in the United States'.

17. Ibid.

18. Calculated based on The Conference Board Total Economy Database, January 2011. http://www.conference-board.org/data/economydatabase/.

19. For more on Electrotherm and Glenmark, see 'India's fastest growing mid-sized companies', 15 June 2008. http://businesstoday.intoday.in/story/indias-fastest-growing-midsized-companies/1/2266.html

20. World Federation of Exchanges.

21. Michael Pettis, 'Don't read too much into the performance of Chinese markets', *Financial Times*, 17 June 2010.

22. The largest Indian corporate fraud in recent history involved Satyam Computer Services, an IT services firm founded in 1980s and taken public in 1991. In January 2009 the company suddenly declared that many of the profits it had claimed on its books were fictitious. The accounting scandal, which led to the arrest of Satyam's founder and other senior executives, caused investors to wonder which other Indian companies might be cooking their books. Satyam was taken over by another Indian IT services company later in 2009. See 'Satyam accounting scandal could be "India's Enron",' *The Telegraph*, 7 January 2009. http://www.telegraph.co.uk/finance/4161198/Satyam-accounting-scandal-could-be-Indias-Enron.html

23. In a 'pump and dump' scheme, owners conspire to inflate the prices of stocks they hold by, for example, spreading false information or otherwise creating new demand for the stock. Then, when the price of the stock has risen, the owners 'dump' their holdings at a profit.

24. 'Global IPO trends 2011', Ernst & Young. http://www.ey.com/Publication/vwLUAssets/Global-IPO-trends_2011/$FILE/Global%20IPO%20trends%202011.pdf

25. 'Global IPO trends 2011'.

26. Ibid.

27. M.T. Raju and Anirban Ghosh, 'Stock Market Volatility – An International Comparison', Working Paper Series No. 8, Securities and Exchange Board of India, April 2004.

28. Hans Bieshaar, Jeremy Knight, and Alexander van Wassenaer, 'Deals that create value', *McKinsey Quarterly*, February 2001.

29. The IMF's forecasts date from September 2011. A slowdown Eurozone economic activity during October and November 2011 due to that region's sovereign debt crisis has cast doubt on the forecast of 1.1% Eurozone growth for 2012. See *IMF World Economic Outlook: Slowing Growth, Rising Risks*, September 2011, Table 1.1

30. Institut für Mittelstandsforschung Bonn. http://www.ifm-bonn.org

31. 'Germany's Mittelstand Still Thrives', *Bloomberg Business Week*, 30 September 2010. http://www.businessweek.com/globalbiz/content/sep2010/gb20100929_905740_page_2.htm

32. Richard Wachman, 'Jaguar Land Rover sees record profits of £1bn as sales soar in China and India', *The Guardian*, 26 May 2011. http://www.guardian.co.uk/business/2011/may/26/jaguar-land-rover-sees-sales-soar

33. 'Consolidated Results for the Year ended March 31, 2011', Tata Motors Group Press Release, 26 May 2011. http://www.tatamotors.com/media/press-releases.php?id=670

34. Promit Mukherjee, 'Tata Steel Europe to cut 1,500 more jobs', *DNA*, 21 May 2011. http://www.dnaindia.com/money/report_tata-steel-europe-to-cut-1500-more-jobs_1545768

35. Terry Macalister, 'Construction slump and carbon costs blamed for 1,500 steel job losses', *The Guardian*, 20 May 2011. http://www.guardian.co.uk/business/2011/may/20/tata-steel-job-losses-yorkshire-teesside

36. Abhineet Kumar, 'Tata Motors may seek rollover of JLR debt', *Business Standard*, 19 January 2009. http://www.business-standard.com/india/news/tata-motors-may-seek-rolloverjlr-debt/346492/

37. Michiyo Nakamoto, 'Mass market appeal with the scent of prestige', *Financial Times*, 1 June 2010.

38. Financial Report 2010-11, Godrej Consumer Products. http://www.godrej.com/godrej/Godrej-ConsumerProducts/cpreportdetail-1011.aspx?id=381&menuid=2296

39. 'M&A Strategy', Godrej Consumer Products, Analyst Call, 7 June 2010. http://www.godrej.com/godrej/Godrej-ConsumerProducts/download/GCPLMAStrategyJune%2007_FINAL2010.pdf

40. Financials and Presentations, Godrej Consumer Products. http://www.godrej.com/godrej/Godrej-ConsumerProducts/fy1011.aspx?id=381&menuid=2296

41. 'Competition for Design', Department of Economic Affairs, Ministry of Finance, Government of India, February, 2009. http://finmin.nic.in/the_ministry/dept_eco_affairs/currency_coinage/Comp_Design.pdf

42. William L. Watts, 'China repeats call for "super-sovereign" currency', *MarketWatch*, 26 June 2009. http://www.marketwatch.com/story/china-repeats-call-for-new-reserve-currency

43. 'RMB Cross Border Settlement: Origins, Mechanics and opportunities', BBVA Research, 9 March 2011. http://www.bbvaresearch.com/KETD/fbin/mult/110309_China_RMB_settlement_EN_tcm348-249217.pdf?ts=2842011.

44. 'China, Brazil reported planning currency trade deal', *MarketWatch*, 28 June 2009. http://www.marketwatch.com/story/china-brazil-plan-currency-trade-deal-reports

45. 'China, Brazil reported planning currency trade deal'.

46. 'Changing patterns of trade give new momentum to emerging markets', *International Herald Tribune*, 4 August 2010.

47. Ibid.

48. Martin N. Baily, Susan Lund, and Charles Atkins, 'Will U.S. consumer debt reduction cripple the recovery?' *McKinsey Global Institute*, March 2009. http://www.mckinsey.com/mgi/reports/pdfs/us_consumers/MGI_US_consumers_full_report.pdf

49. Job creation and investment figures include both Indian companies' greenfield investments as well as their Mergers and Acquisitions in the United States. See Vinod K. Jain and Kamlesh Jain, 'How America benefits from Economic Engagement with India', India-US World Affairs Institute, 2010, p. x.

50. 'Number of poor in India has gone up: World Bank'.
'Report of the Expert Group to Review the Methodology for Estimation of Poverty'.

51. The UN estimates a decline in India's poverty rate from 51.3 percent in 1990 to 41.6 percent in 2005. Ten percent of India's population over that time equates to roughly 100 million people. See Jayati Ghosh, 'Poverty reduction in China and India: Policy implications of recent trends', United Nations Department of Economic and Social Affairs, DESA Working Paper No. 92, January 2010. http://www.un.org/esa/desa/papers/2010/wp92_2010.pdf

Chapter 7

1. 'Chinese, Sri Lankan workers mingle at sprawling Hambantota port site', *Sunday Times* (Sri Lanka), 5 October 2008. http://sundaytimes.lk/081005/FinancialTimes/ft343.html

2. 'Chinese help for Hambantota port for "commercial purposes"', *Zee News*, 18 February 2010. http://zeenews.india.com/news/south-asia/chinese-help-for-hambantota-port-for-commercial-purposes_605128.html

3. The name 'Adam's Bridge' derives from the legend that the Christian Bible's Adam crossed the 'bridge' on his way to present-day Sri Lanka.

4. Robert D. Kaplan, 'The Geography of Chinese Power: How Far Can Beijing Reach on Land and at Sea?' *Foreign Affairs*, May/June 2010.

5. Vikas Bajaj, 'India Worries as China Builds Ports in South Asia', *The New York Times*, 15 February 2010. http://www.nytimes.com/2010/02/16/business/global/16port.html
See also Corey Flintoff , 'Indians Uneasy As China Builds Ports Nearby', *NPR*, 20 June 2011. http://www.npr.org/2011/06/20/137061379/indians-uneasy-as-china-builds-ports-nearby

6. Kaplan, 'The Geography of Chinese Power'.

7. 'Insular Area Summary for the U.S. Virgin Islands: History and Political Status', U.S. Virgin Islands, Office of Insular Affairs. http://www.doi.gov/oia/Islandpages/vipage.htm

8. 'Mission and Vision', Naval Support Facility Diego Garcia. http://www.cnic.navy.mil/DiegoGarcia/About/MissionAndVision/index.htm

9. Donald L. Berlin, 'India and the Indian Ocean', *Naval War College Review*, Spring 2006, Vol. 59, No. 2. http://www.dtic.mil/cgi-bin/GetTRDoc?AD=A DA519745&Location=U2&doc=GetTRDoc.pdf
   See also Christopher J. Pehrson, 'String of Pearls: Meeting the Challenge of China's Rising power across the Asian Littoral', Strategic Studies Institute, United States Army War College, July 2006. http://www.strategicstudiesinstitute. army.mil/pubs/display.cfm?pubID=721

10. The so-called Monroe Doctrine, named after American President James Monroe

11. Federal Depository Library Program Electronic Collection Archive. United States Government Printing Office. http://permanent.access.gpo.gov/lps17563/ www.nsgtmo.navy.mil/hischp3.htm

12. Broadcasting Board of Governors Fiscal Year 2010 Budget Request, p. 37. http://media.voanews.com/documents/bbg_fy10_budget_request.pdf

13. Article V of the North Atlantic Treaty: 'The Parties agree that an armed attack against one or more of them in Europe or North America shall be considered an attack against them all and consequently they agree that, if such an armed attack occurs, each of them, in exercise of the right of individual or collective self-defence recognised by Article 51 of the Charter of the United Nations, will assist the Party or Parties so attacked by taking forthwith, individually and in concert with the other Parties, such action as it deems necessary, including the use of armed force, to restore and maintain the security of the North Atlantic area'. http://www.nato.int/cps/en/natolive/official_texts_17120.htm

14. 'Free Trade Agreement Between the Republic of India and the Democratic Socialist Republic of Sri Lanka', Department of Commerce, Ministry of Commerce and Industry, Government of India. http://commerce.nic.in/ilfta. htm

15. B. Muralidhar Reddy, 'India, Sri Lanka finalise trade agreement', *The Hindu*, 10 July 2008.

16. European Trade Commission. http://trade.ec.europa.eu/doclib/docs/2006/ september/tradoc_113449.pdf

17. 'Trade in Goods with Sri Lanka', United States Census Bureau. http://www. census.gov/foreign-trade/balance/c5420.html

18. 'Imports, exports and trade balance of goods on a balance-of-payments basis, by country or country grouping', Statistics Canada, Government of Canada. http://www40.statcan.gc.ca/l01/cst01/gblec02a-eng.htm

19. 'Top Trading Partners – Total Trade, Exports, Imports', United States Census Bureau. http://www.census.gov/foreign-trade/statistics/highlights/top/top1012yr. html

20. 'India in the Super-Cycle', Standard Chartered Global Research.
21. Daniel Markey, 'Developing India's Foreign Policy "Software"', *Asia Policy* 8 July 2009.
22. 'Catching up', *The Economist*, 26 May 2011.
23. 'Outcome Budget 2010-2011', Ministry of External Affairs, Government of India, p. 6. http://meaindia.nic.in/meaxpsite/budget/MEAOutcomeENG2010-11.pdf
24. *Foreign Affairs*, July/August 2011.
25. World Development Indicators 2011.
    See also OECD National Accounts Data Files. http://www.oecd.org/topicstat sportal/0,3398,en_2825_495684_1_1_1_1_1,00.html
26. 'Members, Observers and Guests', XV Summit of the Non-Aligned Movement, Sharm El Sheikh, 11-16 July 2009. http://www.namegypt.org/en/AboutName/MembersObserversAndGuests/Pages/default.aspx
27. India's population was 436 million in 1961. See 'India's Population According to the 1961 Census', Current Science, Indian Academy of Sciences. http://www.ias.ac.in/jarch/currsci/30/00000195.pdf
28. 'PM's statement prior to his departure to France and Egypt', Office of the Prime Minister, 13 July 2009. http://pmindia.nic.in/visits/content.asp?id=267
29. 'China and the Non-Aligned Movement', Ministry of Foreign Affairs of the People's Republic of China, 27 September 2003. http://www.mfa.gov.cn/eng/wjb/zzjg/gjs/gjzzyhy/2616/t26347.htm
30. 'Support for India's bid for permanent UNSC seat growing: PM', *SIFY News*, 17 April 2011. http://www.sify.com/news/support-for-india-s-bid-for-permanent-unsc-seat-growing-pm-news-national-leralmchaid.html
31. 'Remarks by the President to the Joint Session of the Indian Parliament in New Delhi, India'.
32. Winston Churchill called the First and Second World Wars together 'another Thirty Years' War', in a reference to the (original) Thirty Years War, which took place in Europe during the first half of the seventeenth century.
33. For First World War deaths see 'World War I Casualty and Death Tables', *PBS*. http://www.pbs.org/greatwar/resources/casdeath_pop.html
    For Second World War deaths see 'The Oxford Companion to World War II', I.C.B. Dear and M.R.D. Foot, eds., Oxford University Press, 2002, Demography, Table 1, p. 225.
34. 'Pilot killed in MiG-27 crash', *The Times of India*, 17 February 2010. http://timesofindia.indiatimes.com/india/Pilot-killed-in-MiG-27-crash/articleshow/5581367.cms
35. 'Pilot killed in MiG-27 crash', *The Times of India*.

36. 'Background paper on SIPRI military expenditure data, 2010', Stockholm International Peace Research Institute, April 2011. http://www.sipri.org/research/armaments/milex/factsheet2010

37. 'Background paper on SIPRI military expenditure data, 2010'.

38. Ibid.

39. Ibid.

40. Kaplan, 'The Geography of Chinese Power'.

41. Ibid.

42. Ibid.

43. Ibid.

44. Ibid.

45. 'India to spend $200 billion on defence systems by 2022', *Economic Times*, 15 February 2010. http://economictimes.indiatimes.com/news/politics/nation/India-to-spend-200-bn-on-defence-systems-by-2022/articleshow/5573160.cms

46. 'Text of the Address by President Eisenhower', The White House, 17 January 1961. http://www.eisenhower.archives.gov/research/digital_documents/Farewell_Address/1961_01_17_Press_Release.pdf

47. For total manufacturing employment see United States Bureau of Labor Statistics. http://www.bls.gov/iag/tgs/iag31-33.htm
    For defense share of manufacturing jobs see Charley Keys, 'Defense industry braces for shutdown', *CNN Money*, April 7, 2011.

48. World Development Indicators 2011.

49. Guy Anderson, 'India's Defence Industry', *RUSI Defence Systems*, Royal United Services Institute, February, 2010, pp. 68-70. http://www.rusi.org/downloads/assets/anderson_RDS_feb2010.pdf

50. Vivek Raghuvanshi, 'Fighting for Greater Access', *DefenseNews*. http://www.defensenews.com/story.php?i=4518237&c=FEA&s=SPE

51. Raghuvanshi, 'Fighting for Greater Access'.

52. Keys, 'Defense industry braces for shutdown'.

53. Manufacturing employment in India as of 2010 is 25.5 million people. See 'Economic Census' 2011, Chapter 13, p.164. http://mospi.nic.in/Mospi_New/upload/statistical_year_book_2011/SECTOR-3-INDUSTRY%20SECTOR/CH-13-ECONOMIC%20CENSUS/ECONOMIC%20CENSUS-WRITEUP.pdf

54. 'Highlights of Union Budget 2011-2012', *The Times of India*, 28 February 2011.

55. 'US gives India policing power in the Indian Ocean', *Economic Times*, 3 February 2010. http://economictimes.indiatimes.com/news/politics/nation/US-gives-India-policing-power-in-the-Indian-Ocean/articleshow/5529836.cms

56. Santanu Choudhury, 'India Approves $4.1 Billion Boeing Order', *Wall Street Journal*, 6 June 2011. http://online.wsj.com/article/SB10001424052702304432 304576369183889074472.html
57. Choudhury, 'India Approves $4.1 Billion Boeing Order'.
58. K.V. Prasad, 'U.S. "deeply disappointed" by thumbs down to fighter jets', *The Hindu*, 29 April 2011. http://www.hindu.com/2011/04/29/stories/2011042966311500.htm
59. Danny Fortson, 'BAE results reflect profit from US wars', *The Independent*, 10 August 2007. http://www.independent.co.uk/news/business/news/bae-results-reflect-profit-from-us-wars-460949.html
60. 'Mahindra, BAE Systems to invest $21.25 million in defence JV', *Business Standard*, 9 February 2010. http://www.business-standard.com/india/news/mahindra-bae-systems-to-invest-2125-million-in-defence-jv/16/51/385098/
61. 'BAE, Indian co to jointly supply bullet-proof jackets', *Business Standard*, 11 February 2010. http://www.business-standard.com/india/news/bae-indian-co-to-jointly-supply-bullet-proof-jackets/85578/on
62. Anderson, 'India's Defence Industry'.
63. Edmund Morris, *The Rise of Theodore Roosevelt*, Modern Library, 2001, p. 582.
64. 'Brilliant End of World Cruise', *New York Times*, 22 February 1909.
65. 'Pay Scale – Officers', Indian Navy. http://indiannavy.nic.in/pay.htm
66. 'A Brief History of U.S. Navy Destroyers Part I – The Early Years', The United States Navy. http://www.navy.mil/navydata/navy_legacy_hr.asp?id=141
67. Jon Swaine, 'Georgia: Russia "conducting cyber war"', *The Telegraph*, 11 August 2008. http://www.telegraph.co.uk/news/worldnews/europe/georgia/2539157/Georgia-Russia-conducting-cyber-war.html
68. 'Industry Trends', NASSCOM.
69. 'War in the fifth domain', *The Economist*, 3 July 2010.
70. Ibid.
71. 'India needs tools for cyberwarfare', *India Today*, 6 April 2010.
72. 'Cyber war: Indian Army gearing up', *The Times of India*, 19 July 2010.
73. 'Mobilization in World War II', United States Army. http://www.history.army.mil/documents/mobpam.htm
74. Anne Leland and Mari-Jana 'M-J' Oboroceanu, 'American War and Military Operations Casualties: Lists and Statistics', *Congressional Research Service*, 26 February 2010, Table 1. http://www.fas.org/sgp/crs/natsec/RL32492.pdf
75. 'To infinity and beyond', *The Economist*, 7 August 2010.
76. Wendell Minnick, 'PLA 20 Years Behind U.S. Military: Chinese DM', *Defense News*, 7 June 2011.

77. U.S. Casualty Status, United States Department of Defense. http://www.defense.gov/news/casualty.pdf

78. For India's estimated population in 2030 see 'India in the Super-Cycle', Standard Chartered Global Research, 2011.
   For geographical data see The World Factbook, Central Intelligence agency. https://www.cia.gov/library/publications/the-world-factbook/geos/in.html

79. Erica Downs, 'Inside China, Inc.: China Development Bank's Cross-Border Energy Deals', Brookings, 21 March 2011. http://www.brookings.edu/~/media/Files/rc/papers/2011/0321_china_energy_downs/0321_china_energy_downs.pdf

80. Annie Kelly, 'Who really benefits from China's trade with Latin America', *The Guardian*, 16 February 2011. http://www.guardian.co.uk/global-development/poverty-matters/2011/feb/16/china-latin-america-trade-benefit

81. Ian James, 'China shopping for Latin American oil, food, minerals',*Associated Press*, 6 June 2011. http://www.msnbc.msn.com/id/43293236/ns/business-world_business/t/china-shopping-latin-american-oil-food-minerals/

82. James, 'China shopping for Latin American oil, food, minerals'.

83. Kelly, 'Who really benefits from China's trade with Latin America'.

84. 'China Said to Have Bought Argentine Soy Oil After Six-Month Curbs Lifted', *Bloomberg News*, 15 October 2010. http://www.bloomberg.com/news/2010-10-15/china-said-to-have-bought-argentine-soybean-oil-after-import-curbs-lifted.html

85. Kaplan, 'The Geography of Chinese Power'.

86. 'China calls on world to normalize ties with Sudan', *Reuters*, 13 July 2011. http://www.reuters.com/article/2011/07/14/us-china-sudan-idUSTRE76D04A20110714

87. Kaplan, 'The Geography of Chinese Power'.

88. 'The Indispensable Economy? *The Economist*, 30 October 2010.

89. 'Catching up', *The Economist*.

90. 'The Chinese are Everywhere', *The Economist*, 7 August 2010.

91. 'Catching up', *The Economist*.

92. Y.P. Rajesh, 'Nuclear Deal crucial to meet India's energy needs: Kakodkar', *Indian Express*, 10 July 2008. http://www.indianexpress.com/news/nuclear-deal-crucial-to-meet-indias-energy/333705/

Chapter 8

1. The agreement on intelligence sharing among the five nations formally relates to signals intelligence only, but according to a press release from the United States National Security Agency may encompass other forms of intelligence as well: 'The UKUSA agreement, first called the BRUSA Agreement, was

signed in March 1946 and continues to serve as the foundation for cooperation in signals intelligence between the two nations. The agreement was later extended to encompass former British Dominions: Canada (1948), Australia and New Zealand (1956). Collaboration in various areas of critical intelligence between each of the five partner-nations continues to the present day.' See 'Declassified UKUSA Signals Intelligence Agreement Documents Available,' Press Release, United States National Security Agency, 24 June 2010. http://www.nsa.gov/public_info/press_room/2010/ukusa.shtml

2. Jyoti Thottam, 'Afghanistan: India's Uncertain Road', *Time*, 11 April 2011.

3. 'Anti-Indian militants step up activity in Afghanistan', *International Herald Tribune*, 16 June 2010.

4. Jayshree Bajoria, 'RAW: India's External Intelligence Agency', *Council on Foreign Relations*, 7 November 2008. www.cfr.org/india/raw-indias-external-intelligence-agency/p17707

5. John Garnaut, 'China won't take the Cairo route', *Sydney Morning Herald*, 15 February 2011. http://www.smh.com.au/business/china-wont-take-the-cairo-route-20110214-1atq4.html

6. Chris Buckley, 'China internal security spending jumps past army budget', *Reuters*, 5 March 2011.

7. News Release, Office of the Director of National Intelligence, Washington, D.C., 28 October 2010. http://www.dni.gov/press_releases/20101028_2010_NIP_release.pdf

8. For general background on Headley, see 'David C. Headley', Times Topics, *New York Times*, 24 May 2011. http://topics.nytimes.com/top/reference/timestopics/people/h/david_c_headley/index.html?scp=1-spot&sq=david%20headley&st=cse

9. Ginger Thompson, Eric Schmitt and Souad Mekhennet, 'D.E.A. Deployed Mumbai Plotter despite Warning', *New York Times*, 8 November 2010.

10. Ginger Thompson, 'Mumbai Plotter Testifies about Training', *New York Times*, 25 May 2011. http://www.nytimes.com/2011/05/26/world/asia/26headley.html?ref=davidcheadley

11. 'David C. Headley', *New York Times*.

12. Thompson, Schmitt and Mekhennet, 'D.E.A. Deployed Mumbai Plotter despite Warning'.

13. Thompson, 'Mumbai Plotter Testifies about Training'.

14. 'US shared no specific info on Headley: Pillai', *Financial Express*, 28 October 2010. http://www.financialexpress.com/news/us-shared-no-specific-info-on-headley-pillai/703393/0

15. 'David C. Headley', *New York Times*.

16. Thompson, Schmitt and Mekhennet, 'D.E.A. Deployed Mumbai Plotter despite Warning'.

17. 'Indo-US intelligence sharing improved after 26/11: Roemer', *OneIndia News*, 19 October 2010. http://news.oneindia.in/2010/10/19/indous-intelligence-sharing-improved-after-2611roemer.html

18. 'Intelligence sharing with United States has improved in recent times, says G.K. Pillai', *The Hindu*, 29 October 2010. http://www.thehindu.com/news/article855453.ece

19. The term 'Indian Americans' in this work refers to those whose ancestry is from the Republic of India. In this work the term is intended to encompass all legal Indian American residents of the United States, whether United States citizens, Green Card holders, or temporary visa holders.

20. 'Indian Americans: Demographic Information Updates', USINPAC. http://www.usinpac.com/indian-americans/demographic-info.html

21. Richard Springer, 'Indian American Population in U.S. Jumps 69%', 3 June 2011, indiawest.com. http://www.indiawest.com/readmore.aspx?id=3430&sid=1

22. Springer, 'Indian American Population in U.S. Jumps 69%'.

23. 'Indian Americans: Demographic Information Updates', USINPAC.

24. 'Indian Americans: Education Levels', USINPAC. http://www.usinpac.com/demographic-info/education-levels.html

25. Hillary Clinton, 'Closing Remarks at the African Growth and Opportunity Forum', Lusaka, Zambia, 10 June 2011. http://www.state.gov/secretary/rm/2011/06/165924.htm

26. David Stout, 'Ex-Louisiana Congressman Sentenced to 13 Years', *New York Times*, 13 November 2009. http://www.nytimes.com/2009/11/14/us/politics/14jefferson.html?ref=williamjjefferson

27. 'Tom Delay,' Times Topics, *New York Times*, 10 January 2011. http://topics.nytimes.com/top/reference/timestopics/people/d/tom_delay/index.html?inline=nyt-per

28. Steven R. Weisman, 'The Vice President in Exile', *The New York Times*, 29 December 1996. http://www.nytimes.com/1996/12/29/magazine/the-vice-president-in-exile.html?ref=spirotagnew

29. Douglas Waller, 'India Plays the Lobbying Game', *Time*, 12 March 2006. http://www.time.com/time/magazine/article/0,9171,1172247,00.html

30. Gregor Peter Schmitz, 'Genocide Resolution Risks Shattering Relations with Turkey', *Der Spiegel*, 12 October 2007. http://www.spiegel.de/international/world/0,1518,511210,00.html

31. Obama has not, as of this writing, kept his promise to use the term genocide as United States President to describe the massacre of Armenians. See 'Obama shuns "genocide" label for Armenian killings', *AFP*, 23 April 2011.

32. Ibid.
33. Schmitz, 'Genocide Resolution Risks Shattering Relations with Turkey'.
34. 'Trade in Goods with India', United States Census Bureau.
35. Includes exports from India. See Neha Singh, 'Ford India sales growth seen at 12-15 pct in 2011: exec', *Reuters*, 3 June 2011. http://in.reuters.com/article/2011/06/03/idINIndia-57482220110603
36. 'PepsiCo India Region: Leadership through Performance with Purpose', PepsiCo India. http://pepsicoindia.co.in/company/about-pepsico.html
37. 'GE aims $6 billion revenues from India in 3-4 years', *Business Standard*, 2 October 2009. http://www.business-standard.com/india/news/ge-aims-6-billion-revenuesindia-in-3-4-years/74879/on
38. Homepage, U.S.-India Business Council. http://www.usibc.com/
39. Ajai Shukla, 'Arms spending: India grows as west shrinks', *Business Standard*, 17 June 2010. http://www.business-standard.com/india/news/arms-spending-india-grows-as-west-shrinks/398519/
40. Background paper on SIPRI military expenditure data, 2010.
41. 'Country Policies and Embargoes', Directorate of Defense Trade Controls, United States Department of State, updated 26 October 2009. http://www.pmddtc.state.gov/embargoed_countries/index.html
42. 'Fact Sheet: Counter-Proliferation Investigations', United States Immigration and Customs Enforcement, United States Department of Homeland Security, 14 January 2011. http://www.ice.gov/news/library/factsheets/counter-proliferations.htm

Chapter 9

1   Angus Maddison estimates the population of the Roman Empire in the first century after Christ to have been approximately 44 million and the population of the world at that time to have been approximately 230 million. For the world population estimate, see Maddison, *The World Economy: Historical Statistics,* Table 8a. For the Roman Empire population estimates see Angus Maddison, *Contours of the World Economy 1-2030 AD: Essays in Macro-Economic History*, Oxford 2007, p. 35.
2. For the population of the British Empire at the outbreak of the Second World War (454 million), see Mark Harrison, *The Economics of World War II: Six Great Powers in International Comparison*, Table 1.1. For the world population in 1950 (2.5 billion), see Maddison, *The World Economy: Historical Statistics*, Table 8a.
3. For India's population at Independence, see Maddison, *The World Economy: Historical Statistics*, Table 5a.

4. http://www.guardian.co.uk/politics/2005/nov/07/uk.usa
5. 'Forget the Great in Britain', *Newsweek*, 1 August 2009. http://www.newsweek.com/2009/07/31/forget-the-great-in-britain.html#
6. 'Background paper on SIPRI military expenditure data, 2010'.
7. Kaplan, 'The Geography of Chinese Power'.
8. Mukul Devichand, 'Is Chittagong one of China's "string of pearls"?' *BBC News*, 17 May 2010. http://news.bbc.co.uk/2/hi/business/8687917.stm
9. 'India to give Bangladesh $1bn line of credit', *Times of India*, 12 January 2010. http://articles.timesofindia.indiatimes.com/2010-01-12/india/28124448_1_sheikh-hasina-tipaimukh-dam-project-sheikh-rehana
10. 'Indian commitment to Afghanistan touches USD 2 billion: PM', *Press Trust of India*, 13 May 2011.
11. Sandeep Dikshit, 'Japan to take part in India-U.S. naval exercises again', *The Hindu*, 16 February 2011. http://www.thehindu.com/news/national/article1459041.ece
12. 2009 figure. See World Development Indicators 2011.
13. Ibid.
14. 'PM declares no-first strike', *Indian Express*, 5 August 1998. http://www.expressindia.com/ie/daily/19980805/21750694.html

Epilogue

1. Barack Obama, 'Remarks by the President to the Joint Session of the Indian Parliament in New Delhi, India'.
2. Krittivas Mukherjee and Andrew Quinn, 'Clinton pushes India on nuclear law, market access', *Reuters*, 19 July 2011. http://www.reuters.com/article/2011/07/19/us-india-clinton-idUSTRE76I10720110719
3. Maureen Dowd, 'In Search of Monsters', *New York Times*, 12 March 2011. http://www.nytimes.com/2011/03/13/opinion/13dowd.html?_r=1&scp=1&sq=monsters%20to%20destroy&st=cse
4. The Five Pillars of the Strategic Dialogue are: Strategic Cooperation (encompassing nonproliferation, counterterrorism and military cooperation); Energy and Climate Change; Education and Development; Economics, Trade and Agriculture; Science and Technology, Health and Innovation. See 'U.S.-India Agreements and Achievements: Fact Sheet', Bureau of Public Affairs, United States Department of State, Washington, D.C., 20 July 2009. http://www.state.gov/r/pa/prs/ps/2009/july/126229.htm

LIST OF ACRONYMS

ADB	Asian Development Bank
BJP	Bharatiya Janata Party
BoP	Balance of Payments
BSE	Bombay Stock Exchange
CBI	Central Bureau of Investigation
CCCF	Compensatory and Contingency Financing Facility
CDB	China Development Bank
CERT	Computer Emergency Response Team
CIA	Central Intelligence Agency
DEA	Drug Enforcement Agency
EBLs	Energy-backed Loans
ECG	Electrocardiogram
EIC	East India Company
EU	European Union
FBI	Federal Bureau of Investigation
FDI	Foreign Direct Investment
FTA	Free Trade Agreement
GDP	Gross Domestic Product
GE	General Electric
IAF	Indian Air Force
IIT	Indian Institute of Technology
IMF	International Monetary Fund

IOC	Indian Oil Corporation
IPKF	Indian Peace Keeping Force
IPOs	Initial Public Offerings
ISI	Inter-Services Intelligence
JVs	Joint Ventures
LeT	Lashkar-e-Tayyeba
LoC	Line of Control
LTTE	Liberation Tigers of Tamil Eelam
M&A	Mergers & Acquisitions
NAM	Non-Aligned Movement
NPT	Non-Proliferation Treaty
NSE	National Stock Exchange
ONGC	Oil and National Gas Corporation
PBOC	Peoples Bank of China
PMO	Prime Minister's Office
R&AW	Research & Analysis Wing
R&D	Research & Development
RBI	Reserve Bank of India
SBI	State Bank of India
SDRs	Special Drawing Rights
SEBI	Security and Exchange Board of India
UID	Unique Identification
UNSC	United Nations Security Council
USIBC	US-India Business Council
USINPAC	US India Political Action Committee
UTN	Ummah Tameer-e-Nau

INDEX